UNDERSTANDING
SHAKESPEARE

UNDERSTANDING
SHAKESPEARE

BY

E. F. C. LUDOWYK

Professor Emeritus of English in the
University of Ceylon

CAMBRIDGE
AT THE UNIVERSITY PRESS
1962

PUBLISHED BY
THE SYNDICS OF THE CAMBRIDGE UNIVERSITY PRESS
Bentley House, 200 Euston Road, London, N.W. 1
American Branch: 32 East 57th Street, New York 22, N.Y.
West African Office: P.O. Box 33, Ibadan, Nigeria

©

CAMBRIDGE UNIVERSITY PRESS

1962

Printed in Great Britain at the University Press, Cambridge
(Brooke Crutchley, University Printer)

51,505

CONTENTS

LIST OF ILLUSTRATIONS

PLATES

The plates are bound in between pages 80 and 81.
There are notes on the plates on pp. 77–9.

FIGURES

PREFACE

This book has an ambitious title, but a fairly simple aim. It is meant as a general introduction to Shakespeare for the ordinary reader, the student, or the teacher without the benefit of a university course in English, who feels the need of some direction in presenting Shakespeare to his classes.

It is not easy to claim to understand anything at all. But there is a sense in which Shakespeare can be understood, even by schoolboys whose native language is not English but who have been studying it at school. School levels vary and every teacher knows of cases as desperate as that of the English candidate at G.C.E. (A level) whose 'own words' for Macbeth's lines were: 'O for tomorrow, tomorrow and tomorrow, these days give me the creeps', and also of work as good as any commended in the published reports of examiners. Between these extremes the plays, as they have been cultivated, have bloomed surprisingly and hopefully. One such flower is in the testimony of a seventeenth-century sea-captain, whose record will be found in Chambers's *William Shakespeare*. In September 1607 the ships of William Keeling and William Hawkins stood off Sierra Leone. The crew of Keeling's ship, the *Dragon*, played Shakespeare's *Richard II*, and later *Hamlet*, for their own delectation and for the benefit of Hawkins's crew. Keeling permitted these performances, as he said, to 'keep my people from idleness and unlawful games, or sleep'.

If common sailors 350 years ago could, without special training and knowledge, play one of the most difficult of Shakespeare's tragedies, is it too much to believe that any reader today, suitably instructed, can understand and appreciate him too? It is towards the understanding of Shakespeare as a popular dramatist that this book is intended.

A book of this kind is naturally under very considerable debt to the work of numerous scholars. I owe particular indebtedness to

ix

the work of L. C. Knights, D. A. Traversi, J. Dover Wilson and G. Wilson Knight. I am specially grateful to John Speirs for his criticisms of the opening chapter, to Dr T. W. Craik for his suggestions on the staging of *The Cradle of Security* and to Maria Clark for her interest and help. I am conscious, too, of all I learnt from classes in Ceylon in the twenty-five years of trying to understand Shakespeare there. To them, therefore, I should like to inscribe this book.

All quotations and references are to the Cambridge Pocket Shakespeare (General Editor, J. Dover Wilson). Its glossary, with its lists of various senses of a word and its careful references to the text, deals admirably with one obstacle to understanding Shakespeare—the unfamiliarity of his language to the speaker of modern English.

E. F. C. L.

LONDON

PART I

THE BACKGROUND

1. THE MAN SHAKESPEARE

So little is known of the man Shakespeare that it has even been possible for various people to assert that someone else is really the author of the plays which we call his. It has never been denied that the man William Shakespeare really lived, but it has been claimed that the plays were really by Bacon, or the Earl of Oxford, or some other Elizabethan. The frequency of such claims is due to the hold of Shakespeare's work on the minds of men, and to the extreme meagreness of incontrovertible information about his life. Since almost nothing is known, it is possible for the partisans of the various theories of authorship to assign the plays to some other Elizabethan.

We do not even know the exact date of Shakespeare's birth. The official date—23 April—is St George's day, which, as the day of the patron Saint of England, is appropriate for the birthday of England's greatest dramatic poet. All that we know, which can be attested by document and legal proof, could be written down on the back of a postcard.

The facts about Shakespeare

Baptized on 26 April 1564 at the parish church at Stratford on Avon.

Married very shortly after 27 November 1582 by special licence from the Bishop of Worcester, to 'Anne Whateley' of Temple Grafton, as her name appears in the licence. In the bond of sureties the name is put down as 'Anne Hathwey' of Stratford.

His daughter, Susanna, was baptized in Stratford church on 26 May 1583.

Twins—a son and a daughter—Hamnet and Judith were baptized in Stratford church on 2 February 1585.

In 1593 his name appears as author of *Venus and Adonis*, dedicated to the Earl of Southampton. After this his name appears in various actors' lists.

In 1599 he was a 'sharer' (shareholder) in the Globe Theatre on the Bankside.

In 1602 he purchased freehold land in Stratford, and thereafter his name appears in various documents relating to the ownership of land, tithes and legal disputes.

On 25 March 1616 he signed his will.

His gravestone in the chancel of Stratford church has four well-known lines of unknown authorship:

> Good friend for Jesus sake forbeare,
> To dig the dust enclosed here!
> Blest be the man that spares these stones
> And curst be he that moves my bones.

On the memorial tablet placed in the church it is stated that he died at the age of fifty-three on 23 April 1616. The Stratford Parish Register gives the date of his burial as 25 April 1616.

In 1623 his actor friends and 'fellows' whom he had mentioned in his will—John Heming and Henry Condell—published an edition of his plays in folio—a large-sized volume. It was dedicated to the earls of Pembroke and Montgomery, and contained a tribute in verse by Ben Jonson 'to the memory of my beloved, the author, Mr William Shakespeare, and what he hath left us'. Before 1623 nineteen of the plays had appeared in smaller quarto editions.

Personality in the Elizabethan age

There is a singular lack of information about most famous Elizabethans as persons, or personalities. There is hardly anything written by them, or by others, about themselves which can tell us what sort of persons they were. There were no diaries, no autobiographical notes, no interviews, no newspapers and therefore no gossip columns. If little of this kind exists about the great, it is not surprising that there should be next to nothing in the way of contemporary record about a mere writer of plays and an actor on the popular stage. Both these 'professions', as we call them now, were looked upon as of little worth, and even as degrading. Actors, in

the legal enactments of the time, were classed with rogues and vagabonds, and to write for money was thought to be beneath the dignity
of a gentleman.

It is to be expected, therefore, that we should have little in the way
of authentic contemporary information about the man Shakespeare,
or about the plays he wrote. There is nothing like a review of any of
his plays, though there are notes made about the performance of a
few of them. Nor do we find anybody's record of what Shakespeare
said or thought of any of his plays.

Forty years or more after his death, when Shakespeare's reputation
as a dramatist was beginning to develop, visitors to Stratford began
to interest themselves in him and his connections with the town. But
the information they scraped together contains very little that is
likely to help in judging the plays, or even in saying much about the
man who wrote them. Of course, it is understandably disappointing
that we lack Shakespeare's notes on the plays he wrote. But even if
we had them, we should still have to work on the plays ourselves,
for what a writer says about his work, informative though it might be,
will not absolve us of the necessity of examining his work ourselves
if we wish to understand it.

Shakespeare's upbringing

Of Shakespeare's parents we know even less. His father, John
Shakespeare, was a trader, an owner of property who held civic
office in Stratford, a person not of gentle birth, but of some standing
in the social hierarchy of a small country town. In 1596 Shakespeare's father was given by the College of Arms the right to a coat
of arms and a crest. His status was now advanced to that of a
country gentleman. He would belong to the upper class of rural
society. Above this class would be the knights and the nobility to
which the country gentleman could hope to belong if he made
money in trade or the law, and had influence at court.

Freedom from civil war and the increasing prosperity of the
country gave many opportunities to men of this class of country

gentlemen to improve their status. They could indeed, in their increasing numbers and influence, be thought of as a new class.

Shakespeare's mother, Mary Arden, came of a family described as being both wealthy and gentlefolk. There were eight children born to John and Mary Shakespeare.

Shakespeare probably had a grammar school education at Stratford, which would have given him some familiarity with the major Latin classics, and, in addition, a training in the arts of speech and eloquence.

He did not go to either Oxford or Cambridge, probably on account of his father's financial difficulties. Had his father's prosperity continued, Shakespeare might have been a country gentleman. But it did not. He spent the first eighteen years of his life at Stratford among people who had connections with land and with trade. He knew the sights and sounds of the countryside, as his poems and plays show. Life in Stratford must have given him contact with almost all classes in sixteenth-century England, except the great nobleman and the courtier. This contact with such a wide range of persons in the country was an advantage to Shakespeare, and gave added strength to his knowledge of life and his language, as we shall see when we consider his plays.

Shakespeare in London

Like other young men, Shakespeare was probably drawn to London by the prospect of the fortune to be made there. It may be that, according to a later legend, he had got into trouble at Stratford, and flight to London was the best way of evading its consequences. He must have tried his hand there at both acting and the writing of plays, for in 1592 Robert Greene, the playwright and pamphleteer, makes a reference to a player who had made a success of writing plays. This can be none other than Shakespeare, for Greene puns on Shakespeare's name, and quotes a few words from an early play in which he must have had a hand.

It was not unusual for a young man with some education to have tried to write plays, for drama was popular entertainment at the time, and the first public theatres had already been built in London: the Theatre in 1576, the Curtain in 1577, the Rose in 1587, all of them in the suburbs outside the jurisdiction of the city. There was a theatre in Newington Butts, and in London and all over the provinces plays were being performed.

There was a demand for plays, and Shakespeare had had sufficient education to undertake to supply them. He had been to a grammar school at Stratford, and he knew the life of a country town. He was now in London, making his living and learning by experience. What both these 'schools'—formal education and life in a small community and the metropolis in sixteenth-century England—taught Shakespeare is to be found in his plays. It used to be assumed that the 'small Latin and lesse Greek' with which Ben Jonson credited him, in a remark meant as a commendation of his genius, amounted to a negligible quantity. But it has been shown by experts that, even if Shakespeare did not go to a university and there get the education in which many of his contemporaries took such pride (Greene claimed a special distinction as being a Master of Arts of both Oxford and Cambridge), his schooling in Stratford provided him with a fair education in the classics.

It is useful to remember, then, that Shakespeare was not an unlearned and untutored genius. His education would certainly have made him familiar with modes of argument, with the art of speaking and writing in such a way as to plead a cause or persuade an audience. Books, as well as life—in the countryside (the stones and the running brooks he mentions in As You Like It) and in London pouring out its citizens on some ceremonial occasion (as he remembers it in the Prologue to Henry V)—formed a part of his schooling.

2. THE ELIZABETHAN AGE

It would be useful now to place William Shakespeare, the son of John Shakespeare, 'yeoman' of Stratford on Avon, in the country and in the era to which his parents and himself belonged. What a man writes does not depend only on the time and place in which he lived, but these have their importance, and to forget that Shakespeare was an Englishman living at a particular period in England's history would be to overlook one factor in his development. Not to know that he lived in a country which was, for the greater part of his lifetime, ruled by a Tudor monarch, Queen Elizabeth, or that the people he knew and the life he portrays in his plays had a distinctive stamp given to them by the changes which took place in the fifteenth and sixteenth centuries, is a handicap. Much in Shakespeare belongs to the age in which he lived, and it is necessary to bear in mind certain things about his times.

One side of the picture

The England in which Shakespeare grew up was a small kingdom, with a population of about four or five million people. It was, by modern standards, undeveloped, but its capital London was by far its largest town, and was fast becoming an important European centre of trade. To the north lay the kingdom of Scotland with which there was a tradition of warfare. Across the sea to the west lay Ireland, of which England held only a small area known as 'the Pale'. With its numerous villages and its rural character, England resembled those parts of the world today where industrial and commercial change have not yet transformed the land. The wealth of England then lay in its agriculture and the wool trade. If we speak of England's wealth today, we would be thinking of industrial output. The difference indicates the change there has been in three hundred years.

8

The land, without large coalfields, steelmills and other factories, and without large industrial towns, was dotted with small country towns and villages. The old castles and fortified places, built in the time in which the private armies of powerful nobles carried on their forays, were giving way to a more peaceful type of building. And all about him, whether he lived in village or town, or even in the metropolis, the Englishman had the countryside. Shakespeare knew all its varied life of plants, trees, animals, birds and people. In his plays his characters spontaneously express their thoughts and feelings in terms of country life and scenery. One of the strongest sources of Shakespeare's feeling must have been the remembrance of the country round the small town of Stratford. Quite often the moments of strong tension in his plays are marked by a touch which brings to mind the English countryside he knew. To take one example: Duncan is about to enter the castle of Glamis. He praises its pleasant situation, and Banquo adds

> This guest of summer,
> The temple-haunting martlet, does approve,
> By his loved mansionry, that the heaven's breath
> Smells wooingly here: no jutty, frieze,
> Buttress, nor coign of vantage, but this bird
> Hath made his pendent bed and procreant cradle:
> Where they most breed and haunt, I have observed
> The air is delicate.

The bird that lives in churches and sanctuaries is seen as a builder going lovingly about his task—that of building himself a home. In this image we see natural surroundings and human activity combined to present a strong suggestion, with pictorial associations, of the sanctity and the tenderness of the home, and of the continuation of families ('procreant cradle'), just at the moment when the king is entering the home where he is going to be killed. It is a moment of tension, of excitement, for though the audience know what Duncan's fate is likely to be, Duncan and Banquo do not, and to the audience these simple words with their touching reference to the peaceful

9

home-building of the birds form a striking contrast to the dramatic situation: Lady Macbeth, the subject, cousin, and hostess, welcoming her king to the home which is going to be a slaughter-house.

By 1564 England had enjoyed nearly seven decades of comparative peace and security from civil strife. The Tudor monarchy was well established, and the chief source of internal dissension in other countries—the religious factions aroused by the Reformation— seemed by the time of Elizabeth's accession, in 1558, to have been ended by the success with which the religious and economic changes made by her father, Henry VIII, had been accepted by the majority of people. These changes were far-reaching, and they constituted the biggest break so far with the older order which was still remembered, and which still lingered here and there.

England had cut itself off from religious community with Roman Catholic Europe. The Supreme Head of the Church in England was no longer the pope but the English monarch. The great monastic establishments had been dissolved and their properties confiscated. In 1559 two Acts, the first authorizing the Prayer Book of 1552 and the second giving Elizabeth supreme authority in all ecclesiastical matters, laid the foundations of the Church of England.

England was becoming a great trading country. It is true that fortunes were being made by farming, but much more spectacular fortunes were those of the speculators, above all of those who in- vested their money in a voyage often combining trade with some piracy. Portuguese and Italian mariners had discovered both a new way to the old continent of Asia as well as a whole new continent, America. Through the exploitation of these discoveries every country in Europe was to be affected, and just as the peasant in Ghana or Malaya is rich or poor today according to the price of cocoa or rubber in the markets of London, so the ordinary man in England, in Shakespeare's time, found the purchasing power of his money diminished by the silver from the mines in Potosi in South America and the wealth being brought from the new world and the old into Europe and England. In spite of Henry VIII's debasement of the coinage which had sent prices up, and increased taxation, Englishmen in the reign of Elizabeth were living in an era of comparative prosperity.

The other side

But there was another side to the picture. Throughout Elizabeth's reign there were repeated plots against her, aimed at killing her and putting her cousin, Mary Queen of Scots, on the throne. All over Europe there was war between Roman Catholics and Protestants, on religious and political grounds. There was fighting between some German principalities and the Spanish king. Between 1560 and 1598 there was intermittent war in France between Catholic and Protestant factions. From 1568 till 1609 there was continual fighting in the Low Countries, where Protestant and Catholic were up in arms against their Spanish overlords. England had actively helped the Dutch rebels, and there were Englishmen fighting in the Netherlands. Sir Philip Sidney died in a battle at Zutphen in 1586.

Elizabeth had no alternative but to help, whenever it was politic, the enemies of the powerful king of Spain, whose commander in the Netherlands was organizing an army for the invasion of England. After 1570 when she had been excommunicated and 'deposed' by the pope, it was expected that invasion of the country by the Spanish would follow. Throughout the greater part of her reign there were threats of foreign invasion. Though the full-scale Spanish attempt, the Armada, was defeated in 1588, others were being planned. The courage and daring of the English seamen, the exploits of commanders like Drake, Hawkins and Grenville and the intrepidity of the numerous discoverers celebrated by Richard Hakluyt in his *Principal Navigations, Voyagers, Traffics, and Discoveries of the English Nation* enabled English sea-power to maintain English prosperity and independence.

Towards the end of Elizabeth's reign there were fears of the recurrence of civil strife in the possibility of disputed succession at her death. At the end of the century she had been on the throne for forty-two years. It is easy to understand the great affection her subjects had for her. The patriotism which speaks in Shakespeare's plays of England in previous reigns derives most of its strength and meaning from the feeling of English people in his own time.

In his play of *Henry VIII*, written at the end of his life, Shakespeare, looking back over the past, put into the mouth of Cranmer a 'prophecy' about the royal babe, Elizabeth, he had held in his arms at her baptism:

> This royal infant,—heaven still move about her!—
> Though in her cradle, yet now promises
> Upon this land a thousand thousand blessings
> Which time shall bring to ripeness: she shall be—
> But few now living can behold that goodness—
> A pattern to all princes living with her....

Shakespeare had 'beheld that goodness', and some part of the glory attached to the Elizabethan age was given it by his work.

Change in England

Cranmer continued his 'prophetic' speech in *Henry VIII* with an idyllic picture of England in Elizabeth's reign:

> In her days every man shall eat in safety
> Under his own vine what he plants; and sing
> The merry songs of peace to all his neighbours....

But as we have indicated, there was another side to the picture. Important changes had taken place in England during the sixteenth century, and there was uneasiness and disquiet at their consequences. By the middle of the century a great alteration in the holding of land in England had taken place: the monasteries had been dissolved, the Church was dispossessed of much of its estates, and a great deal of 'common land' (which had been open for use by the ordinary man) came to be enclosed as private property. And at this time, too, the new owners of land turned their lands either to new use, or farmed it in new ways. It could be said that as the largest owner of property—the Church with its monasteries and chantries—was stripped of its land, a new class of property owner came into being, and the economy of the country presents a changed picture. As this happened, men's ideas of the world changed too.

Old and new—deserted abbeys and the new homes of country gentlemen—were to be found side by side, the old sometimes maintaining an unequal struggle with the new, sometimes seemingly vanquished and gone for good. The Tudor monarchy was both old and new; it might have seemed to be as autocratic and arbitrary as it had always been, but on the other hand Parliament, particularly in the last years of Elizabeth's reign, claimed rights which might have been thought of as outrageously new. To the queen certain subjects like religion and the issue of monopolies (giving exclusive right to trade in a particular commodity which the holder could sell) were matters of royal prerogative, yet Parliament attempted to bring them under its control. The old nobility were very much diminished in numbers, and new men arose on whom the Crown relied for the business of government. This was a trend noticeable throughout the century. The most influential men in England, on whom the Tudors could depend and whom they used, were 'upstarts' in the opinion of the old nobility. Men like Wolsey, Cromwell, the Cecils were tried and experienced administrators and diplomats. Cromwell and William Cecil, who became the first Lord Burleigh, the father of Sir Robert Cecil, were lawyers. Polonius in *Hamlet* may be a caricature of some such loyal servant of the monarch. There were the old servants and the new—quite definitely contrasted in *King Lear* in the figures of Kent and Oswald. In *Twelfth Night* the steward Malvolio may be a picture of the new, while Sir Toby may be a type of the useless old retainer still found in the houses of the great.

Reading Shakespeare's plays we see how much he is aware of the way in which his world had changed. After all he lived in an age in which printing, the use of gunpowder, the discovery of America were still comparatively recent additions to the store of common knowledge. He knew the newest maps of the world, he could see all around him an England different from that which his parents knew.

And yet his attitude to the world and man's position in it is not greatly different from theirs or from that of a man to whom all such things as printing, gunpowder, the roundness of the earth, the sequestration of Church property, the refusal to acknowledge the supremacy of the pope, would have been the work of the devil, and impossible to conceive of or to accept.

A poetic vision of change

Some lines in 2 *Henry IV* show what is running through the mind of the king as he considers the times in which he has lived. To us, 'the revolution of the times' (3. 1. 46) would perhaps simply mean one kind of political change, but Shakespeare's king sees it as the toppling over of all the most solid and fixed things in the world as if by some natural catastrophe:

> O God! that one might read the book of fate,
> And see the revolution of the times
> Make mountains level, and the continent,
> Weary of solid firmness, melt itself
> Into the sea! and, other times, to see
> The beachy girdle of the ocean
> Too wide for Neptune's hips; how chances mocks
> And changes fill the cup of alteration
> With divers liquors!

The tempestuous force of the sea is connected in Shakespeare's mind with human distress and the uncertainty of human happiness. The image of the sea had been haunting the king's mind; contrasting his inability to sleep in his rich soft bed of state with the discomfort of the shipboy up on the heaving mast and yet sound asleep, he pictures the sea in its angry mood so forcibly that we are made aware simultaneously of the shipboy's ability to sleep and of the king's desire for rest, but above all of the ocean's elemental power:

> O thou dull god, why li'st thou with the vile
> In loathsome beds, and leav'st the kingly couch
> A watch-case or a common 'larum bell?
> Wilt thou upon the high and giddy mast

Seal up the ship-boy's eyes and rock his brains
In cradle of the rude imperious surge,
And in the visitation of the winds,
Who take the ruffian billows by the top,
Curling their monstrous heads, and hanging them
With deafing clamour in the slippery clouds,
That, with the hurly, death itself awakes?

These lines come from a play about the England of the early fifteenth century, but change in the world Shakespeare knew was just as elemental a force. There was change and yet there were people like the shipboy who could sleep through it all, unaware that storms were ranging round them.

The subject-matter of the plays

Not one of Shakespeare's plays is set in the England of his own time. He is apparently dealing with Venice, Athens, Illyria, France, classical Rome and so on. He makes no explicit reference to contemporary events or people, except for a few allusions in *Henry V* and *Henry VIII*. But there seem to be two related subjects which arise out of contemporary English life as it impressed itself on him, as on numerous other writers and thinkers. The first is the preoccupation with the conflict between the old or the traditional and the new. Sometimes this is seen as a tussle between persons— as between Edmund and Edgar in *King Lear*—sometimes between groups, or in the ideas which animate persons or groups—as in *Macbeth* where the forces of darkness appear to be in conflict with those of light. Secondly, arising out of this preoccupation, a particular question is often debated: who or what is right? What is justly mine or yours? Have I a right to this, or have you? It is significant, surely, that in so many of the plays, not only in the histories, the heart of the matter seems to be a legal dispute; and a trial or a scene in a court of law is one of the play's climaxes.

In the histories the action is often concerned with the conflict between two rivals, each with his band of supporters, and the

15

matter at dispute is the succession to the throne, which is the whole of England, and really therefore the whole world, as far as an Englishman of that time was concerned. Whose is the rightful claim? How does a man decide whose cause is the just one? Who is the good king? In a play like *Richard III* we have, besides, the man with a new philosophy of life who sets himself up against the old and traditional order.

In *Julius Caesar*, a play about classical Rome, we see that there is a similar conflict between two notions of what is right government for a country; we see that this conflict is waged between two sets of people, both politicians with arguments of political expediency, and that involved in it is a figure very different from them, that of 'the noblest Roman of them all'. Was it right or just or necessary that Caesar should have been killed? The central scene of the play is really a trial, where the two counsel, Brutus and Antony, face the tribunal of the public of Rome, and mould the opinions of their audience.

Or in material very different from both histories or Roman plays, in the romantic world of *The Merchant of Venice*, we see that the trial or the test—who has the right to the pound of flesh, to the fabulous heiress, Portia—is the driving force. There are really two scenes of trial here, not only the judgement of the Duke in the court of law, but also that of the suitors before the caskets.

3. THE ELIZABETHAN WORLD

Changed notions of the world

Whatever the setting of the plays, and whatever their real subject, Shakespeare was writing about people with attitudes to the world very different from ours. In the sixteenth century the very picture of the physical world had changed. The world of medieval maps, with angelic faces blowing the winds from its four corners towards a single central land-mass, might be met with in Shakespeare together with the new map with the 'augmentation of the Indies'. His contemporaries knew that the world was round, that whole 'new' continents existed, and that, far from being the centre of the universe and a fixed, flat mass, the earth on which they lived was one of many planets spinning in space. How many of them were able to grasp or describe this changed notion of the world correctly would be difficult to say. Probably just as few of us today would be able to describe the new universe and the world the physicists have revealed to us in recent years. We know that we can no longer think of space and matter as people at the beginning of the century thought of them. We know, because we see the results of new scientific discoveries in such things as aeroplanes, radio and nylon, that the world has changed, but we may not be able to describe these changes coherently, and some of us may not understand their consequences. What is more, our ideas of the world in which we live may not, in spite of all the change, be very different from those of our grandparents and great-grandparents.

Shakespeare's ideas about his world

It would be useful, then, to know how Shakespeare looked at his world, and what his ideas were, so that we may better understand what he is conveying in his poetry. His world was that of the Christian of his time, a world created by God, lying at the centre of the universe, in which God had placed his special creation, man. The history of man was to be found in the Bible and would be completed by the Second Coming of Christ and the Last Judgement. Its prominent events were the Fall of Man through Original Sin; the coming of Christ on earth to redeem man; Christ's life on earth with his passion, death and resurrection; the Church he established, and the necessity put upon men so to live that they should inherit at the Last Judgement eternal life in heaven, and not the torments of hell. Man, as God's special creation for whom his son had suffered, had

17

something of the divine in him, but as a sinner after his seduction by the devil, he had something of the enemy of God in him too. If he was to save himself, man had constantly to be on the alert against the wiles of the devil and call upon God for protection. The earth on which man lived and everything in it were God's creation too, and part of a universal plan and an order which God foresaw and directed.

How different this would be from the view of man and the world today held by numerous people of our time. To them man would be an animal evolved as a result of thousands of years on a planet of whose origins we are not quite certain, but which we may put down to an explosion on the sun millions of years ago. For these people man is biologically no different from the animals. Like every other biological organism, man has a life-cycle, and his death is simply an event like any other stage in it, all of it being governed by natural laws.

The ordered pattern

The Elizabethan looked on his world as manifesting the order which God had brought into being. Order, the disposition of all things in a fixed pattern, was the keynote of all things, whether they were in heaven, or on earth. This order was both simple and complex. It was clear, and yet it included a multiplicity of gradations and ranks which were fore-ordained. Its picture of the universe and of every part in it was of a system of carefully arranged ranks, which could be seen wherever man chose to look. Shakespeare inherited this traditional hierarchic notion of the world, or of the various worlds—of man, of heaven, of the sea, of the air, of the animals, of vegetables, of minerals, and so on—of which the universe was composed. These worlds resemble each other in that there are five common points to be noted.

First of all they are God-created; their disposition into grades or ranks one beneath the other is God's ordering too; a mutual system of duties and obligations, God-ordained, links the divisions together and makes for the harmonious working of the whole; any disturb-

(relatedness of whole)

ance of one particular link in the system throws the whole into confusion and disorder; and such action is abhorrent to God, the creator of the ordered scheme.

So in the political order, or the world of the state, the ruler (king, prince, duke, or general) is the divinely appointed head and chief, as the lion is among animals, the rose among flowers, the sun among planets, the dolphin among fishes, and the eagle among birds. To him all his subjects, his brothers no less than his humble dependents, owe prescribed duties. He also has certain obligations to perform, and the health of the body politic depends on this constant two-way traffic of duties and obligations. In its carefully ordered gradation of ranks there is an interdependence of parts like that in the mechanism of a watch or an internal combustion engine, except that the two latter are human constructions, while the former is the creation of a God who rules the universe. For one part or one member, therefore, to arrogate to itself what was not granted by the divine plan, was to jeopardize the whole, and to produce disorder. Such actions as the usurpation of the kingship, or a subject's rising up against his immediate superior, were really sacrilegious, contrary to God's law.

Menenius Agrippa uses an analogy similar to this in the fable he relates to the plebeians in *Coriolanus*:

> There was a time, when all the body's members
> Rebell'd against the belly; thus accus'd it;
> That only like a gulf it did remain
> I' the midst o' the body, idle and unactive,
> Still cupboarding the viand, never bearing
> Like labour with the rest, where the other instruments
> Did see, and hear, devise, instruct, walk, feel,
> And, mutually participate, did minister
> Unto the appetite, and affection common
> Of the whole body. The belly answer'd...
> 'True is it, my incorporate friends', quoth he,
> 'That I receive the general food at first,
> Which you do live upon; and fit it is,
> Because I am the store-house and the shop

Of the whole body: but, if you do remember,
I send it through the rivers of your blood
Even to the court, the heart, to the seat o' the brain....

To the other members of the body who do its work, the stomach may seem lazy and inactive; but it has its fore-ordained function to perform, and if it does not do this, if the rest of the members of the body do not act as they are expected to, then the whole organism—the human being—would starve and cease to exist.

This order, with the interdependence of its parts, was fore-ordained by God, yet no man was without hope that his fate was sealed for ever, and that it was useless to try to alter it. Man was endowed with his God-given soul, and with reason. He had, too, a lower part of his nature which was prone to sin. In the perpetual conflict between these two parts of his nature, man could, even at the very last moment, be master of his fate.

Other views

This was the Christian view; yet at the same time there was another attitude to human beings which saw them tossed about as the sport of some Fate or blind necessity. According to this point of view, men prosper or fall according as Fortune turns her wheel. Princes, no less than the most humble, were the playthings of Fortune. A large number of medieval and Elizabethan plays and tracts were based on these ideas of the wheel of Fortune and the fall of princes. These ideas were pagan but, as they were applied, they could illustrate Christian truths, for the awful spectacle of the ruin of the great or the daring could be taken as examples of God's judgements.

One code of conduct recommended Christian charity and mercy to human beings if they wished to live in accordance with God's law. Another, the philosophy Elizabethans associated with the vile politician (both strong terms of reprobation) Machiavelli, advised the man who wished for power and success to unite the strength of the lion and the cunning of the fox, in a world in which all men strove for their own advantage. To the traditionalists of the time this was a shocking doctrine, although Machiavelli was only stating as a realist what he had observed in the successful careers of the military leaders of his age—objective data which the traditionalists had themselves noticed. To the Elizabethans Machiavelli became the symbol of everything devilish.

On p. 16 *Richard III* was referred to as a play in which a man with a new philosophy of life set himself up against the traditional order. Richard, duke of Gloucester, is one of Shakespeare's earliest sketches of the Machiavellian. (Aaron in *Titus Andronicus* is another.) In 3 *Henry VI* Richard describes himself as a man who could teach Machiavelli. There is a great deal of the Machiavellian in Iago in *Othello* and Edmund in *King Lear*. When Edmund invokes Nature as his 'goddess':

> Thou Nature art my goddess, to thy law
> My services are bound...

he thinks of that part of his nature which he shares with beasts— that which naturally leads them to attack others and to satisfy their appetites. This is the Nature which he worships and will live by. In opposition to it is that part of human nature which links man with God, which makes him respect the traditional ties of kinship, of society, and of the order God has created. For this conception of Nature Edmund has only contempt.

Ideas in Shakespeare

Shakespeare's ideas about the world and about man's destiny were compounded of notions such as these. Some of his ideas may seem to us to be more medieval than was appropriate to the experience of a person living at the end of the sixteenth century. Our own notions of the world in which we live might similarly be shown to be outmoded and antiquated. Our concern, however, is not with the truth or the validity of Shakespeare's ideas, some of which may be antipathetic to us.

It is not sufficient to say that the idea itself does not matter if its expression is moving or impressive, for it is difficult sometimes to separate ideas from their expression. It would be truer to state that the ideas—the items of belief or knowledge, the propositions—are transformed by the power of the writer. The words he has used have changed an idea into—in Shakespeare's case—a poet's experiencing of the idea; as Keats said, he does not just feel it 'in his head', but in his blood as well. It is not that Shakespeare dresses up his idea attractively with all the resources of the poet—imagery, rhythm, rhetoric and whatever else we will—but that the idea loses its identity as idea, and is transmuted, through the poet's imaginative power as he considers human experience, into poetry with its own unique way of expressing itself. An item of belief changes into a poetic statement which we can accept whatever our own ideas or beliefs. We make contact not with an idea as a mental process, but with poetry which can alter our own way of looking at the world.

We may not believe in witchcraft, be completely uninterested in sacramental notions of kingship, think of ghosts as childish superstition, but *Macbeth* will still move and excite us as a study of the ambiguousness of evil, and its threat to our moral being.

4. THE ELIZABETHAN STAGE

Actor and playwright

It should not be forgotten that Shakespeare was both actor and playwright in London. So he belongs to that group of people who wrote as professionals, knowing the stage, actors and the mode of translating written text into theatrical performance. Whether such people do, or must, write better than the playwright who has never known the stage from the inside or from behind the scenes is hardly worth discussing. But it is important to remember that Shakespeare, the dramatist, was like Molière or Sophocles or

Ibsen, a man who had been associated with the performing and presentation of plays. The plays he wrote would therefore bear the marks of the kind of stage performance for which they were destined. To forget this, or to refuse to consider it, is to risk misunderstanding the play.

In any case a play is written for performance on a stage, and however much we feel that it means more to us when we read it than when we see it in actual performance, we must bear in mind what it was meant to be, and how it was given life on the stage. The stage is a complex organism, whether we think of the most recently built American university drama department's million-dollar theatre or the platform in a school hall. Both use the same basic means for the purpose of engaging the attention of an audience.

A play is not only the written words, the text, or the book which in writing, type or print represents the work of the playwright. This is only one element—though to most people the most important, and to some the only interesting element—in what constitutes a play. The play comes to life as the result of the work of several kinds of people. It is a text intended for acting on the stage by actors, and this involves the interaction of other arts besides those of writer and actor—of music, of dance, of painter, of designer, of costumier. When all these things combine, performed before an audience, it becomes a play.

A play

That a play is not the words alone will readily be granted if we think what would be left out if we concentrated on the written or spoken words, forgetting, for instance, that they are meant to be accompanied by gesture and action, and that they are spoken by one actor to others. There is a scene in *Macbeth* (4. 3. 159 ff.) which shows how important in a play are those things which are not said, but are acted.

Malcolm, talking of the miracle-working king of England, has called up the picture of a country full of grace because of the virtue and goodness of its king. This creates in the minds of the audience, and of Macduff who is with him on the stage, the implied contrast with Scotland, ruled by the tyrant and murderer Macbeth. Ross enters, and at once Scotland is brought to mind by the very costume he wears. The dramatist draws particular attention to him, for he is seen coming across the stage, and is unrecognized until he comes up to Macduff ('My countryman, but yet I know him not'). When he enters, the audience knows that he is the last person to see Lady Macduff and her child alive, and that they were killed in the previous scene; so at some moment they must expect him to inform Macduff of their murder.

We notice that Ross first gives only a general picture of the suffering of Scotland under the tyrant. He faces Macduff and speaks to him, but says nothing about his family. When directly questioned about them, Ross replies laconically with 'why, well', and again with 'well, too'—words which, to the audience, must have a grim ironic undertone, for to the Christian believer the dead, being at rest from the troubles of this world, could be described as being 'well'. Forced to reply to Macduff's question 'The tyrant has not battered at their peace?', he again replies briefly and equivocally, with the same word 'well': 'No; they were well at peace when I did leave 'em'. To which Macduff impatiently replies: 'Be not a niggard of your speech: how goes it?'

There is much more than the words here. If we try to remember the stage on which the play is performed we can see how important is the rising tension, how Ross's nervousness, his obvious uneasiness, have communicated themselves to his audience and to Macduff. We see how excited and irritable the latter is when Ross, glad to be able to turn away from him, but yet overpowered by the 'weight' of the 'tidings' he brings, returns to their dreadfulness: 'But I have words.' There is a quick exchange with Macduff, who grows more and more excited and impatient until his feverish anxiety reaches the pitch of 'If it be mine...let me have it'. After this, when Ross, ready to broach his tidings, begins, Macduff is quieter, obviously suspecting and fearing what he is about to hear, and as Ross goes on, we see literally how he pulls his hat over his brows to hide his tears, and says nothing. We know this from Malcolm's words, but the effect of his presence there, what he does, and his silence, all this can only be conveyed by the actor.

There are two things to be noted here: first, the extent to which the tones of the human voice and its varying speeds as emotion changes them—everything in fact which we could call the music of speech—contribute a quality and significance which the printed words alone cannot give. And, secondly, we realize how much the presence of the actor, even when he says not a word, is effective. Such things are the actions, situations and gestures naturally used by the dramatist. We who read the plays should remember them. To leave them out, or to disregard them is to lose something of the effect which has been intended. Shakespeare was not only a poet, he was a dramatic poet, working for stage, actors and audience, as he knew them.

Let us therefore recall what goes into the making of a play: the writer of the text, whose life and world and ideas we have been considering; his text; the stage for which he wrote; the actors who play the roles written for them; all the various arts assembled in the performance; and lastly the audience, for whom writer, players and other artists work.

The Elizabethan stage

In spite of the labours of scholars on Elizabethan stages, we cannot be sure about many details in their structure. The contract for the Fortune Theatre (1600), to be built by Peter Street for Philip Henslowe and Edward Alleyn, specifies dimensions and materials, but does not say very much about the stage which was 'to be in all other proportions contrived and fashioned like unto the stage of the said playhouse called the Globe'. There are woodcuts in printed plays showing scenes performed on the stage, but these are artists' impressions. They were not intended to provide a picture accurate in every detail, and raise more problems than they solve. There is

Fig. 1. A reconstruction, based on the researches of Richard Southern, of a typical Elizabethan theatre, from the outside. The plan (top) shows the upper floor on the left, the ground plan on the right.

Fig. 2. The same theatre, from the inside, with a performance in progress.
Compare the drawing by De Witt (Plate III).

27

the drawing of the Swan Theatre on the Bankside made in 1596 by a Hollander who worked on the information given him by his friend de Witt, who had visited London and seen it. As public playhouses were unusual institutions to a foreigner they were one of the sights of London. It is difficult to understand in this well-known drawing who the people sitting in the *mimorum aedes* (the house of the actors) are, and what was their relation to what is taking place on the stage. As it was drawn by someone who had not himself seen the stage, helped by a friend whose memory might have been at fault, we can hardly expect it to provide a satisfactory picture for after times.

Shakespeare's plays were performed on various stages—the Elizabethan public theatres, at inns in London, in great halls, at court, in provincial towns. In thinking of his stage it is therefore best to consider only the most general features of the Elizabethan stage, those about which scholars are in agreement. Some of these are to be found in stages used in previous centuries.

Earlier stages

For several centuries before theatres were built in Europe strolling players—groups of actors, tumblers, dancers and jugglers— travelled from place to place performing improvised sketches and entertaining audiences with their tricks. In England strolling players set up their stages at the well-known London 'fairs', or markets, of Bartholomew, Southwark and Greenwich. They travelled to country 'fairs' too. Their stage was a platform of boards on trestles, raised high above the audience. Essentially this was all that was required for the performance of a play—an acting area in full view of an audience. The younger Dumas said that only four boards and a passion were needed: the four boards for the raised platform, and the 'passion'—the play, with the author's and the actors' emotional involvement in what they are engaged in putting before the audience.

In medieval times plays on religious subjects had been performed in churches and cathedrals. In order to enable the congregation to see them, raised platforms were specially constructed. As these plays increased in popularity, they moved out of church into church precincts. In 1311 the institution of a new church festival, Corpus Christi, celebrated on the Thursday following Trinity Sunday, gave an impetus to the guilds, the associations of workers and traders in medieval times, to undertake the production of plays illustrating events from Bible history. These plays continued till the end of the sixteenth century, though after the English Reformation their magnificence had gone.

They were performed on specially built structures, platforms which were sometimes elaborately furnished. There is a description of those used at Chester in 1594: 'Every company had his pageant or part, which pageants were a high scaffold with two rooms, a higher and a lower, upon four wheels. In the lower they apparelled themselves, and in the higher room they played, being all open on the top, that all beholders might hear and see them.' This was another stage known to Elizabethans.

Plays were performed throughout the sixteenth century in great halls, like the dining-halls of Oxford and Cambridge colleges and those of the professional bodies of lawyers in London—the Inns of Court. The inn-yard stage was yet another platform on which players performed. They were still in use in Shakespeare's time, and some of his plays were performed at Cross Keys Inn in Gracechurch Street in London. Their main features are worth noting for they contributed to the development of the stage of the English playhouse.

The inn-yard stage. The English inn in the sixteenth century (and later) was built round a yard used by vehicles and their passengers. The yard was surrounded on three or all four sides by a first floor gallery which communicated with the rooms for the guests. There was the main entrance to the yard from the road outside, and another from yard to the inn proper. A platform, projected into the yard and built opposite its main entrance, would give actors a playing area with plenty of room in front for the spectators, who either stood in the yard or watched the performance seated in the gallery. The inn itself provided a back-wall for the stage, and served as dressing-room for the actors; the gallery above could give another position on which the actors could perform. Here we have an early version of some of the features of the Elizabethan playhouse. On such stages actors performed in London and the provinces, and when the first London playhouse was built in 1576, it naturally incorporated some of the features of the inn-yard stage.

A performance of a play in Shakespeare's childhood

Before we enumerate some of the features which the Elizabethan public playhouse inherited from the older stages, it would be interesting to consider a record of a performance on one of the latter which took place when Shakespeare was a child. The extract which follows is well known, and provides evidence of the broad details of Elizabethan staging. Its writer, John Willis, was born in 1564, and he describes a performance he remembered seeing as a boy in Gloucester, which is not far away from Stratford, so any plays Shakespeare might have seen in his native town would have been of this kind:

In the city of Gloucester the manner is (as I think it is in other like corporations) that when players of interludes come to town they first attend the Mayor to inform him what noblemen's servants they are and so to get license for their public playing; and if the Mayor like the actors or would show respect to their lord and master, he appoints them to play the first play before himself and the aldermen and common council of the city, and that is called the Mayor's Play where every one that will comes in without money, the Mayor giving the players a reward as he thinks fit to show respect unto them. At such a play my father took me with him and made me stand between his legs as he sat upon one of the benches where we saw and heard very well. The play was called *The Cradle of Security*, wherein was personated a king or some great prince, with his courtiers of several kinds, amongst which three ladies were in special grace with him, and they keeping him in delights and pleasures, drew him from graver counsellors, hearing of sermons, and listening to good counsel and admonitions, that in the end they got him to lie down in a cradle upon the stage, where these three ladies joining in a sweet song rocked him asleep that he snorted again; and in the meantime closely conveyed under the clothes wherewithal he was covered, a vizard [mask] like a swine's snout upon his face, with three wire chains fastened thereunto, the other end whereof being holden severally by those three ladies, who fell to singing again, and then discovered [uncovered] his face that the spectators might see how they had transformed him, going on with their singing; whilst all this was acting there came forth of another door at the farthest end of the stage, two old men, the one in blue with a sergeant at arms, his mace on his shoulder, the other in red with a drawn sword in his hand, and leaning with the other hand upon the other's shoulder, and so they two went along in a soft pace [slowly] around by the skirt [edge, where there was a rail] of the stage, till at last they came to the cradle, when all the court was in greatest jollity, and then the foremost old man with his mace struck a fearful blow upon the cradle, whereat all the courtiers, with the three ladies and the vizard, all vanished, and the desolate prince starting up barefaced and finding himself thus sent for to judgment, made a lamentable complaint of his miserable case [fate], and so was carried away by wicked spirits. This prince did personate in the moral the wicked of the world, the three ladies, Pride, Covetousness, and Luxury; the two old men, the end of the world and the Last Judgment. This sight took such impression in me that when I came towards man's estate it was as fresh in my memory as if I had seen it newly acted (*Mount Tabor: Or Private Exercises of a Penitent Sinner*, 1639, pp. 110–14).

Willis was seventy-five years old when his book appeared. He described a moral interlude, an extremely popular form in the first half of the sixteenth century. Its serious subject-matter, its moral intention, its set debates, the personified virtues and vices as characters, were taken up and transformed by popular dramatists like Shakespeare when the moral interlude had gone out of fashion. Traces of it are to be found in the way characters in Elizabethan plays seem to represent some generalized abstraction. For instance, Richard II could well be thought of as a wanton young man.

It should be noted that Willis, writing of what took place in the late sixties presumably, describes the players as 'noblemen's servants'. By the second half of the century some groups of players had succeeded in obtaining the patronage of noblemen. Called their 'servants', or members of a nobleman's household, they could be thought of as their retainers. Some of them wore their lord's livery. This would give them status, protection from the law which otherwise could proceed against them as 'vagabonds', and the right to perform in certain places. The company to which Shakespeare belonged was that of the Lord Chamberlain, an important palace official. In 1603 King James I gave Shakespeare and various actors named the right 'freely to use and exercise the Arte and faculty of playing Comedies, Tragedies, histories, Enterludes, moralls, pastoralls, Stageplays...as well for the recreation of our loving Subjects as for our Solace and pleasure when wee shall thincke good to see them duringe our pleasure'. They were now the King's Men.

Some features of this performance

The broad open stage. From the older stages the Elizabethan playhouse derived the deep and broad stage which projected into the audience, round three sides of which the spectators stood. The stage at the Fortune projected 27½ feet into the yard. The 'yard' in which they stood is the term borrowed from the familiar inn-yard. No curtain separated stage from audience. In the description above, we see that the small boy stood between his father's legs as he sat on a bench, where 'they saw and heard very well'. In the Elizabethan playhouse, the favoured members of the audience (and those who paid more), were provided with seats in the galleries running round the playhouse, as in the old inn-yard.

The cellarage. Below the main stage was what was called the basement or cellarage, from which voices or persons might issue, and into which persons would 'disappear' or 'vanish'. In the extract above we note that some people 'vanished'. Did they use a trap-door? It is doubtful whether this could have been provided on the trestle stage of the inn-yard. In any case in the public play-house, where trap-doors were well known, they could hardly have taken six or seven people. Perhaps in his description of a play he had seen decades earlier Willis credited it with much more adroit staging than it was really given. The area below the stage was used in many Elizabethan plays. It must have been used in *Macbeth* for the disappearance of the cauldron, and also for the vanishing of the Weird Sisters.

Doors. There were doors at the 'farthest end of the stage' in Willis's description. These would have been the doors leading to the inn, or, if the play was given in the hall of a building, those from it to the other rooms. It is from these doors that the actor appeared as he came on the stage. As he walked across its whole width down-stage another actor already on the stage could draw the audience's attention to him. In the scene from *Macbeth* we have considered, we noted how Ross is seen arriving, so far back that he cannot immediately be recognized. All his friends could say of him is that he is wearing the clothes of a Scot.

Properties and costume. How would location be indicated on this stage? Willis writes of the play as being set in a court. Through the use of properties and hangings the easiest kind of verisimilitude could be provided. That the scene presented a court was surely made clear by the costume of the actors, the crown worn by the main character, and such things as a throne or chair of state.

There is a further point of interest. The scene probably changed from the presence chamber or hall, where the king heard good counsel and admonitions and listened to sermons, to his private room to which the three ladies enticed him. The cradle, an important property because it ironically illustrated the transformation of the king, now an infant in the power of the three sirens, would show that the stage now presents a bedroom or private apartment. The costume of the two men who appeared enabled Willis to identify them as End of the World and Judgement. The former with his sergeant's mace destroys the world and summons souls to judge-ment, Judgement himself carries the sword of Justice. When they speak their identity is confirmed. How readily and naturally figures from the life of the times (e.g. the sergeant or sheriff's officer) vitalize abstractions in moral play and allegory.

Processions. The deep Elizabethan stage lent itself to formal processions. When we remember that civic pageants, royal 'pro-gresses' (tours), shows, church festivals gave occasion for stately marches we see how the stage supplied an element of public taste.

Describing the two people who appeared on the stage, Willis writes: 'And so they went along in a soft pace around by the skirt of the stage, till at last they came to the cradle.' In other words they proceeded in their array, not straight to the cradle from the door at which they entered, but made a detour about the stage walking slowly by its rail, and so to the cradle which must have been in a central position. Judgement leans on End of the World's shoulder with his free hand, a symbolic gesture, showing the dependence of one on the other. These movements are reminiscent of the mode of entry of the chief characters on the Chinese stage, or the way in which the characters in the Japanese Kabuki play progress formally on the 'flower passage' by the side wall of the theatre, and eventually arrive on the main stage.

The flexibility of the stage. As the stage was not an area with settings intended to represent one particular place at one particular time, it could be any place at all, or even one place at one time, and immediately after some other place at some other time. As long as the cradle was on the stage, it could be the king's chamber or apartment; when the old men enter, some part of the stage would be the world through which these dread characters are stalking. When the procession reaches the cradle the whole stage is, once again, the chamber of the king.

This flexibility of the Elizabethan stage is important. The Elizabethan dramatist was not using the realism of our contemporary stage. Yet his audience would have no difficulty in accepting what was familiar to them. They had to make no special effort of the imagination to grant anything the dramatist, using the convention of the time, required. Nor would the dramatist feel that he was putting a special strain on his audience when he used the conventional means of indicating locality. For instance, on some Elizabethan stages it used to be the practice to affix boards to various parts of the stage announcing locality. But this was commoner on school and academic stages where classical comedy used to be performed. It is not likely that it was regular on the public stage. Dover Wilson, in his note to

34

The Comedy of Errors, suggested that that play was arranged for something corresponding to a classical stage, with doors labelled 'The House of Antipholus', 'The Street to the Bay', etc.

To Elizabethan spectators the way locality was indicated was probably not important. Certainly they went to the theatre both to hear and to see, as Willis is careful to point out. But we should not forget that the stage setting (scenery, etc.) was not like a picture, unvarying in every detail, and presented to an audience some distance away and entirely in front of the stage, as is the practice in modern theatres. The audience then was on three sides of the stage; they saw quite clearly from wherever they were, but they did not all see from the same viewpoint. What they saw was dramatically effective to them, but it did not have the realism of a picture or a photograph. The stage provided another kind of dramatic reality, which the audiences were accustomed to. This was given above all by the words the actors spoke and by such things as costume and properties which acted as visual aids. The words mattered more than anything else, and it is not strange that Marlowe, when he invited the audience in the prologue to his very successful play of *Tamburlaine*, should have said that they would '*hear*' the mighty Tamburlaine. They would certainly see him too, and see, too, the magnificence of the way in which he puts on the various crowns which symbolize his position as world conqueror drawn in his chariot by kings. But that he was a world conqueror would be proved much more effectively by his vauntings and by Marlowe's 'mighty verse' than by elaborate scenery, properties, lighting and sound-effects.

So the dramatic effect of the Elizabethan stage was created by the dramatist's power of words, and by his making use of the potentiality of that stage—its presentation of the actor in a position of vantage and speaking with a passion, in tones and gesture attuned to the part he was playing.

Soliloquy. One more reference to *The Cradle of Security* will show the importance of remembering another convention of the Elizabethan stage, and lend further weight to what has been said about the central importance of the actor speaking on that stage. Before the prince, or king, is finally 'carried away by wicked spirits'—an enactment of the Christian belief that this was the punishment of the wicked—he is alone on the stage. Here he speaks to the audience. He makes, in Willis's words, 'a lamentable complaint of his miserable case'. Here is the final underlining of the document of admonition the play must have been. The wretched prince, alone and 'barefaced', finding himself in the dire situation of one about to be judged, informs the audience of his plight. His words would be signed with the authority given to the last speeches of those about to die.

We have here the perfect naturalness of the Elizabethan soliloquy. The dramatic effect of the play, or the realism of its presentation, does not 'distance' the actor from the audience, holding him apart as something to be seen away from them. At all times it keeps him in touch with them as a person to be both seen and heard in their midst. On that stage it is only logical that the actor should address the audience, speak to it directly and take it into his confidence, for he was in the middle of it. As a result, what was spoken in these direct statements to the audience has to be taken as conveying the truth about the matter.

On a modern stage dominated by pictorial realism, where the actor appears to be part of a reconstruction of actuality, it is different. But in all folk drama, where there is a straight communication between actors and audience, the characters quite naturally address, exhort, and make jokes with the audience. The soliloquy, like much else in folk drama, should be seen as part of the 'realism' of its stage, and not as one of its awkward encumbrances. It is a vital part of the play.

The public theatre stages. Willis wrote of a performance given by a group of players who performed in an inn-yard, or hall, in a provincial town. His account does not enable us to see what stages on the London public theatres could provide. As there was no single type of theatre or stage, it is possible to speak only in the most general terms. In theatres like the Fortune and the Globe, to which reference has already been made, where three galleries apparently ran right round the building, and the 'tiring-house' (dressing-rooms) was an architectural feature of the building at the back of the main stage, there would be what would now be called a permanent set on the stage. There would be the galleries, the 'heavens' as they were called; the pillars supporting them; the 'shadow' or 'cover'—the canopy—which gave some protection to the players; and very probably beneath the gallery and at the back of the main stage a curtained recess with access to the dressing-rooms.

'*Inner stage*'. This curtained acting area has been called the 'inner stage'. The term was not used in Elizabethan times, but the frequency of the stage direction 'within' suggests such an acting area at the back of the main stage, separated from it by curtain or hangings. The strolling-players must have used a curtain stretched across the back of the platform, enabling them to change their costumes and to store properties out of sight of the spectators. This feature of early stages must have developed into the 'inner stage' of the public playhouse—the smaller acting area cut off from the main stage by a curtain ('arras') or hangings, which could be parted to reveal another scene or place set differently—very often a bed-chamber, or cave, or inner room. In *Othello* the stage direction in the Folio at the opening of 5. 2 is 'Enter Othello and Desdemona in her bed'. The bed on which Desdemona was asleep must have been at the back of the stage cut off from the main stage by a curtain, for at the end of the play (5. 2. 365–7) Lodovico says to Iago:

> Look on the tragic loading of this bed—
> This is thy work. The object poisons sight;
> Let it be hid.

Obviously at this point the curtain must have been drawn, and the bed on which Desdemona, Othello and Emilia lie dead cut off from the audience.

'*Upper stage*'. The stage direction 'above' would refer to the 'upper stage', either a platform raised higher than the main stage, or, on stages where this was an architectural feature, the gallery above the stage. The Swan drawing shows people seated in the gallery. Favoured spectators were often accommodated here. It was also used by musicians. When in the *Merchant of Venice* the quarto stage direction at 2. 6. 25 states 'Jessica above', she would have appeared on this 'upper stage'. Similarly, when in *Henry V* 3. 1 the Folio stage direction has 'Scaling ladders at Harflew', it is clear that these are intended to scale the walls of the besieged town, represented by the 'upper stage' on which the citizens are to appear in 3. 3. In *Richard II* 3. 3. 61 the Folio stage direction gives Richard an entry 'on the walls' of Flint Castle. He would have appeared with his train on the 'upper stage'.

Turret or hut. In some public playhouses there was a turret, or hut, above the gallery or galleries in which a few simple machines were placed, one of which must have been a crane, or hoists, with a chair, or some special piece of property, which could be lowered on to the main stage. Above this turret would fly a flag which announced to the citizens of London that a play was to be given that day. That stage machinery was used on the public and private stages is clear from Shakespeare's later plays. In *Cymbeline* (5. 4) the god Jove descends in thunder and lightning, sitting on an eagle, from turret to main stage where he addresses the sleeping Posthumus. We know that Ben Jonson in his Prologue to *Every Man in his Humour* is scornful of such things as the 'creaking throne' which descended on the main stage to the delight of the apprentices in the audience.

The machine, or crane, which lowered the actor on to the stage and drew him up again, was located in the turret, visually the most prominent feature of these Elizabethan public playhouses. In Visscher's drawing of London in 1616 we see in the foreground the polygonal structure of the Globe—the theatre where Shakespeare's plays were performed, and in which he owned a share—with a large flag flying from its turret.

A private theatre—the Blackfriars

In 1608 Shakespeare's company acquired the lease of the Blackfriars theatre, a private playhouse in the city, which up to that time had been used by a company of boy players. Here the King's Men, the company to which Shakespeare belonged, played in the winter months.

The main differences between the private and the public playhouses was that in the former the whole area of stage and auditorium was covered. In fact the private theatre was a large hall with a stage resembling that of the public theatres, but artificial lighting was used and stage properties and production were more elaborate. As higher rates of admission were charged at the private theatres, its audiences were not quite the same as those of the public theatres.

Properties on private and public stages

We have seen that properties were used by the players who presented *The Cradle of Security* in Gloucester. It is hardly possible to perform a play on a stage without them, and a number were used on Shakespeare's stages. Most of them were simple and necessary aids to the course of the action on the stage—the mirror for Richard in *Richard II* 4.1; a tree for the scene out of doors in *Twelfth Night* (Maria asks Sir Toby, Sir Andrew and Feste to get 'into the box-tree', 2. 5. 16); a cauldron for the Witches in *Macbeth*; the caskets in *The Merchant of Venice*; the wine and the tapers in *Julius Caesar* 4. 3, and so on.

Properties would also be used to suggest what the scene required—a throne making it clear that the stage is the 'presence chamber' where the king gave audience—as in *Henry V* 1. 2. Such properties, like some of those listed above, need not have been realistically designed or painted, for they were not going to be used on a stage which aimed at presenting a picture of life.

Noises off occur frequently in the plays—*Macbeth* has numerous examples of such things as bells, of thunder, of notes on trumpets.

These would have needed properties in charge, most probably, of the prompter.

As more and more money was spent on stage shows, particularly in the private theatres where lavish sets and spectacle gradually crept in, properties would become more elaborate. *The Tempest*, a play performed at Blackfriars Theatre and the Court, would have needed, among other things, a banquet in 3. 3. 19. How elaborately this was presented we do not know, but Sebastian (*The Tempest* 3. 3. 21) describes it as 'a living drollery'—a puppet-show resembling those given at the London fairs, but with live actors instead of marionettes.

Recent investigators have suggested that 'mansions' or 'houses' ('cunningly hinged frames—filled either with painted canvas or with curtains running on rods—fitted with cloth roofs or tops, and measuring about seven or eight feet in height') were used to represent in miniature whatever localized scenes the play called for: such as Brutus's tent in *Julius Caesar*; the tents of Richmond and Richard in *Richard III* 5. 3. The Elizabethan stage therefore was certainly not completely bare or unadorned.

Costume

The costume worn by the actors could be both rich and expensive. Sir Henry Wotton described a performance of Shakespeare's *Henry VIII* at the Globe in 1613, when the thatched roof of the theatre caught fire. It was presented 'with many extraordinary circumstances of pomp and majesty...the knights of the Order with their Georges and Garters, the Guards with their embroidered coats'. Thomas Platter who visited England from Switzerland in 1599 commented on the fine costumes worn by the actors: 'The actors are most expensively and elaborately costumed.'

Like properties, costume helped to build up theatrical illusion. But it did not always, as Wotton's description might suggest, make a point of historical accuracy. Shakespeare's Romans, for instance, did not wear Roman costume, as we shall see. Conventional details of costume and make-up would help in differentiating certain characters from others: Morocco 'all in white' in *The Merchant of Venice* must have had, in addition to his scimitar, something Moorish in his attire; Feste must have been in 'motley', the parti-coloured costume worn by the jester. In *The Tempest* the use of a special robe or cloak, according to the convention, made its wearer invisible. The craftsmen in *Julius Caesar* did not wear their conventional aprons, and this is remarked on by Marullus.

The colours of the materials used were often symbolical: that Malvolio should wear yellow stockings (a colour detested by Olivia) would denote that he was in love. Characters playing such roles as Rumour in 2 *Henry IV*, or the Prologue in *Henry V*, would wear conventional garb.

Not a primitive stage

We have now reached the point when we can see that the Elizabethan stage was not as primitive and ill-equipped as it has often been made out to be. Leaving out of consideration other stages known to Elizabethans, such as the special stages built for the production of masques at the court—stages on which elaborate spectacles were given to the accompaniment of music and dancing—we can say that the public playhouse provided Shakespeare with a medium full of resources which he, like any other dramatist trained in the theatre, knew how to exploit. That public playhouses were built in England (they were not known elsewhere in Europe in the sixteenth century except in Spain) shows that there was both a demand for plays and the existence of a tradition of playing which could satisfy it. Plays were performed elsewhere in Europe in the palaces of princes, in great halls, or out in the open, but a building intended for the performance of plays, which anyone who paid the rate of admission could enter, was not known in Europe until it was first built in England.

These playhouses were built by actors who were also good business men. They had, in spite of the patronage of the great, the opposition of the local government authorities to contend with, for plays were thought of as irreligious and licentious by Puritans, and players were among the lowest in the commonwealth. So all the public play-houses had to be built outside the city, for the city authorities would not allow them within the limits of their jurisdiction.

The illusion of reality

The Elizabethan public playhouse, like all other stages, whether we think of the classical Greek, the medieval Japanese, the ancient Indian, or the modern Chinese, had its own modes of creating the illusion of reality. What happened on it during the performance of a play was accepted as a representation of living persons and their actions in a particular place, this representation being governed by the known theatrical conventions of the time. On the Chinese stage, and in a great deal of Eastern folk drama, a masked and costumed actor appearing on the boards of the stage will tell us who he is and what he is about to do. Through those conventions, of the mask and the introductory speech, is established the kind of realism the play demands. So, too, on Shakespeare's stage, the dramatist, using the conventional means at his disposal, creates the representation of the world of the persons and the place he wants.

The conventional means used by Shakespeare on his stage differed from those in use today. The soliloquy (see p. 35), the aside, dialogue setting out what is shortly to happen on the stage—as at the opening of *Cymbeline*—the use of a chorus as in *Henry V*, set speeches of description or narration, were some of the conventions he used in common with other Elizabethan dramatists. Of course, Shakespeare used, too, the universal mode of producing the illusion of reality on the stage—through the use of costume, properties and the miming of his actors.

He is sometimes critical of his own practice. In his chorus in *Henry V* he apologizes for disgracing 'the name of Agincourt' by putting

<blockquote>
four or five most vile and ragged foils,
Right ill-disposed, in brawl ridiculous
</blockquote>

on the stage.

Criticism of the Elizabethan stage

Some of the criticism of the Elizabethan stage in its own time was the result of the desire of the critic for a greater degree of 'realism'. He was unable to accept the old convention that the platform on which the play is performed can be any place the dramatist wishes it to be. Sir Philip Sidney objected to contemporary plays on this ground:

For where the stage should always represent but one place, and the uttermost time presupposed in it should be...but one day, there is both many days, and many places, inartificially [crudely] imagined...where you shall have Asia of the one side, and Africa of the other, and so many other under-kingdoms, that the player, when he cometh in, must ever begin with telling where he is, or else the tale will not be conceived. Now ye shall have three ladies walk to gather flowers, and then we must believe the stage to be a garden. By and by we hear news of a shipwreck in the same place, and then we are to blame if we accept it not for a rock. Upon the back of that comes out a hideous monster, with fire and smoke, and then the miserable beholders are bound to take it for a cave....

If, like Sidney, we are troubled by the flexibility of the Elizabethan stage with regard to the localities it represents, our difficulties are partly due to editors of the text of Shakespeare from the eighteenth century onwards. They divided up the plays into acts and scenes, and gave careful directions for setting each scene. Shakespeare's texts have no such stage directions, and what is more, acting the plays right through without a break would have made the careful reconstruction of each scene division impossible. Take *Macbeth*—it opens with three women who speak of their meeting again on a heath, but there is no indication where they are now. When they next meet, we are to suppose that they have met on a heath. Indeed Macbeth asks (in 1. 3. 77) why they stop Banquo and himself 'upon this blasted heath'. The scene is, therefore, a heath, but no further stress is laid by Shakespeare on the actual spot. When Macbeth and his friends leave the stage and the king enters we know that we are now in the royal palace.

43

Where place and time are essential to his purpose, the dramatist will indicate them, as for instance later in *Macbeth* (3. 2. 40), where the onset of night is referred to. But to Shakespeare these lines were much more important than an indication of the time of day. They have much more to do with the evocation of the ambiguous world of evil they so powerfully suggest. The lines are there, not to make good the deficiencies of his stage, or even to make it clear that the darkness of night is gradually closing in, because these are the only means Shakespeare had at his command. Had he wanted to, he might have used another convention, that of having people arrive on the stage with torches or candles in order to show that it was dark (the plays were performed in the afternoons, in daylight). But he wrote his lines because he wanted them. They are there in order to create a poetic effect; they suggest through the reference to darkness another stage in the progress of the human being who has given himself to the spiritual darkness of evil. The poetry is there on its own account. It is both poetry and dramatic poetry. If it were mere added ornament, then dramatic effectiveness would suffer. There would be a break between the poetry the dramatist uses only to indicate what the scene or the time may be, and the rest of his medium.

It may be that it was much easier for people at the Elizabethan theatre to accept speech as the vital element in the play than it is for us at the present time. We are less ready in our reactions to speech. William Archer found it a fault in Elizabethan drama that its characters possessed a strangely unrealistic ability in speech. He praised what seemed to be the greater realism of the characters in late nineteenth and early twentieth-century plays, tongue-tied at climactic moments. Their silence was, to him, more realistic than the rhetorical blank verse periods of the Elizabethan.

Archer's objection, too, was framed in the name of realism. It is the same thing as asking whether it is natural that Macbeth should, when he is given the news of his wife's death, react to it in the way he does—with a magnificent passage of blank verse. Does this seem real? Is this the kind of thing which would come readily to any of us? Archer would feel that in a similar situation in real life the character would be silent, or hardly say more than a word or two.

Archer misdirected himself in his criticism of the characters of Elizabethan plays, for he looked at them as if they had to behave like people of his own time, reacting to their experiences as if they had been Edwardians. It is unlikely that we shall make this demand of the persons of Shakespeare's plays, but we should be on our guard against expecting from them consistent motivation according to our notions of behaviour.

Besides, Archer found Shakespeare unsatisfactory for not writing the type of play he was interested in. Archer wanted plays which were slices of contemporary life, with careful psychological probing into the characters of recognizable individuals. Shakespeare was not writing as Ibsen wrote. He used the psychological notions of his own time in presenting his figures on the stage. They are much more generalized, more types than characters in nineteenth-century plays and novels. The representation of reality Shakespeare was interested in did not depend on the projection of ordinary human beings on the stage. His themes are grander, his figures more impersonal, and his language more heightened than that of nine-teenth-century realist drama.

Elizabethan actors

The actors who presented the plays on the stage contributed something to them too. Legend has it that Shakespeare played Adam in *As You Like It* and the ghost in *Hamlet*. Whether he was good actor or bad, he is, in the plays, always alive to the transforming and creative power possessed by the player. In *Julius Caesar* Cassius, after the murder of Caesar, sees how this episode will live on stages all over the world, immortalized by the actor's genius:

> How many ages hence
> Shall this our lofty scene be acted over
> In states unborn and accents yet unknown!

45

If Shakespeare was thinking of their own production at the Globe in England, he was, with a good dramatic instinct, fulfilling his prophecy as soon as it was uttered.

The actor, or the player as he was called in Elizabethan times, was just beginning to acquire a social importance which, very slowly, enabled him to live down the bad name of his profession. Not until the end of the nineteenth century, however, did the actor in England succeed in clearing himself of this unsavoury reputation. Some players, like Shakespeare and Alleyn, did so well out of their playing and their financial interest in the theatre that they became respectable and wealthy, but most lived a hard life, like Robert Kempe who played many of the clowns in Shakespeare's earlier plays.

Companies of players. Each company would have its actors who were cast in the roles which best suited them, some of these being so typical that they could be thought of as stock parts. An Elizabethan company was not big enough to provide as many players as there would be parts in the play, so doubling of parts was frequent. The actor would not therefore be unduly restricted to the one stock part. In organized companies there would be a hierarchy similar to that of the trade guilds with a master who knew the craft, journeymen and apprentices. Masters would be actors of senior status, as Burbage was in Shakespeare's company—permanent members of the company who, besides playing the chief roles, had a share in the business. Journeymen were those who had graduated from being apprentices, but had yet to acquire more experience. They were generally players hired from time to time. Last of all were the young men and boys still in training.

Their training. Actors were professionals who had from an early age studied their craft under accredited masters. By the time their experience qualified them to hire their skill to a group of players they would have received a practical training in all the varied activities of a theatre. As actors they would have been trained in speech, in movement, in dancing, in singing, in music, and in acrobatics.

The English actors of this time were renowned for their talents,

46

and wherever they travelled in Europe they were a sensational success, even though most foreigners did not understand a word of what they were saying. There is a record in the chronicle of the city of Münster in Germany—26 November 1599—which deals with the visit to the town of eleven young English players. They spent five days there, and gave five plays in English. They played on several musical instruments like the lute, cithern, fifes, and pipe. They danced many kinds of new dances at the beginning and the end of their plays. Their fool, who knew a bit of German, made the crowd laugh with his jests and his interruptions of the actors. The chronicle ends with a remark on the money they made during their five days' stay, charging one shilling for admission. Another reference to their popularity in Germany speaks of their drawing greater crowds than the preachers, people preferring to stand for four hours at their shows to spending one hour sitting in the church, dozing on the hard benches. (Similar remarks made of the players in England show that the popular preachers regarded them as dangerous and formidable rivals.)

Their popularity must have been due, not only to the splendour of their costumes, often commented upon, but to their song and dance, their skill in all the branches of acting, and to their use of a language of gesture which, though it did not compensate for the German audience's ignorance of English, could yet make clear what the play was about to those who knew the bare outlines of the story. One part of their ability, their elocution as we would call it now, would be lost on a foreign audience because it had to do with the management of voice in speaking English. Actors were trained in the art of speaking. Their delivery was likely to be more florid and more carefully produced than that of the ideal recommended for the orator of the time, because theirs was intended for the stage. Rhetoric, which included both composition and the art of speaking, was a subject in schools. Those who had had some schooling, and even those who had not, but who listened to the preachers, would have been able to appreciate this part of the actor's accomplishment.

Gesture. Another part of the actor's study was the language of gesture. The motions of the hands, the use of the body, feet, head, and eyes, were all carefully studied and described, so that there was a gesture appropriate to every mood, and even to particular persons, all of which would be known and understood. Those who know formal dance modes, like ballet and the Indian *Bharata Natyam*, will know how expressive gesture can be, and how carefully it is differentiated, and how the test of the performer is in his execution of the conventional mode. When in *Bharata Natyam* the dancer places her fingers in a certain position we know at once what she intends to convey; so on the Elizabethan stage the player would reveal his mood, not only by the tones of his voice and the delivery of his words, but also by the gesture suited to it.

It was the actor's business to train himself in formal gesture and to develop finish and style in it. This language of gesture might seem to us both unnatural and over-conventionalized. But as it had meaning, and was considered appropriate and 'decorous' (that is, fitting), it was used quite naturally by the Elizabethan actor as part of the 'realism' of his performance. Gesture can still vary very much from culture to culture. How would we call someone to us? If we used a hand to beckon to a person, would we raise it, palm facing us, and move the fingers held upwards back towards us? Or would we turn the palm outwards, holding the fingers down, and so move them towards us? In the East we might offend the person we called if we used the first gesture. It might be resented in democratic Australia too. Would most people in the West attract the attention of someone by clapping? This would seem queer and unaccountable behaviour in England, but quite normal in India and Ceylon.

So gesture and speech on the Elizabethan stage would not be natural according to our notions of the word 'natural'. It is very likely that if it were possible for us to hear Shakespeare spoken and acted as the Elizabethan actor did it, we should think the performance unbearable. So when we read of Burbage in Flecknoe's *Short*

Discourse of the English Stage (1664) that 'he was a delightful *Proteus*, so wholly transforming himself into his Part, and putting off himself with his Cloathes, as he never (not so much as in the Tyring-House) assum'd himself again until the Play was done', we ought not to expect that he played his roles according to our notions (or Stanislavsky's) of how the characters he portrayed would behave. What he gave to his roles belonged to the notions of speech and gesture appropriate to them at his time. These were very different from ours.

There is a scene in *Hamlet* which forcibly convinces us of what the actor's art must have been in Elizabethan times. Let us look at the lines. Hamlet has had the players provide a sample of their skill, and the first player continues the speech which Hamlet has begun 'with good accent and good discretion', as Polonius puts it. When the player concludes, Polonius draws attention to the fact that he is in tears and that the passion he has simulated has made him pale. The praise Hamlet gives the players is that they are 'the abstracts and brief chronicles of the time', that is, a play can succinctly present to us the people of an age through the actor's skill. When he is alone, he calls up for us a picture of the actor speaking the lines which so moved both of them—actor and spectator:

> this player here,
> But in a fiction, in a dream of passion,
> Could force his soul so to his own conceit
> That from her working all his visage wanned,
> Tears in his eyes, distraction in his aspect,
> A broken voice, and his whole function suiting
> With forms to his conceit.... (*Hamlet* 2. 2. 554–60)

As Hamlet saw it, the actor's imagination ('conceit') so worked on him that he grew pale, tears started in his eyes, he looked distracted, and his voice broke. His 'whole bearing or action during the performance' ('function'), his 'gesture and facial expression' ('forms') were in accord with his imagination of the part.

Now this might seem to be as good a rule of how a role should be conceived and played by the actor as anything we know in the naturalist method of Stanislavsky. But it is important to note that we are not told *what* action, gesture or facial expression seemed to the actor appropriate to the role. Nor is it likely that the Elizabethan actor thought of the person telling the tale of the fall of Troy as a character in the real life of Trojan times, as Stanislavsky would have done. Action, gesture and facial expression on the Elizabethan stage were much more likely to have been formal and conventional than naturalistic.

Besides all this, the Elizabethan actor would have had to be expert in fencing, and a fair acrobat. Duels are a feature of action on the stage in the plays. Indeed, most battles resolve themselves into encounters between two combatants, as *Macbeth* shows.

Stock parts. There were stock parts for members of the company: the chief roles of the tragedian; the chief comic character. Shakespeare had Burbage for his chief tragic roles and two versatile players, Kempe and Armin, in some of his best-known comedies. Kempe combined skill in dancing with a talent for buffoonery; Armin, who succeeded him, was a singer and composer, and is likely to have played Feste in *Twelfth Night*, a part which bears traces of its player's singing genius. Among comic characters there were those who tended to pair off through some oddity of physical appearance; for instance, the fat man, whether he was really corpulent or only padded out to look enormous, and the incredibly thin figure of a man (Sir Toby Belch and Sir Andrew Aguecheek in *Twelfth Night*). Then there were the rustics who belonged to the lowest stratum of life, and had to be differentiated from the noblemen and gentlemen. Often in Shakespeare's plays the ordinary man gives a feeling of greater depth and roundedness to plays which would otherwise be confined to courts and the great houses of nobles. We shall notice this particularly in the history plays. Then there are the 'humour' characters (in both the Elizabethan sense of the over-development of a single trait and also the modern sense of the laughable), and the national types like Jamy, MacMorris, Fluellen and Gower in *Henry V*.

Boy players. Last of all there were the women, played throughout the sixteenth century and up to Restoration times in the seventeenth century by young boys and the younger journeymen. The boys, of whose prowess we read in *Hamlet*, had it in them through their training and their natural grace to give Shakespeare's women all he wanted of them. They were skilled in speech, in mime, and in grace of movement.

Perhaps those who believe that Shakespeare expressed a deep knowledge of the psychology of women are logical in insisting that his women should be played by mature actresses, but it seems more likely that the young boy player could provide just as much as Shakespeare expected of him. That men and boys should play female roles would seem today, except in school performances, a blemish on the performance. It was normal practice then, as it is in folk plays in the East, and on the classic Japanese and Chinese stages.

It would be wiser if we did not involve ourselves in the modern psychological appraisal of the characters of women, but remembered that what Shakespeare would naturally demand of his boy player would be what that player could obviously give to the interpretation of his role. The lines he gave his player to speak would have to be rendered with all the skill expected of him. That it could, or should, contain much more than we, or even the Elizabethan, believe could be conveyed by voice, gesture and bearing, was the result of Shakespeare's art. We shall find this not only in the lines he gave his boy players, but in those he gave his chief actors, the adult males in his company.

In the repertoire of roles for the boy player there were stock parts too. There was the soft-voiced, gentle woman, like Portia in *Julius Caesar* and Cordelia in *King Lear*. There was her opposite—the shrew or the termagant, the woman who was assertive and wished to rule instead of accepting, as she should, the rightful overlordship of the male. Such were Katherine in *The Taming of the Shrew*, and Margaret in *Richard III*. Then there were all the young women who put themselves in men's attire—a frequent device in Elizabethan drama. As the women were played by boys it was a pleasant irony to have a double pretence. There were the clever and witty women; and there were specifically boys' parts like Ariel or the diminutive pages, Moth in *Love's Labour's Lost* and Falstaff's page in 2 *Henry IV*.

Song

Another excellence was associated with the boy players, and particularly with the boys who were members of the choir schools—their singing. Two groups of such boys—the Children of the Chapel Royal and the Children of Paul's—performed plays with great success at the court and privately in London. Their success threatened the prosperity of the companies of players at the public theatres. Lyly and Jonson wrote plays for these boy players.

It is proper to consider here how naturally and frequently the Elizabethan play uses song and assumes the existence of a culture of song in both players and audience. How natural it was in the Elizabethan home we see in books of a practical nature which instructed the Elizabethan. There is one such book, the dialogues of a Huguenot refugee called Hollyband, who taught French and composed conversation manuals in order to give practice to his pupils. In one of these dialogues, describing the citizen at home, the father asks: 'Roland, shall we have a song?' to which Roland replies, 'They bee in my chest...you shall find them in a little til at the left hand.' When he asks who is to sing with him, Father says: 'You shall have companie enough: David shall make the base: Jhon the tenor: James the treble.' So they sing and agree that it is a good song. One of the guests present says, 'I do marvell who hath made it', to which Father answers, 'It is the maister of the children of the Queenes chapel...Maister Edwards'. Of him Father says: 'Truelie it is pitie [that he is dead]: he was a man of good wit, and a good poete: and a great player of playes.' Richard Edwards, who was Master of the Children of the Chapel Royal from 1561 to 1566, wrote plays for them. He was one of the persons to whom the

'Children' owed their skill in song and their vogue as professional actors.

To some extent the readiness of a people to sing depends on a lack of sophistication, on the presence of a tradition in which the professional singer is not clearly distinguished and set apart from a general public not very familiar with song. This is something which apparently tends to dry up as we get more and more civilized. People used to sing at work in the fields, they knew what their fathers and mothers sang throughout the year at their work and at play, and singing became a part of their lives. Some of the strongest emotional associations of their life in the community are bound up with song. We still have the chance of observing this in communities where new techniques have not yet driven out older ways of life.

The Elizabethan play is full of this kind of popular song. There is hardly a character of any resourcefulness in Shakespeare, but we shall see that he knows tags of old song and can use them appositely. Falstaff, Hamlet, the fool in *Lear*, Sir Toby, Feste, Autolycus in *The Winter's Tale*, all share in this. They occur spontaneously in Shakespeare's plays, and we find him using songs dramatically to get contrasts and stresses into his themes in a way that is effective and economical.

There are a number of things to be noted of Shakespeare's songs: their words; their relevance to the action; and the skills required of the performer. All these have their part to play in the drama, and are as important as anything else in it. Song is no more tossed in for the pleasure it gives the audience than Shakespeare writes some fine poetry to keep them quiet.

The classic instance of the integration of song and drama is in *The Merchant of Venice*, where the song 'Tell me where is fancy bred' is sung while Bassanio is left on the stage to make up his mind about the caskets. It is no interlude, but moral example to which he listens. Had it been merely an occasion for the skill of an entertainer, something would have been wanting in the meaning and point of the scene. Bassanio chooses the leaden casket because 'the whilst (he) comments on the caskets to himself' (as the stage direction has it), he is supported in his train of thought by the song. It is perhaps more dramatic than if he had been told what to do by a character called Good Counsel, as might have happened in a morality play.

Song is used dramatically in *Twelfth Night* to reveal the attitudes of one character to the others. Feste, who sings to the Duke in 2. 4 a song very different from its description as an unsophisticated ditty sung by girls making bobbin-lace, hints at the Duke's romantic melancholy. The snatches of ballads and songs from jigs, sung by Sir Toby and Feste in 2. 3 deliberately to anger and fool Malvolio, would at once have made clear to the audience that the words and tunes they sang were intended as an attack on the Puritan's scorn of popular merriment.

Dance

Shakespeare's actors were trained dancers too. The Elizabethan actor in the words of a book published in 1616 was noted for his 'dancing, activity (acrobatics), music, song, elocution'. Dance entered so naturally and frequently into the life of courts that if the player had been ignorant of the formal dance of the time he would not have been able to perform in Elizabethan plays. Dance is frequent in Shakespeare's plays: in *Love's Labour's Lost*, in *Much Ado About Nothing*, in *Romeo and Juliet* formal dance helps the dramatic action.

One of the plays, 2 *Henry IV*, had an Epilogue which was spoken by a dancer, and the play ended with a dance. The jig, a dialogue with song and dance, was a popular form, which developed into an after-piece at the public playhouses. We shall see how Platter, who was present at a performance of *Julius Caesar* at the Globe Theatre, was greatly impressed by the dance which followed the play.

Would the parts as Shakespeare wrote them have been specially intended for the actors who were going to play them? This is so commonplace in theatres that it is difficult to believe, for instance, that Shakespeare, knowing he had a Burbage as the chief actor of tragic roles, did not have him in mind when he wrote his plays.

54

To grant this is far from assuming that the lines in the play were there because Shakespeare wrote the part for Burbage. No single cause would decide this. As the actors were there, Shakespeare would write for them.

The actors in the plays must have left a great impression on the minds of their audiences, as one reference will show. Many years after both Shakespeare and Burbage were dead, the poet Richard Corbet relates how the guide who conducted him over Bosworth Field, where the battle which ended in the defeat of Richard III was fought, pointed out the very spot where Burbage had cried, 'A horse! A horse! My kingdom for a horse!' The resounding line and the actor's performance in the title role made him the living person for the guide and not the historical king.

5. SHAKESPEARE'S AUDIENCE

As important as the actors of the plays were their audiences. It is difficult to believe that Shakespeare, a popular dramatist who made money by his plays, did not consider those who paid their pennies and their shillings to see and hear them. There were plays written at the time which were not intended to be performed before audiences but only to be read. There were other plays intended for special audiences at schools and universities, but Shakespeare's were written for the common audience of that time. The plays were popular, so whether Shakespeare, in our phrase with its derogatory senses, gave his public what it wanted, or not, it paid to see his plays.

People at the plays

First of all: who composed the audiences at Shakespeare's plays? There were a number of audiences for Shakespeare's plays. We know that some of the plays were given at one or other of the royal palaces, and that at the court of both Elizabeth and James I were noblemen and courtiers who at least knew the plays. Court audiences would include the most eminent, and among them the most highly educated, people in the realm.

We know, too, that some of the plays were performed at one or other of the Inns of Court (the 'colleges' in London which provided a legal training and were virtually the third university). Whether they were specially commissioned for these occasions or not, they would draw audiences composed almost entirely of professional lawyers, courtiers, and their guests. The plays were performed, too, at the great houses of noblemen who were patrons of the arts, or who wished on special occasions to present or enjoy a dramatic performance. *A Midsummer Night's Dream* was probably played in some nobleman's hall. On such occasions, and at the two universities of Oxford and Cambridge, the audiences would be largely composed of the well educated.

At the public theatres of London, like the Globe, which was built by the Burbages, would be found all those who belonged to the population of a capital city—a small town by present-day standards, but still the great city of the kingdom. In these audiences there would be a sprinkling of the nobility and the gentry, there would be the citizenry, the young apprentices who often played truant to go to the theatre, and a goodly section of the crowd to be found in a port—some foreigners, and a fair section of characters from low life. Most of these members of the audience would have been, by our tests, illiterate. Some of them would be there not so much to see the play, as to take advantage of the chance to ply their trade among the crowds drawn to the theatre—pickpockets, thieves, prostitutes and all the other low-life characters mentioned by the preachers who denounced plays.

It would be true, therefore, to say that the audiences of Elizabethan plays included almost every stratum in the population of the larger towns of England. And as these towns, like London, were continually drawing people from the country, and even the remote country, practically every element in the population of the nation might be found in the audiences of the public theatres at the end of the sixteenth century and the beginning of the seventeenth. (The only people not to be found there would be those who objected to playgoing on religious grounds.) People from the countryside, where there were no theatres, would know folk-plays, would have seen processions and shows, and would have taken part in games and festivities which had a markedly dramatic character, so that to go to a 'theatre' in a town like London would mean not so much a completely new mode as something fairly familiar in a new setting. Certainly the London theatre was a new thing. It was so new and surprising that as we have noted it was one of the sights of the town which visitors from Europe had to see. What the countryman would see there would be different from what he already knew—in so far as a play of Shakespeare's differs from a moral interlude or the last lingering remnants of a Miracle play. But it would not be totally strange to him.

In short, theatre-going was popular, or indeed universal, entertainment in the seventeenth century. Ben Jonson, in commendatory lines prefaced to the play of a friend, refers to the various people who were to be found in theatre audiences: gamester, captain, knight, knight's man or servant, lady, woman of doubtful reputation, shop's foreman, brave sparks. All of them having paid to see the show sat in judgement on the life and death of plays.

As there are no statistics available we cannot say what proportion of the population went to plays 350 years ago. The closing of the theatres in 1642 after the Puritan revolution is an indication of their hold on the populace, and their threat to the moral order which Puritanism was determined to maintain.

What the plays provided

Ben Jonson, who, like Shakespeare, was a man of the theatre with experience of a number of stages, praises Shakespeare as a popular dramatist, the man whose plays drew crowds to the theatre: 'The applause! delight! the wonder of our Stage!' The audiences at Shakespeare's plays were drawn to the plays by one, or all, of the many things provided by them. There was a great deal of action which must have been both exciting and dramatically important. The plays are full of duels as we have noted. There is a wrestling match in *As You Like It*, scenes of fighting in the streets in *Romeo and Juliet*, a riot in *Julius Caesar*. Ghosts and the supernatural were another element which must have appealed strongly—the ghost in *Hamlet* was a memorable figure and was often referred to in the literature of the time. Audiences accustomed to the show and pageantry of stately processions, as accounts of the reception of foreign notabilities and the sovereign in London and other cities prove, would have their appetite for spectacle gratified by the attention paid to ceremonial processions in the plays. From *Titus Andronicus* to *Henry VIII* Shakespeare uses the opportunities provided for solemn and dignified movement on the stage. The close of *Hamlet*, with the four captains bearing Hamlet's body off the stage to the accompaniment of 'the soldier's music and the rite of war', shows how dramatic such spectacle can be. There was a great deal of clowning, which called not only for acrobatic skill and miming, but also for witty speech. There is a long list of clowns, jesters, fools, comic serving men like Lancelot Gobbo in *The Merchant of Venice*, to be found in Shakespeare's plays. Some of the jests of the clowns may seem unintelligible now, but there is no doubt that the role was a popular one, for in his advice to the players Hamlet warns the clown not to indulge in such tricks as laughing simply to set some people in the audience laughing too. Popular drama, such as Shakespeare's, must have had all that life of excitement, laughter, violence and spectacle which appeals to our physical senses.

But were these the only things which brought them to the theatre? Were the tastes of most people in the audience like those Hamlet scornfully attributed to Polonius: that he enjoyed only a play with something bawdy in the plot or a jig ('He's for a jig, or a tale of bawdry, or he sleeps', *Hamlet*, 2. 2. 504)?

58

The words of the play

If this were so Shakespeare's audiences would have had to endure a great deal of poetry, of speech, of dialogue between the characters on the stage, for there was very much more of this than of the fireworks, the knock-about and violence. The words of the play—its text—were its largest part, and indeed it is through its medium of dialogue that a play differs from other forms of art like dance or novel. All three can tell you a story, but what marks a play is the fact that movement and life are given through the words spoken by the actors—the dialogue. Shakespeare used words because they were his rightful medium. Action, spectacle, song, may have been extraordinarily diverting, but a play stands or falls by virtue of its words.

Shakespeare uses his words as a poet, as a poet of his time, and as an ordinary man who shares with his audience an attitude to words, an enjoyment of them, and facility in them which changes in our way of life have largely destroyed today. We can readily understand that such attitudes and interests were common among the educated in this time. But that the ordinary person at that time had something of this ability might require a little explaining.

The 'educated' playgoer

To take the 'educated' playgoer first of all: we can, perhaps, see where their education tended, if we reflect on the great difference between our education and that of the sixteenth and seventeenth centuries.

A large number of us still receive what is called a literary education; it has to do with words, but not so much with the spoken word as with the written word—the texts we study, the books on these texts which we read. Good or bad though literary education may be, it is our ability to read and write and to think through the skills of reading and writing which makes the difference between those of us who succeed, and those who are merely average. But in Elizabethan times the key which opened all doors—apart from accidents of birth, favouritism, etc.—was one's ability in speech, the power of words one possessed and could use as a speaker. The boy in grammar school was trained in writing and in composition too, but it was in speech that the young scholar could show his pre-eminence. There were few careers, in the sense in which we know the word today, open to young men who went up to university from grammar school, and had nothing to depend on but their talents. But those which existed turned on whether the young man—as priest, as lawyer, or in the diplomatic service—could handle speech convincingly and persuasively. All those branches of learning which we know now as 'science' did not belong to the courses of study at a university. As for teaching, the Church controlled the best posts in the profession. Those who went from university to teach as 'gentle-men ushers', or assistant teachers, certainly did not think of them-selves as being successful. Those who had ability, and again this would mean ability in speech or writing, might hope to attract the notice of some noble and obtain preferment through him.

That there should have been this test of a man's ability is not strange, for education at a time when printed books were still not readily available, and when knowledge was communicated orally, had to depend on the student's powers of speaking, arguing, dis-puting and persuading. One survival of the old medieval and Renaissance practice is still found in European universities, where the degree of doctor is not awarded until the graduate is questioned in public on his thesis, and is expected to support, by his answers to questions and his argument, the case he has made out in his written work. Medieval education was comprehended in four branches of knowledge which required skill in speech. Degree examinations took the form of disputations, where the candidate was given a subject on which he had to argue.

Exercises like these played a large part in the school curriculum. Such a discipline would not seem very different from the ancient and medieval Indian for instance. It laid the same stress on speech, and on learning by rote. It was conservative, it admired philosophical speculation, and it found no place for any training in handicrafts, manual skills or technical knowledge. Without taking the resemblance too far we could say that in the East at the present time there is just as much interest as there used to be in Elizabethan times in such things as oratory, and persuasive speech, largely because less of the old has been destroyed in the field of education.

Books were part of education in the sixteenth century, certainly. The classical authors were read, and their modes of writing were formally studied. The schoolboy would have his attention directed to the figures of speech used by the poet and the orator, he would be made to try them out in his own writing and speech, so that familiarity with the best models could be expected to improve his own mode of speech and writing. Though this discipline seems dry and formal, it should be remembered that it was used for the practical purpose of improving the learner's own skills. Carrying over what was learnt in Latin to composition in a living and developing language like English would remove a great deal of the profitless memory work involved. The writer (or the speaker) would not be wasting his time copying, he would be exercising himself in a medium which gave him opportunities for originality.

In the last 150 years, with the development of industrial processes, there has been such a mass diffusion of reading-matter that the reading of those times becomes so different from ours in degree that it must be thought of as an entirely different kind. When we speak of reading now, or when we ask for something to read, most of us probably think of fiction. But reading to Shakespeare's contemporaries would not have meant that at all. They would have read romances, but these would not belong to the same category as fiction today. They would also have read poetry, sermons, philosophy, translations from the classics and from contemporary European languages, especially Italian, history, the records of voyages, and some miscellanea. Reading of this kind would certainly call for more vigilance, more attention to the word than is at present given in the reading of novels.

The 'uneducated' playgoer

As for the 'uneducated', we should remember that the word today most often means those who have not had the education provided in a school. It is easier for those who do not live in an industrial civilization to understand that there are 'educated' people who have had no schooling, but have gained traditional knowledge and skills from the life they have led. To have spent six or seven years at school is a matter of legal compulsion now, but it is neither proof nor test of education.

The 'uneducated' Elizabethan was much more dependent on the spoken word than his educated counterpart today. The life he lived gave the Elizabethan some training in the ability to listen to words and to be interested in their use. Information, controversy, political opinions, and philosophical speculation were transmitted not by radio, newspaper and television, but through the spoken word in public square, pulpit, theatre. Two decades ago when a king of England abdicated, newspaper and radio informed people of what was happening. Contrast this with the arrangements being made in *Richard III* to ensure the succession of Richard, duke of Gloucester, to the English throne. Buckingham will 'play the orator' and secure the allegiance of the mayor and the corporation of London; for the rest, preachers at various positions in the city would present the case to the people. It might be objected that there seems to be some similarity of intention in these different approaches to the populace. We can, however, without discussing this, state that there is a difference between following an argument in a sermon and listening to an announcement on the radio.

The part played in Shakespeare's plays by arguments, special pleading, debate, effective turns of speech, the cut and thrust of speakers quarrelling, or determined to score off each other, should be remembered. For instance, the opening of *Richard II* is a series of angry speeches, of persons defying and accusing each other in a strain of eloquence which quite obviously appealed to the audience.

Hamlet in his soliloquies addresses the ordinary Elizabethan play-goer, and the Archbishop's long exposition of the Salic law in *Henry V* is an important part of a play which must have been popular, because it was described as 'sundry times played by the Right honourable the Lord Chamberlaine's servants'. In the comedies we shall see how much depends on the wit of his main characters, on a professional jester, or clown, who wears the garb of fool, but is paradoxically wiser than most of the others in the play, and on characters from low life who seem to have all the flexibility of speech of their betters. The language is so deftly united with the turn of the plot and the amusement of the situations that we cannot say 'let's take out the witty language which seems difficult, and then we shall have a manageable unit'. Present-day English productions of the comedies, sensing that the audience is going to be in difficulty with the 'wit', often romp through the play with some advertised novelty as justification for the production, the words being given at such high speed that there is no telling what has been said, though the audience is conscious through its style and gesture that it must have been fine and elegant. It may be claimed in extenuation that the commercial theatre generally has some difficulty in drawing people to a play of Shakespeare's.

The Elizabethan audience, boisterous, restless, 'nut-cracking', or interested in private amours—we are given all these descriptions of it by contemporary writers—would surely not have stood for long plays like Shakespeare's, not even if there was always hope that in a minute there would be some rough and tumble on the stage, some hair-raising thrill, or some lewdness from the clown. Would it be wrong to believe that what they were given in the theatre was what they were, on a slightly different level, accustomed to in life around them? Let us not forget that popular 'entertainment' included listening to sermons. In fact, a play might be a sermon, and there are descriptions of Elizabethan plays which show how plainly they are regarded as moral allegory. Sermons then were an important part of open-air social events, but the opponents of the theatre—the divines and the Puritans—felt that people at their time were tending to prefer the theatre to sermons.

Consider the great appeal of the public speeches in such plays as *Julius Caesar* and *Coriolanus*, of the numerous trial scenes in the plays with the addresses of the participants in the case, of set pieces of debate, of dying speeches. All these naturally belong to a culture where speech was valued and ability in it highly esteemed. In some of these cases the dramatist seems to be saying how easy it is to influence the crowd through some specious argument, or some emotional appeal, but still we see that, though crowds might have been notoriously fickle and unstable, they were receptive to the spoken word, and were prepared to listen to and enjoy the masterly orator.

We have already referred to the dialogues of the Huguenot refugee with their description of the English family at home, and their four-part singing. The family was in good circumstances, and its members were certainly not illiterate. We see in these dialogues some of the activities of the Englishman of that time. The son sets out for school; father and his friends go out to see the Maypole which has been set up in the town with the usual merrymaking which accompanied it. There is a wedding procession in the street, and learning that it is on its way to Saint Paul's, father and his friends follow, for, after the wedding, there will be a sermon at Paul's Cross. This reference is most interesting, for with the rites of May and a social event like a wedding, a sermon is quite naturally linked. Listening to them, was, on this evidence, as popular an entertainment as either of the others. The sermons, and the Elizabethan homilies, strongly influenced not only the way people wrote, but also their background of imagination, for the preacher was providing for the public benefit knowledge, news, admonition and education.

It would be wrong, therefore, to think of Shakespeare's audience as a rough set of groundlings who forced the greatest poet in the world into giving them what they wanted, so preventing him from being the greatest artist in the world as well. It would be more reasonable to think of Shakespeare as a popular artist and a popular dramatist. He could have been neither had he not shared a great deal with his audience.

6. HOW SHAKESPEARE WROTE

Shakespeare and dramatic tradition

Shakespeare must have begun writing for audiences early in the 1590's, for the first records of payments made to players for the performance of plays later claimed to be his—such as the three parts of *Henry VI*—occur in 1592.

How would a young man at that time—or at any other time—have begun to write except by working upon what others had written? We are creatures of our environment, and how we write belongs as much to how others at the time are writing as to our own decided notions of what we want to do. There is no writer, even the most original, who in his beginnings does not write in one of the established modes of the time. The young writer will tend to write as one or the other of his great contemporaries has written. It is interesting to see how the writing of the young in the East, whether we look in India or in Japan, is what it is because Eliot and Joyce have written in certain ways.

So Shakespeare would write like one of those contemporaries of his who had developed an individual style and made his own reputation. In the drama that was filling the London 'theatres' there were two contemporaries of his, not much older than himself, who had already made a reputation for themselves and had achieved an individual medium of expression: Kyd and Marlowe.

Thomas Kyd's *The Spanish Tragedy* (1589) was one of the great popular successes of the Elizabethan stage. Its exciting story of murder and revenge, and much more strikingly its impassioned speech, its ghosts, and its Machiavellian character Lorenzo made it one of the most memorable plays of its time. Christopher Marlowe's hero Tamburlaine and his 'high-astounding terms' have already been referred to. Marlowe's success as poet and dramatist, the beauty of his flexible verse line, his interest in the figure of the man with an aspiring mind, the grim sardonic humour of some of his characters could not have failed to impress a young poet and dramatist. In his early plays Shakespeare must have gone to school to playwrights like Kyd and Marlowe.

The young Shakespeare must have so easily and naturally picked up their way of doing it that Robert Greene, writing in 1592, is probably referring to him as 'an upstart crow, beautified with our feathers', who, unabashed at being an actor, actually had the arrogance to believe he could write like his educated betters. Greene's words show the exasperation of the university man at the conceit of the player who imagined he could write. It is clear that Shakespeare was writing very successfully as his betters wrote, or Greene would not have been outraged. Shakespeare's success shows that he had something more than a dull repetitive talent. Most of us, when it comes to writing, may be able to produce something in the current mode, but only a few can do it so well that it could sting an established writer into protest at unfair competition.

A large number of plays at that time were put together by the revision of older plays. A play might be the joint work of two or three people, who either worked together throughout, or divided it between them. Shakespeare might, through his apprenticeship as 'botcher' (mender of plays), or through collaboration with others, have learned how to write like his contemporaries. It is, particularly in the earliest plays, difficult to separate his work from that of others. All we can say of his prentice work is what has by common experience been observed of the growth of the poet. In the course of time, a writer who begins with a poetic idiom formed by others, if he has the power, soon begins to develop his own, and we catch in his work new tones, and a speech mode which he is able to bring to life out of others' idiom in order to express what is distinctively his own.

Current dramatic modes

Between 1592 and 1612, when Shakespeare was writing for the public theatre, playwriting was not confined to the professional dramatist who worked for the public playhouses; there were other forms which Shakespeare must have known, ranging from archaic dramatic modes tending to obsolescence, the strict imitation of classical Latin plays, to the numerous shows which, as they were popular, could not be ignored by the playwright. Among archaic dramatic modes was the moral interlude, the form Willis described in his account of *The Cradle of Security*. This kind of play was superseded by new developments, but it was never entirely forgotten. Its moral intention and structure are still to be traced beneath plays seemingly far removed from its simplicity and transparency.

Similarly, popular modes like pageantry sometimes enable Shakespeare to express his attitude to his material dramatically. *Richard II* often comes close to pageant. The king is divine, and the sequence of events in the play recalls ceremonial and religious rites. The Chronicle play, to which the patriotism of the times gave a special vogue, was a dramatic mode very early employed by Shakespeare. His earliest work in the theatre must have been *Henry VI*, which was a popular success. And of course there were the eminent modes of comedy and tragedy, eminent because of Greek and Roman examples and of the attention paid to their theory and practice in academic and literary circles.

Like other popular dramatists, he knew and was sensitive to fashions in plays, though it cannot be said that he slavishly copied them. The Revenge play, for instance, was Kyd's successful transformation of earlier tragedy through impressive verse and a keen sense of dramatic situation represented on the stage. Shakespeare's *Hamlet* might be reckoned a Revenge play. Yet it transcends whatever debts it might have owed to Kyd and the fashion he started. Shakespeare was one of the actors in *Every Man in His Humour*, and he knew the humour plays of Jonson very well. They were very much in vogue, and in some of his characters—for instance, Nym in *Henry V*, Malvolio in *Twelfth Night*—he may have been in Jonson's debt. But again there is no simple following of an established precedent. Certain things in Shakespeare's plays could be linked up with Elizabethan and Jacobean trends in drama. The popularity of the court masques—aristocratic entertainment at which nobles disguised and masked danced and performed a short play—is undoubtedly reflected in the element of masque in plays like *The Tempest* and *Henry VIII*. But maskers and disguisings are to be found even in early plays. The young men in *The Merchant of Venice* who prepare for 'a masque tonight' (2. 4. 22), are only doing what young Elizabethan gallants in aristocratic circles must have been doing.

'Kinds' of play

Shakespeare, like many other popular dramatists of the time, constructed his plays quite arbitrarily out of various materials, with an apparent unconcern for authority or critical rules. There was in his time a respectable body of opinion which stated that the various kinds of play—tragedy and comedy for instance—should be kept apart and not be mixed. The various kinds of play, on which academic criticism was busy, are referred to in Polonius's recommendation of the players: 'The best actors in the world, either for tragedy, comedy, history, pastoral, pastoral-comical, historical-pastoral, tragical-historical, tragical-comical-historical-pastoral. . . .' Of course, Shakespeare is making fun of Polonius, and this description is not to be taken as a list of the various kinds of drama known at his time.

Shakespeare did not set much store by critical notions of good art, and Jonson, who was a friend of his and praised his work warmly, never could get over his feeling that Shakespeare's plays would have been better for more attention to the rules. *Macbeth* and the other tragedies are quite obviously not contemporary imitations of the classical, nor would the 'hero' have fitted the formulae of contemporary critics on how tragedies should be written. Shakespeare's forms are generally mixed forms. This is the virtue they derived from being popular drama. We should, therefore, think of them as popular Elizabethan and Jacobean plays, and hold in abeyance older notions, and even present-day ideas, of what is tragedy and what comedy, and how they should be written, when we consider Shakespeare's work.

Shakespeare's language

Shakespeare's language, too, differs from ours. It is simple enough to see that the meanings of words change, for in a living language nothing remains static. The senses of many of Shakespeare's words are different from what would immediately be associated with them today. Words like 'fancy', 'conceit', 'mere', 'proper', 'quick' are only a few which would come to mind at once. This is a difficulty which can only be dealt with by reference to the glossary of the text we use.

We ought to remember the great variety of Shakespeare's language. It has been estimated that the average man at the present time gets along reasonably well with a vocabulary of some 3000 words which serve him for all the occasions of speech and writing. The educated man—arts man more likely than scientist who uses an international language for most of his writing—*may* know some 40,000 words, most of which are unlikely to be used frequently by him. Shakespeare had a vocabulary of 24,000 words.

His was an age in which all languages in Europe were extending their resources by borrowings and coinages from the classical, and some of the senses of these newly coined words would be different from ours. A large number of coinages never took root and survived, but it was a time of great inventiveness in language.

His language gives us a wide range of special interests, and individualized speakers. Formal speech, affected Latinized diction, slang, snatches of popular song, coarseness, words and phrases soaked in religious associations, are all used by him to develop what he wants to say. He is careful to avail himself of the various tones language offered him.

As he is an ingenious user of language, he is a critic of it too, and very often character and situation are presented through a language style. What is Osric in *Hamlet* but the affected and pretentious reflection of the preciousness of his language? Hamlet himself is a critic of language, just as much as Shakespeare was.

His attitude to language. More important than the range of his vocabulary is Shakespeare's attitude to language. Like writers and speakers of the time he uses it with great virtuosity. He deliberately plays upon the associations of words; he draws out their emotional significances; their ambiguities are savoured; he relishes the possibilities offered him for puns, overt and concealed. His attitude is that of the poet who has an extremely sensitive instrument with a wide range of tones, producing an effect akin to the musical, not in its sound alone (though this could be one part of the total effect), but in the organization of the parts which make up the whole.

Coleridge in his elucidation of Shakespeare's powers as revealed in his poems of *Venus and Adonis* and *The Rape of Lucrece* (1592 and 1593), drew attention to the way in which the poet's imagination fused Shakespeare's sense of musical delight with the power of producing it, his images and his thought into a new whole. Coleridge rated this creative power of the imagination as the highest excellence of the poet.

We shall see again and again in the plays how the poetry, using the sounds and suggestions of the words, the rhythms of impassioned utterance and the speaking voice, reveals dramatic situation and the poet's experience of the world which is embodied in his imagined creations. Take Macbeth's words in 3. 2. 46–50:

> Come, seeling night,
> Scarf up the tender eye of pitiful day,
> And with thy bloody and invisible hand
> Cancel and tear to pieces that great bond
> Which keeps me pale! Light thickens...

His mind is brooding on the murder of Banquo and Fleance which he has planned; Lady Macbeth is on the stage, obviously moved not only by Macbeth's words which refer to something of which she knows nothing, but also by their incantatory power. (He says 'Thou marvell'st at my words' in line 54.) The poetry builds up an atmosphere full of the suggestions of evil contrasted with kindly humanity which are linked with what has gone before. Shakespeare develops the ambiguities of the words he uses: so 'seeling' through the concealed pun in its sound suggests 'sealing' too. We have both the Elizabethan technical term from falconry for the operation of blinding, or sewing up, the eyelids of the falcon (an act parallel to the murder of Banquo and Fleance), and the senses of 'seal'—to set one's seal to, to close up, as night closes up and puts an end to day. The second sense ('seal') lingers in the poet's mind, for the 'great bond' is a reminiscence of a legal document, signed and sealed. 'Seeling' as image is connected with all the images of blood (think of molten red sealing-wax dripping on to paper) and violence which run through the play. The dramatic poetry works by bringing into our own awareness of Macbeth's state of mind suggestions of his own attitude revealed by the words: his horror and fear of having to repudiate (again) all the obligations religion and social order lay upon him; his consciousness of what he is doing; the ambiguity of his own world in which night is invoked to cover up a deed which he knows to be evil. The phrase 'bloody and invisible hand' recalls the scene after the murder of Duncan. It also keeps in tension together Macbeth's awareness of his crime—it is 'bloody'—and the self-deception to which he is prone after he has been deluded by the agents of evil—the feeling that if it is not seen ('invisible'), then he is safe.

All this is conveyed in an evocation of a particular moment of time—twilight, when darkness is engaged in overpowering and destroying day. This recalls not only the darkness of the world of evil soon to assume control over the world, but also that uncertain half-light when 'nothing is but what is not'. 'Light thickens'—the strong emotional suggestions in this phrase give us the atmosphere of the whole play in miniature. Professor Empson's analysis of the lines in *Seven Types of Ambiguity* should be consulted.

In form the Shakespearean play could be thought of as a musical composition, where out of the themes which are enunciated, repeated and varied, the whole effect is being built up, the impression left on the hearer depending on the co-ordination of the various parts. His words should be thought of as the musical phrase, their suggestions and images being responsible for the structure of the play.

To those accustomed to a plain and straightforward manner of speaking and writing on all occasions, Shakespeare's may seem too figurative, too much dependent on the significances derived and pressed deliberately out of the words he uses. The single word and the phrase may light up, in the context in which they appear, the meaning of the whole play, and just as the musician's use of a phrase may enable us the more easily to grasp the structure of the composition, so the image in the play may reveal to us the writer's attitude to his material. Shakespeare could do this because, as we have seen, his audience would have been only too ready to listen to plays with the attention that such a use of language demanded.

The text of Shakespeare's plays

No manuscript of the plays or poems in Shakespeare's writing has survived, though it is fairly certain that about three pages in the manuscript of *Sir Thomas More*, a play to which a number of unidentified writers made additions, are in Shakespeare's handwriting.

Some of Shakespeare's plays were published in Quarto form in his lifetime. Those printed with the authority of his company are likely to have been set up from his own manuscripts, which must have been, as was the custom then, used in the theatre by the prompter while the play was being rehearsed and performed. The printed text as a result sometimes reveals the prompter's own brief notes on the manuscript he was using, as for instance in the illustration of the page of the first Folio (Fig. 3).

See, and then fpeake your felues : awake, awake,
      Exeunt Macbeth and Lenox.
Ring the Alarum Bell : Murther, and Treafon,
Banquo, and *Donalbaine* : *Malcolme* awake,
Shake off this Downey fleepe, Deaths counterfeit,
And looke on Death it felfe : vp, vp, and fee
The great Doomes Image : *Malcolme, Banquo,*
As from your Graues rife vp, and walke like Sprights,
To countenance this horror. Ring the Bell.
    Bell rings. Enter Lady.
 Lady. What's the Bufineffe?
That fuch a hideous Trumpet calls to parley
The fleepers of the Houfe? fpeake, fpeake.
 Macd. O gentle Lady,
'Tis not for you to heare what I can fpeake :
The repetition in a Womans eare,
Would murther as it fell.
    Enter Banquo.
O *Banquo, Banquo,* Our Royall Mafter's murther'd.
 Lady. Woe, alas :
What, in our Houfe?
 Ban. Too cruell, any where.
Deare *Duff,* I prythee contradict thy felfe,
And fay, it is not fo.

    Enter Macbeth, Lenox, and Roffe.

 Macb. Had I but dy'd an houre before this chance,
I had liu'd a bleffed time : for from this inftant,
There's nothing ferious in Mortalitie :
All is but Toyes : Renowne and Grace is dead.

Fig. 3. A passage from *Macbeth*, Act 2, scene 3, as printed in the First Folio, 1623.
Note the line which in modern texts is printed

  To countenance this horror   [*Bell rings*

The stage direction has been printed as part of the text. The full line

  To countenance this horror. Ring the Bell.
 Lady M.   What's the Business?

is obviously too long. Modern editors therefore suggest that 'Ring the bell' was written
in the original manuscript as a direction to the prompter who stood off-stage holding his
manuscript prompt-copy, ready to give the actors their cue, whisper the words to them
if they forgot them, and to perform actions like this of ringing the bell. It is presumed
that the printer set the text from the prompt-copy and failed to notice that these words
are a stage direction.

It is very unlikely that fair copies were made for the benefit of the printer, as these would have cost money, and they would have added to the possibility of the text's falling into the hands of unauthorized persons. As Shakespeare's were popular plays, there was money to be made by printing them; and some plays were obviously 'pirated', or published by persons who printed some kind of text which was not their property. Among methods resorted to by 'pirates' of plays at the time were using a form of shorthand to take down a text during performances, and working with the help of an actor in the company who knew his and others' parts. Quartos so put together and printed have been called 'Bad Quartos' to distinguish them from others presumably printed with the authority of Shakespeare's company and based on good texts—'Good Quartos'.

The First Folio (1623) may have been printed from an assortment of documents: Shakespeare's own manuscripts with his (and the prompter's) corrections, and revisions; printed Quartos already in existence—'Good Quartos' presumably; these printed texts corrected and revised for fresh performances in the theatre. Printer's errors and misreadings have naturally added to the difficulties of trying to discover what exactly Shakespeare originally wrote.

The whole problem of the text of the plays is very complex and cannot be gone into here. These few remarks merely serve as a warning that printed texts of the plays (apart from modernized spellings, act and scene divisions and stage directions) merely represent the nearest that a particular editor has been able to get, by reasoning and research, to the actual words Shakespeare wrote. A good modern text probably corresponds quite closely with the lost original, but we never can claim absolute certainty.

We have tried to see Shakespeare, the Elizabethan playwright, producing his plays in the conditions of his time, in order to enable ourselves to approach his work with the best chance of understanding it. It should be remembered, however, that even if we had been instructed by the experts themselves, we could neither put ourselves back in his time, nor hear and feel the plays as his contemporaries must have done. We belong to our own time, and all the detailed knowledge some of us may possess about a past age will not enable us to look at its artistic creation as if we were the contemporaries of its writers. We both know too much, and too little, to be able to react as Elizabethans must have reacted to the plays. The most we can claim for all the knowledge of the background we acquire is that it is likely to act as a check on hazardous assumptions and prevent wrong attitudes. For all the knowledge we painfully dig out of the labours of others can only help us to work out for ourselves an understanding of the plays. This comes, not from learning this, that, or the other, but from being able to use the tools our knowledge gives us. If some of the hints offered here act as signposts, we can go on more resolutely to take up the major task of examining what Shakespeare wrote and understanding what a Shakespearean play is. We shall miss both if we neglect Shakespeare's words and concern ourselves with what all the experts have said.

If then the distinguishing mark of a play is its words, spoken by its persons in the situations which confront them, then it is obvious that we must turn our attention there. We can see how the words of a dramatic poet like Shakespeare, who used a form more strongly concentrated and textured than the prose of our own day, demand closer attention. They create and keep in motion on the stage everything which belongs to the play. Character, plot, scene, situation, have all to be thought of as a by-product of the words, which as they go on in time, build up, as the images of the cinema do, a picture which is continually changing. As the visual image is to the cinema, so is the word to the play. The words in their progression not only bring character, plot, and situation to life in our consciousness, they also communicate to us whatever the writer in his choice of them is trying to express.

We have therefore to examine what they are saying, what they are suggesting, how, in the moments in which they occur, they are contributing to the creation of a pattern, an attitude. In other words, we see through them what the dramatist's themes are. Earlier we used an image from music to suggest the relationship between the words and phrases as they gave us the total effect of a play. A similar description of the character of a play might be given through an image from weaving. If we look at a silk Bokhara carpet, we are almost at once aware of a pattern, and of its balance and symmetry. Studying it more closely we notice how the single threads, with their colours and their arrangement, provide the total effect of the carpet.

So with the words of the play: they give us all that in the instant of life given them on the stage could leave as strong an impression as *The Cradle of Security* left on Willis. When we return to them we see how in the position in which they occur, in their colour (their emotional associations, their images) and their arrangement (the way they repeat, or vary, what has gone before), they complete the total design. Without the single units of the threads of the warp and weft, and their arrangement by the weaver, there could be no carpet, and without the words no play.

THE PLATES

PLATE I

William Shakespeare. The engraved portrait by Martin Droeshout, on the title-page of the First Folio of the plays, 1623. This is the only authentic portrait of Shakespeare. It can hardly have been made 'from the life', as Droeshout was only fifteen when Shakespeare died. Probably it is a copy of a drawing or portrait made in Shakespeare's lifetime. According to Ben Jonson it is a good likeness:

> This Figure, that thou here seest put,
> It was for gentle Shakespeare cut;
> Wherein the Graver had a strife
> With Nature, to out-do the life:
> O, could he but have drawn his wit
> As well in brass, as he hath hit
> His face; the Print would then surpass
> All, that was ever writ in brass.
> But, since he cannot, Reader, look
> Not on his Picture, but his Book.

PLATE II

(*a*) The courtyard of the New Inn, Gloucester, in the early nineteenth century, its appearance probably comparatively unchanged since Shakespeare's day. This is the inn where *The Cradle of Security* (p. 30) was probably performed.

This is the typical arrangement of the old coaching-inn. Horses and carriage drove into the central courtyard, and travellers entered the inn by the stairs. If a stage were erected at one end of the yard, the spectators could stand around it in the yard, or in the galleries round the side. The actors would have access to the stage from the rear.

(*b*) A primitive fair-ground stage, part of a picture *A Village Fête* attributed to Pieter Breughel the Younger. The stage itself was a rough platform of boards with a curtained enclosure behind; the players made their entrances from behind the front curtain which was able to be drawn for the purpose; and a ladder in the enclosure allowed players to enter 'above', and play some of the action at the top of the front curtain. This very simple structure contained the essential features of the Elizabethan playhouse. Compare the theatres in de Witt's drawing (Plate III) and Figs. 1 and 2 (pp. 26 and 27).

77

PLATE III

The Swan Theatre, London; a drawing made about 1596 by or for a Dutch visitor, Johannes de Witt. This is the only contemporary reproduction of an Elizabethan theatre. It is only a rough sketch, and is full of ambiguities when closely examined. But note the tower, with the banner to indicate that a performance is in progress; the trumpeter (who had the same function); the stage (*proscaenium*); the two doors leading to the 'tiring-house' (attiring-house; dressing-room; *mimorum aedes*); the pit (*planities sive arena*); the entrance (*ingressus*); and the galleries all round. Compare Figs. 1 and 2 (pp. 26 and 27).

PLATE IV

The funeral procession of Sir Philip Sidney, 1587. The whole procession occupied thirty plates in Theodore de Bry's engraved representation. Sheets 13, 14, 15 and 16 are shown here.

The procession must have been the most spectacular of the age; it shows perfectly the Elizabethan love of pomp and spectacle, the habit of symbolic representation and the keen sense of degree or hierarchy.

In sheet 13 are shown knights related to Sidney, or friends of his (including Sir Francis Drake, fourth from the left). A gentleman is carrying Sidney's pennant; he is followed by a footman leading Sidney's warhorse, ridden by a page trailing a broken lance. The page, Henry Danvers, was later Earl of Danby.

In sheet 14 another page, carrying a battle-axe with its head downwards—a sign of mourning—is followed by the ushers of the heralds (next sheet) and by a gentleman carrying Sidney's 'great banner'.

In sheet 15 the heralds and the 'king of arms' carry the emblems of Sidney's knighthood; his spurs, his gauntlets, his helmet and crest, his shield, his coat of arms.

Sheet 16 shows the hearse, covered with velvet and borne by fourteen yeomen. At each corner four gentlemen bear 'bannerols' indicating Sidney's noble ancestry.

Other members of the procession were earls and barons, representatives of the States of Holland, the Lord Mayor and Corporation of London, citizens of London, the London militia, other soldiers. The whole was preceded by thirty-two poor men (one for each year of Sidney's age). In all, some 700 people took part, each section representing some degree or function of society, and bearing the emblems of their sorrow, and Sidney's rank and attainments.

78

PLATE V

London seen from the south bank of the Thames in the year of Shakespeare's death, 1616 (from Claes Jans Visscher's 'Long View of London', British Museum).

(*a*) Off the map, to the left, is Westminster. The royal palace of Whitehall is shown. On the near side of the river is the Swan Theatre.

(*b*) Old St Paul's is clearly shown. Hampstead is on the horizon. On the south bank is the bear-garden and the Globe.

(*b*) and (*c*) show the City of London proper, with all its churches, mostly destroyed in the Great Fire of London, and rebuilt by Wren. London Bridge joins the City to Southwark, and like other great medieval bridges carries houses and shops. At the southern end Bridge Gate shows the heads of executed criminals.

(*c*) and (*d*), then as now, contained the main dock area. Note the Tower of London.

PLATE VI

In this diagram (from Robert Fludd, *Microcosmi Historia*, 1617) note the Elizabethan plan of the universe. Man lies in the centre, in the sphere of earth, surrounded by the spheres of water, air and fire. Above these are the spheres of the planets, and above them the spheres of the seraphim, cherubim, thrones, dominations, princes, powers, virtues, archangels and angels. Above all is the triangular symbol of the radiant Trinity.

Parallel to all these are the intellectual and spiritual concepts labelled A–F, from the simple soul which issues from the hand of God, to the body which is the receptacle of all.

This scheme, similar in its general outline to many other diagrams by Elizabethan thinkers, also gives a mixed geometrical and cosmological counterpart to the theory of harmony, on the right.

The whole system is based on the old Ptolemaic theory of the universe. Nine concentric crystal spheres all revolving make a divine harmony as they move. Note too the four elements, and the hierarchy of heavenly powers.

PLATE I

PLATE II

(a)

(b)

PLATE III

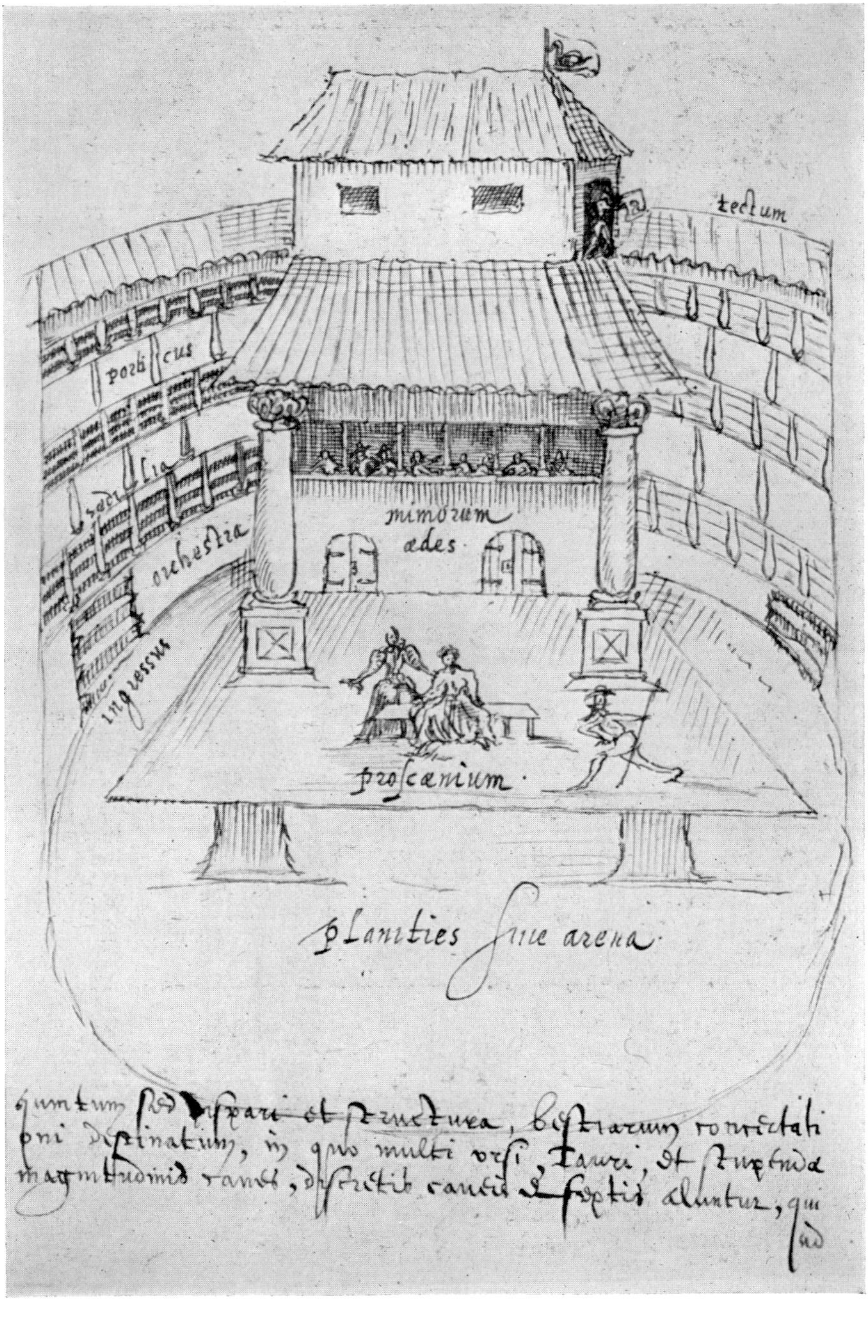

tectum

porticus

sedilia

orchestra

mimorum
aedes

ingressus

proscaenium.

planities sive arena

quintum sedificari et structura, bestiarum conuictati
oni destinatum, in quo multi versi, tauri, Et stupenda
magnitudinis canes, districtis canibus et septis aluntur, qui
sub

PLATE IV

(*a*)

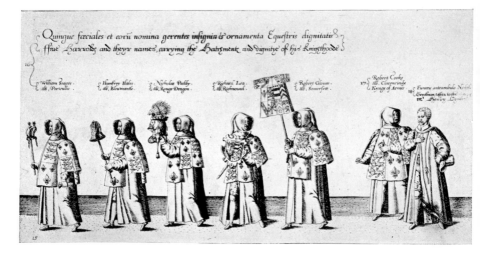

(*c*)

PLATE IV

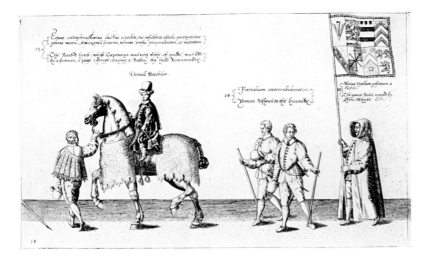

(*b*)

(*d*)

PLATE V

(b)

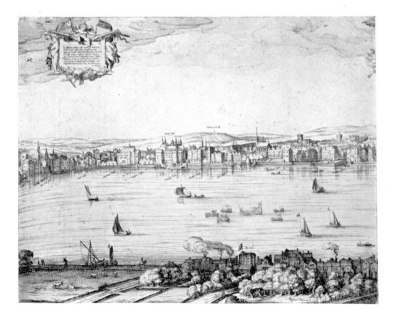

(a)

PLATE V

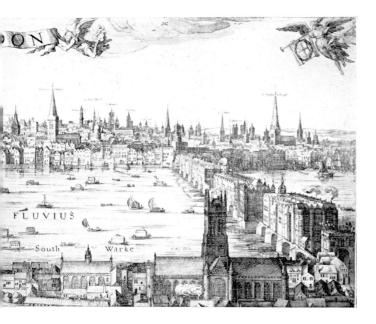

(c)

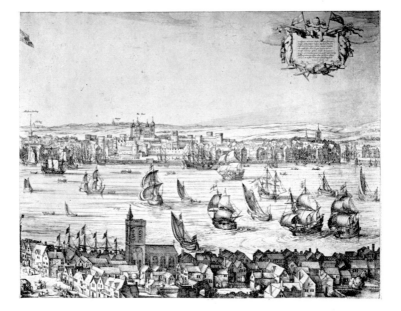

(d)

PLATE VI

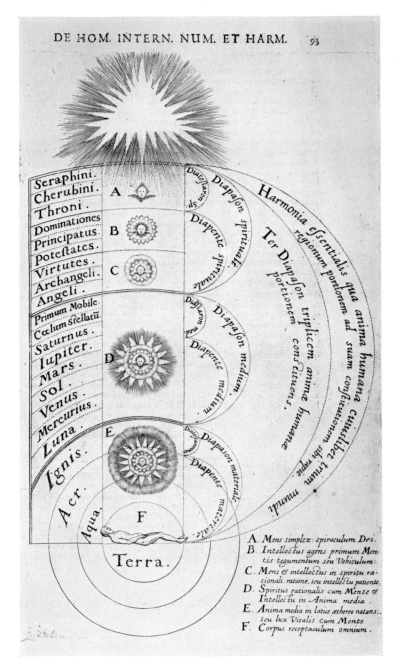

PART II

THE PLAYS

7. A METHOD OF WORK

The foregoing pages have tried to place Shakespeare's plays in their time, the necessary preliminary to work on specific plays. For each of the plays can be better grasped if seen in relation to Shakespeare's work as a popular dramatist.

To suggest a mode of work is always risky, for conditions vary from school to school or from country to country. But as our concern is with the practical matter of studying plays, there may be some common ground in our attitudes to what is a play, which may usefully provide a starting-point. The suggestions which follow are intended as one way of dealing with Shakespeare.

If it is possible the first stage should be listening to a recorded version of the play. A teacher may introduce the recorded version, drawing attention to its method of approach to the play, keeping in mind, for discussion later, any differences between the line of approach of the recorded version and his own. The Marlowe Society's recordings of the plays under the direction of Mr George Rylands should be available wherever the British Council is represented.

Listening to the recorded version one understands that a play is meant to be performed, not just read. A play is a sequence of actions built upon dialogue involving persons, using various visual and aural arts and performed on some kind of stage for the benefit of an audience. The sequence of actions is the plot, which is made up of a series of situations. A situation is one particular moment in the affairs of the persons in a play in relation to other persons and events. A situation may be the whole scene of a play, or a few lines in it. For instance, the whole of I. I of *The Merchant of Venice* could be the opening situation, in which we are introduced to two of the major persons in the play, and shown who they are and how the request of one is met by the other. Equally, lines 135–9 could be a

4-2

situation in which the relation of Antonio to his friend Bassanio is expressed. This smaller situation is part of the larger situation of 1. 1, just as again the latter is a smaller part of one set of situations in the play. Whether we take the whole scene or three lines, we are aware, in recording or in theatre, of words spoken, of dialogue. Antonio is speaking to Bassanio; further, this dialogue not only presents persons, it also states what these persons are doing at a particular moment, and this is related to what will be done in the situations yet to follow. So the dialogue creates characters and moves action.

A situation is a particular selected moment, one of a series which makes up the whole play: so that when we select one we are what is, in the staged or recorded play, in continual motion (just as when we examine a reel of film and view one photographic image, we are isolating for the purpose of study what is in the film one of a series of images in motion). Situation is like the single image in the series. It is linked with what precedes it and what follows it. The link between the situations which make up the play is provided by the words of the dialogue which is its medium, as the photographic image is the medium of the film.

As artistic form a play depends on acted dialogue. Actions and persons without words could be either mime or dance; and action with words which includes dialogue but is not exclusively dependent on it would be narrative. The writer of fiction who tells the story of an action may frequently use dialogue, but he is not exclusively dependent on it. He can describe persons, events and scenes, he can comment on them, he can talk to the reader in the first person, he can take as much time as he wishes over his story, above all it is not represented on a stage.

The dramatist can describe, he can comment, he can make his persons address the spectator, but as the play uses the medium of the theatre it is different from narrative or fiction.

As a play is built up of dialogue and exhibits a series of linked situations involving persons represented on the stage, through which the playwright expresses his experience and ideas, the simplest mode of understanding the latter would be by trying to discover what the situations reveal. What is common to them, what is stressed in them? We should examine the situations for clues to the dramatist's intention. There may be similarities, repetitions, contrasts, emphases which force themselves on our attention. Breaking up the play into certain selected situations we should make it our task to see whether there is any significance in these, and whether our analysis enables us to reassemble the whole in such a way that we do not leave out anything which belongs to the play. We shall have to satisfy ourselves that everything finds a place in our reconstruction, and also that there is nothing in it that cannot be discovered in the play. If we feel that this reconstruction helps us to arrive at the experience the writer has attempted to recreate, then we shall be beginning to understand the play. We can describe the situations which make up the play as its structure, or that arrangement by examining which we arrive at the play's total meaning.

We may be helped in our work on the structure of a play by such things as the play's title, by how it has been described—for instance whether a particular play is listed as tragedy or comedy. There may be, as in the case of some of Shakespeare's original publications, a title-page description which may be useful. Descriptions of the play by contemporary writers or spectators may be useful too.

But these are extraneous aids and not as important as the dramatist's words—his text. For the word, through direct statement, through association, through its connotations, its symbolic force, is the element which brings to life all other elements of the medium of theatrical performance. The question we should always put to ourselves is: do the words in the situations we examine help us to see some pattern or arrangement in the play? This pattern or arrangement is the play's structure. As the arrangement of the bones gives the anatomical structure of the human body, so what we select in the situations of a play gives us its structure. And as there is more to the human being than his anatomical structure, so there will be more in a play than its structure.

Structure in a play, since situations are being investigated, may be made up of particular turns in the action, attitudes in the persons, as they are revealed by the words, phrases and images. So in *The Merchant of Venice* structure seems to depend on the frequency of particular turns in the action which involve situations of test or trial. In *Richard II* the pattern consists of situations marking the progress of the king from the heights to the depths, because as a person he is shown to be incapable of meeting the demands made of him as king.

In *Macbeth* more important than action as an element of the situations—seen either as the rise and fall of Macbeth or the conflict between the forces of good and evil—is the creation of the atmosphere of an equivocal and ambiguous world through the images and the turns of the action of the play. Or structure might be composed of the character brought out by the situations, as in *Henry V*, where everything is subordinated to the process of showing the character of the ideal sovereign.

Using the situations abstracted from the play, we try to build up an awareness and appreciation of what these reveal. Whether the teacher uses the approach suggested here or any other, the clue to the whole play should be given at the time of its very first reading in the class. Some simplification may result, but if structure is presented with flexibility, then insufficiencies or unsatisfactoriness can be made good as the play is worked on and these come to light.

If possible the play should be read aloud by students in class as if at a first try-out of a new play by its assembled cast in the presence of its producer, in this case the teacher. Reading it aloud is much more likely to bring situations to life than any other mode of study. First of all it will transform the words from printed signs on a page to spoken language; it will later, through the contrast of voices and through the identification of voice with speaker, bring the text closer to stage representation.

This first reading must be accompanied by reference to the glossary, and the meanings of unfamiliar (and seemingly familiar) words elucidated. The value of the glossary cannot be overstressed. (It would be useful at the end of the course for the student to go through the glossary in order to make sure that every word glossed has been noted. The assumption that the meaning of Elizabethan words can be guessed from their similarity with contemporary English words is dangerous.)

At this first stage, with its frequent references to the glossary, the over-all impression of the play as provided by its structure should be kept in mind. Later readings would naturally have to be backed up with more extensive comment. If time is available, then some of the major situations in the play, on which its understanding depends, might be staged, primarily for the benefit of the students themselves. But preferable to a full-dress stage show, which might easily involve interests not necessarily related to understanding Shakespeare, is the reading out of the parts in a few selected situations by readers chosen for their skill in speech. For instance, the two trials in *The Merchant of Venice*—that of the suitors and of Antonio before the duke—the two appeals to the Roman crowd in *Julius Caesar*, the gulling of Malvolio, the deposition of Richard II, could be given by speakers reading from their texts on a platform before an audience. This would obviate a few of the burdens of a stage show, notably the learning of parts. The attention of the audience would be drawn to the words of the readers presenting the situation. Through an experience of this kind the class, by now familiar with the meanings of the words, would understand how Shakespeare uses them as one of the great resources of his art. If this is seen, then the class, even without being able to see the play on the stage, could be made to understand how stage presentation fills out what the words convey.

In the study of six plays which follows, attention has been drawn to the structure through which understanding of the play may be secured. Of course, breaking up the play into the parts making up its structure does not reduce it to the units important to the dramatist as he constructed it, or even to the only units of which it could be composed. The plays have been so treated in order to make them better understood. A method of work is suggested; no rule is given.

8. RICHARD II

This play, probably written in 1595, though not the earliest of Shakespeare's plays, is very definitely an early play, both in its verse and its construction. Some of the reasons for its great popular success had little to do with Shakespeare's dramatic or poetic achievement, and belonged rather to the political excitements of those times. On the eve of Essex's abortive attempt to rouse the citizens of London against the Queen's advisers in 1601, Shakespeare's company was persuaded to revive the play, presumably because one of its scenes had to do with the deposition of the sovereign.

It was described at its first printing—in the first of its five quarto editions—as *The Tragedie of King Richard the Second*. Its subject was the tragedy of a king. As tragedy was understood at the time, it would show the fall of the ruler from the height of his power and greatness to the misery of death. Ever since Boccaccio's late fourteenth-century Italian prose work *De Casibus Virorum Illustrium* (Concerning the Falls of Famous Men), European literature looked upon this subject as particularly suited to the grandeur and the moral intention of tragedy. In these stories Fortune, pictured as a woman turning a wheel, on which people were at one moment up and then down, brought down the mighty, through God's judgements on them and through their own fault. From their fate the moral had to be drawn.

Structure

The structure of the play therefore traces the decline of Richard's fortunes. As plot, its succession of scenes represents the movement of Richard from king to wretched and humiliated man. The simple straight line which marks his downward course is defined by two images in the play. In 2. 4. 19–20 Salisbury sees Richard's glory

like a shooting star,
Fall to the base earth from the firmament.

88

And in 4. 1. 184ff. Richard sees his course, as contrasted with Bolingbroke's, like one of Fortune's buckets plunged deep down in the water of the well, while his rival's flies up on high. (The image is of two buckets, one at each end of a rope or chain, which passes over a pulley. As the rope is pulled one bucket goes up and the other must necessarily go down.)

In simple narrative structure Richard's fall is shown us on the visual plane. The play opens with the king, in his role as dispenser of justice, seated high in his glory on the 'upper stage' or on a raised dais or scaffold. His descent and degradation are marked by two scenes particularly insisting on the visual picture of the decline of his fortunes: that of 3. 2, where appearing on the stage, newly landed from Ireland, the king sits on a bank to 'salute' the English soil, and later actually goes down on to the ground to bewail the fates of kings; and that of 3. 3, where from the 'upper stage', on the walls of Flint Castle according to the stage direction, he descends to the 'base court', the main stage, to meet his rival who, as he says, demonstrating it with his hand, aspires as high as his head (his royal crown). The play closes with the king being knocked down and killed, felled to the ground by one of his subjects, and his body in a coffin being borne out in a funeral procession.

In these simple visual terms the 'tragedy' of Richard can be glimpsed. This subject, of the contrast between the height of the great man's felicity and the depths of misery to which he falls, was dear to the imaginations of people at that time. To the medieval mind such a progression of events was enough to make its vehicle— whether story or poem or play—tragedy. The moral of such representations, when acted on the stage, impressed itself on the spectator with greater force, since the events concerned no ordinary persons but emperors, kings, princes, generals and great statesmen. To us, too, though the subject may no longer provide such good opportunities for edification, and the great may be no more than financiers or film stars, it is still interesting.

Yet structure here is not simply a matter of plot, or the progression of scenes. Throughout the play there is a contrast between the role the king is expected to play, or claims to be playing, and his actual performance. In a sense Richard affirms what he has been doing, when in 5. 5. 31 he says 'Thus play I in one person many people'. If he had had any role to play it was that of king. We can see the structure taking up various functions, or aspects, of the role of king, in its record of his decline and fall. More than plot is involved here, for through these contrasts between what a king should be and what Richard is, character and thought are being presented.

We could regard the play then as being devoted to the study of what makes a king, investigating it through the examples Richard provides of the actor unfitted for the role. As dispenser of justice, as steward of the kingdom, as soldier, even allegorically as gardener in 3. 4, he fails to play the part expected of him. So finally, in his moment of humiliation, he is in York's own words (in 5. 2. 23 ff.) treated with no more regard than the indifferent actor on the stage, eclipsed by the great actor who has just left it.

Pageant

If we ask how the play must have been taken by its audience, then one sentence would provide a fair indication of how it was presented and accepted by the theatre-goers of that time. At the end of the long single scene of Act IV, when the deposition has been played out to its finish, and the 'unkinged' Richard is conducted from the stage where he has resigned the robes and the symbols of kingship, the Abbot of Westminster says, 'A woeful pageant have we here beheld' (4. 1. 321). He speaks presumably not only for those on the stage, but also for everyone in the theatre. The decline and fall of the man unfitted to play the role he has been cast for is presented as if it were ceremonial, the solemn grandeur of a show. Like all 'pageants' it offers a moral which its spectators and auditors accept as the purpose of its magnificent array.

The Elizabethan pageant was spectacular. It had, like such examples of present-day pageantry as the Lord Mayor's show or the procession of Dassera in India, some practical point to make clear or some traditional significance to fulfil. In Tudor England the pageant generally propounded some theme, or inculcated some lesson. It often included allegorical figures who recited verses specially composed for this purpose, or painted cloths or arches decking the way with superscriptions in verse. So with the Abbot of Westminster we could see in the play a pageant with a 'woeful' conclusion, in both senses ('ending' or 'inference').

Shortly after the Abbot has spoken, Richard himself comes on stage. As he looks back on what has happened he places a very different valuation upon what has been played and what is still to come. He asks the queen to look back on the past as 'an old wives' tale' of the lamentable fall of a king (5. 1. 40 ff.). Nothing could be further from a pageant than an old wives' tale, yet, with that inability to think of anything but himself which, we shall see, is characteristic of him, Richard hyperbolically assumes that the fire will put itself out and 'sympathize', or be in accord with, the accents of grief which relate the story of 'the deposing of a rightful king' (5. 1. 46–50). He feels his story will be the culmination of all those told by the fire on a winter's night. It will 'quit', both repay and cap, all tales told that night. To the chief actor in these events, their story will really be no old wives' tale at all, but something miracle-working and extraordinary.

If then *Richard II* is both pageant and no ordinary old wives' tale, we should look in it for the magnificence and elaboration of the former, and also for the moral or theme which is the intention of both. We are asked to be impressed by the spectacle of the great man brought to ruin, and also to draw the conclusion from it.

A chronicle play

The play is one of the English 'histories' or 'chronicles'. At this time history was ceasing to be the annalist's simple record of events; it was beginning to be the moralist's study of the past. The historian, with his moral point of view about politics, presented material from the past in such a way that the reader should benefit from it. Such was the theme of a collection of verse 'tragedies' by a number of poets entitled *The Mirror for Magistrates* (1559) to which Shakespeare was indebted for some of the material of his play. A mirror was something into which a man looked in order to see himself as he really was; so a mirror for 'magistrates' (rulers) was intended to enable them to see themselves as they were and also to see for themselves what was amiss and to amend it. Shakespeare had perhaps written four 'histories' before he wrote *Richard II*. It is unlikely that when he began writing his earlier histories he had already in mind how he was going to write his later ones. But it is most likely that, as a good Elizabethan, at whatever point he looked at the events of the past, he would see the processes at work that he depicts in all his 'histories'.

The moral of the play

The moral of the play—and of all the histories—is plain for all to see. It is enunciated in the speech of the Bishop of Carlisle in 4. 1. 114 ff. The king is God's deputy, as Gaunt says quite plainly in 1. 2. 37–8. However weak, corrupt and inefficient he may be, no subject, not even his cousin of the blood royal, has the right to proceed against him. If this happens, then the intricate system of order, or hierarchy, on which the whole kingdom and the whole universe is founded collapses, and the result can only be confusion, and the chaos of civil strife and foreign intervention. This was, to Elizabethans, no mere matter of academic theory about how history should be written, or how the events of the past might be surveyed, it was a fact of grave urgency throughout Elizabeth's reign with its threats of civil strife and foreign intervention. She was, to some people in her kingdom and to a number of European sovereigns, an usurper whom the pope had excommunicated and against whom he called Roman Catholics to revolt. So in English churches, throughout her reign and after, homilies were appointed to be read, insisting upon the divine right of the sovereign and the heinous crime of revolting against her. As we have seen in our examination of Elizabethan beliefs about the world, everything depended on a beautifully regulated order, to disturb which was to bring about ruin. In *Henry V* we shall see how the king, the son of the Bolingbroke of this play, on the eve of his decisive battle at Agincourt, asks God's forgiveness for his father's trespass in depriving Richard of the throne. It is therefore strange that the play should have been regarded as recommending the deposition of the sovereign. That Shakespeare's company was able to clear itself of complicity in Essex's rebellion may have been due to the clear impression left by the play that, however incapable the lawfully crowned ruler might be, right was not on the side of those who proposed to depose him.

The elaboration of pageant

Pageant with a moral would have had to give its audiences both spectacle and a clear insight into the dramatist's intention. To take the former first of all. That magnificence and splendour were produced we can see at once by looking at the list of persons in the play and remembering what passes on the stage. In this tragedy of an English king, practically all the characters are either his royal kinsmen or noblemen, bishops and lords of the church. To the spectator at the theatre the events of the play dealt with persons and institutions of two centuries before. If we consider how we today would present a play which dealt with the characters and happenings of a court two centuries ago, whether of a Moghul emperor, or a Hanoverian king, we could readily grant that the distance of time would add a greater strangeness and a touch of impressiveness to our spectacle. And if we remember that many people in Shakespeare's audience would be simple commoners of Elizabethan London, we can understand how the very names of these characters, like the legendary John of Gaunt, would immediately produce some of the atmosphere the play would require.

Even at the present day, to the simple mind, royalty requires all the panoply of regality associated with it. A king or queen must appear in robes of royal state, with crown, sceptre and orb, for this is how the figure is pictured in the imagination. (It was a disappointment to villagers in Ceylon who lined the track to see the royal train pass by that Queen Elizabeth II was dressed like any other Englishwoman.)

Costume. Pageantry would require these royal personages and courtiers to be costumed magnificently. Richard, who had the reputation of having wasted his revenue on show, refers to what he must have been wearing at the time when he thinks of himself as becoming a humble palmer (3. 3. 147 ff.). The trappings of royalty, apart from their symbolic significance, would be necessary as objects, as props, if the fall, the literal drop in Richard's fortunes, is to be demonstrated. In the deposition scene (4. 1) he gives away everything which symbolizes kingship. There is a strong contrast between him in his brave array at the beginning of the play and the figure who meets his queen in London on his way to the Tower (5. 1). He is shown on the stage, abject, deprived of all which outwardly made up a king. Not only do we see him, we are later given a description of him by York (5. 2. 23–36), who contrasts the new king in his glory with the deposed Richard with dust thrown on his head—a suggestion which seems to recall the biblical story of the passion of Christ.

Not only is the apparel of the king important visually and symbolically, the costume of the other characters should also be remembered. There is the queen, with her attendants. In 5. 1. 16 she is addressed by Richard as 'fair woman', a form of greeting which would have no point if she were not wearing her ceremonial robes, for there is in Richard's words not only a deliberate withdrawal of himself, as if the experiences he had been through had made him someone else and not the king, but also the suggestion of the superior wisdom to which he is now entitled. It is as if he were saying that royal garb means nothing and one must lead one's life so that one might win 'a new world's crown'. What he is saying to her is: The crown I once wore and your regal state now are of little worth compared with a heavenly crown, or our reward in heaven,

94

which we have thought so little of so far. There are, in addition, the nobles richly robed in those scenes which require ceremonial ostentation.

Ceremonial. To the richness of costume, without which pageant could not come to life, ritual adds its characteristic effect of formal grandeur. The substance of scene after scene is based on the traditional splendour of the lists of chivalry (the decorated arena where tilting took place) and court ceremonial. The play opens with the stateliness of the king, high on his throne of justice, with formal challenge and repudiation enacted on the stage below. This is followed by the 'death-scene' (for it is her last appearance) of a royal duchess. The play as it opens is taken up with alternate movement between scenes requiring the 'business' of the ritual of chivalry and the death-scenes of royalty. Throughout its course, whether the scene is at Windsor, Ravenspurgh, Berkeley, or Flint, the staging turns on ceremonial procedure which governs life at court. It is against this background that the character of Richard, as the dramatist presents it, should be seen. The scene of the king's deposition, as Richard plays it, is ritual which parallels the rite of coronation. The last meeting between king and queen, again as Richard contrives it, depends on a formal ceremony of marriage. As that rite once joined them, so their kisses and the words which accompany them undo the marriage bond between himself and the queen.

The verse

The verse most strongly and successfully supports the impression of pageant, with its costume and formal movement. Here the particular excellence of Shakespeare's mode of writing, even in its immaturity, can be seen. The poetry gives an impression of a stiff and elaborate effect, as of a rich brocade, to the scenes and to the persons. Its emotional range is not wide, but this is no great disadvantage, for the effects aimed at are simple. It is either carefully composed regular five-foot Elizabethan blank verse, or rhymed couplets which give a particular formality and emphasis to both speech and occasion. Shakespeare has clearly benefited from his acquaintance with the verse of Marlowe, and there are many reminiscences of both *Edward II* and *Dr Faustus*.

Three strands of verse can be noticed in the play. First of all the proud and angry tones which are distributed among all the characters. This is verse appropriate to their position and the importance of the events in which the characters are involved. Then there is lavished on all the characters without discrimination the elaborate tissue of word play, which heightens the effect. Finally, there is the verse which specially differentiates Richard in his fall from the other characters.

To take the first type of verse: Shakespeare shows that he can write a blank verse line appropriate to the passionate and 'high stomached' (overbearingly proud) speakers of his play. The success of the verse, the way it convincingly pulls it off (if we may use this expression of the way in which Shakespeare is able to rise to the demands he puts upon himself) can be seen in the numerous passages anthologized from it for the collection entitled *England's Parnassus* (1600). They must have been chosen not only because they were thoughts worth treasuring on such subjects as Sorrow, but also because they were so eloquently expressed.

A set piece. In the most famous of such passages—the words of the dying John of Gaunt on England (2. 1. 40–66)—is a beautifully composed set-piece in which the rhetorical piling up of apostrophe after apostrophe is balanced by another set of contrasting references to the 'tenement', 'pelting farm', 'shame', 'inky parchment blots', etc. Shakespeare's verse gives all the occasion demands: it gets the attentive hush which accompanies the dying words of a heroic English figure; the speaker claims prophetic inspiration for them, and they begin with a series of 'sentences', or copy-book maxims, on the subject that excess soon destroys itself. It gets under way with amplification, the loading of line upon line of weighty sentiment, each closed within itself. The strong, hard beat develops into something to which the audience would immediately respond. This is not great poetry, but it is what the pageantry of the play wants, and

Shakespeare providing it shows that he has the required mastery of his medium. These lines, which to most Englishmen suggest the glory and the eminence of England, were intended by their speaker to convey exactly the opposite. What John of Gaunt is saying is 'Alas that this famous and glorious island should be reduced to the wretched state in which it lies'. But such is the strength of the patriotism evoked and the powerful rhythm of the verse that it presents not shame but glory. If we look again at the lines we see how well their contents—England's glory, the references to royalty ('sceptred isle', 'earth of majesty'), to classical legend, to the biblical Eden, to precious stones and silver, to the strength of a fortress, to chivalry with its impressions of stateliness, grandeur, the highest excellence man can think of, are triumphantly rendered by Shakespeare's blank verse line.

Scenes of contention. It is a blank verse line like this, but not so heavy, which gives such an impression of strength to all those scenes in which the nobles defy each other, quarrel, and challenge each other to mortal combat. We might use a homely illustration here to see what Shakespeare is doing. If we see a powerfully built dog we must expect from it a deep full-throated bark. If it could only produce a puny whimper we would feel that something has gone wrong. Shakespeare gets from his verse the tones which we expect from persons and material such as his. A great deal of the content of this play is composed of quarrel between 'mighty opposites'. Almost as soon as the characters appear on the stage, the king says (1. 1. 15 ff.):

> Then call them to our presence—face to face,
> And frowning brow to brow, ourselves will hear
> The accuser and the accused freely speak:
> High-stomached are they both and full of ire,
> In rage, deaf as the sea, hasty as fire.

What is required if such persons are to 'speak freely' what is in their minds is verse appropriate to their overweening pride. Their rage and anger, as Richard puts it, are like the elemental forces of the sea and of fire. The verse has to be strong, heavy, and, since these are formal occasions, rhetorical.

Not only are there scenes of quarrel—we could go through the play and work out how many such situations there are, indeed the whole subject-matter might well be the 'quarrel' or 'contention' between Richard and Bolingbroke—there are a number of scenes of formal adjuration, in which one character conjures another upon oath to a course of action, or prophesies. So the Duchess of Gloucester in her scene with John of Gaunt uses verse similar to that of his dying speech or Richard's opening lines, to urge Gaunt to revenge her husband's death. We notice in her lines (1. 2. 9 ff.) how repetition and amplification go hand in hand with the royal and sacred references of the blank verse to produce an effect of solemn grandeur. So the scene with the dying Gaunt carried on the stage is both adjuration and quarrel, and York in his impatience with Richard's confiscation of Bolingbroke's properties and revenues bursts out into verse of the same kind.

This common language, as we might call it, is the endowment of all the noble characters, whether they are described as 'high-stomached', 'high', 'haught', 'insulting', 'daring' (of tongue) as Aumerle is described by Bagot in 4. 1. 8. Even the two women—the Duchess of Gloucester and the Duchess of York—have it. The Queen has a slight modulation of it in her scolding of the gardener. It might be looked at as the mask in folk plays which gives a kind of megaphonic quality to what the actors say.

Word play. It is not only resounding speech which the dramatist gives his characters. Their talk is also full of rhetorical figures and word-play which gives it an effect of elaborate art. We have seen that rhetoric was part of the general education of the times. In this play, and in some other early plays of Shakespeare's, the kind of word-play and the working out of all the possibilities of meaning in a word or a phrase, show a self-conscious interest which is valued as a thing in itself. Shakespeare is certainly interested in his instrument of speech. What he elects to do with it gives the play just the effect it requires; or to put it in another way, what the play needs in the way of high-sounding speech and elaborate word-play is just what Shakespeare at this time could give. Nothing beyond his ability to produce is demanded of him.

Most of the difficulties of following the speech of the characters in the play are due, not so much to the unfamiliarity of the language, but to the frequency of quibbles upon the senses of words for which the modern reader or speaker of English is unprepared. But both these sources of difficulty provide the texture the play seems to call for. Right through the opening scene we note besides the strong and bitter clamour of two eager tongues, something else too—the wit which can elaborate a thought as astounding as the terms of the speech are clamorous. Take Bolingbroke's words at 1. 1. 188 ff. Its exaggerated terms are backed by images from cock-fighting, from chivalry, from warfare, and from a melodramatic memory of an Elizabethan stage success, when Hieronimo in *The Spanish Tragedy* rather than speak bites out his tongue and spits it at his torturers. This is rhetorical and witty language with a vengeance, but then what is needed here but such high-astounding terms?

Wit. The wit of the language, as the dramatist bestows it on practically all the characters of importance in his play, is shown in the way that the single comparison or analogy can be extended by one speaker and twisted round the other way by another. There is the interesting scene between the queen and Bushy in 2. 2. 5 ff., where both play with an image and quibble with the meanings of a word. The queen begins weakly with the repetition of 'sweet', but her 'yet again' proves that the dramatist's purpose is to elaborate; it is as if he says: 'Watch out, here comes another figure'. Then follows the image of the likelihood of Fate's producing from its womb some sorrow as yet unborn. The proneness to produce figure after figure should not be thought of primarily as a character trait of the queen's, but much more significantly as part of the intention of the dramatist. The queen may be playing with 'images' of grief as Bushy suggests, but this type of wit suits the elaboration of the whole show.

Bushy who replies to the queen is just as ready to play with
'images'. He quibbles with the senses of 'perspectives' in order to
tell her that not reflecting, as she should, on the king's absence, she
has deceived herself by finding imaginary sorrows to bewail. The
general sense of the passage may be difficult, but the tissue of fine
extravagance of language is obvious. Bushy, looking at the tears
which fill the queen's eyes, finds a similitude between them and the
facets of glass or of a precious stone which reflect the single person
or thing mirrored in it a hundredfold. This is one sense of 'perspectives'. (In 1. 3. 208 we see that Richard refers to the 'glasses'
of Gaunt's eyes, not only the lenses of his eyes, but the eyes filled
with tears, and so like facets of glass reflecting light.) From this
Bushy jumps to something else, the perspective or trick picture,
where the painter, as proof of his ingenuity, produces a painting
which has to be looked at aslant, or awry, if his subject is to be
understood, and not by standing in front of it. He quibbles on the
two senses 'awry'—its literal meaning of 'aslant', and the further
moral sense derived from 'improperly' or 'in the wrong way'. The
queen, to Bushy, looking sideways at the perspective picture
distinguishes a shape in it, but at the same time when she does this
she is looking 'awry' at it, or not as she should. The quibble produces some confusion, for as Bushy says if you look at these pictures
'rightly', that is, standing directly in front of them, you can distinguish nothing and all seems confused; on the other hand, the
'right' way of looking at them is to look at them 'awry', from some
prescribed angle at the side. This is not really important, but the
intricacy of the word-play should be noted.

The best example of elaborate word-play is in the last long speech
of the king shortly before his death (5. 5. 1–66). We shall leave aside,
for the time being, its connection with the way the character is
represented by the dramatist. Richard begins 'I have been
studying'. He goes on to say what is the subject of his study—a
comparison between his prison (the room to which he is now confined) and the whole world. His difficulty is that he is the only person

in his cell, whereas there are millions of people in the world, but yet he 'will hammer it out', or try to work it out somehow. The suggestions of both 'studying' and 'hammer it out' are of conscious care and labour given to the work in hand, here that of producing an effective comparison. This fits in with the effect of elaboration of texture given to the whole play. As Richard develops his comparison we see how skilled the dramatist is in getting his verse to perform what he wants of it.

Sentences. Similarly, a number of sententious passages in rhymed verse—some of them anthologized in *England's Parnassus*—such things as 1. 1. 176 ff.; or 2. 1. 5 ff. (where a rhymed quatrain is worked into ll. 8–12) show Shakespeare's artistry. The effect of these, as that of the sestet in 3. 2. 76–81, is to heighten, through the finish and flow of the verse, the emotional situation of the speaker. Richard's lines in 3. 2. 76 ff. are strengthened by the two images of colour (the healthy red of his complexion, which might recall the colours of the troops, now pale and deathly since all his forces are gone), and those connected with 'blot', stain or smudge, in their literal and moral senses, which recur in the play. These two images, besides being worked into verse of the texture the play requires, are part of the pattern of its thought. The king's ruddy complexion links him with the 'rose', the chief of all the flowers, while the words 'time hath set a blot upon my pride' indicate in clear terms the simple moral or lesson of the play. 'Blot', the black mark of disgrace, obscures and spoils his reputation, in the same way that the rose is attacked by the black canker. Richard's tragedy is referred to here. It is that of the man who cannot fulfil the demands made of the king. In other words, there is a 'blot' upon his reputation. There is a 'blot', too, on the reputation of those who deposed him. So Richard's murder has, as its instigator quite rightly points out, wrought a 'deed of slander upon my head and all this famous land'. Bolingbroke, in these lines in 5. 6. 34–6, thinks of himself as bearing the brand of the criminal on his forehead. This was the 'blot' on his character.

The elaboration of the speech medium, in the interests of providing a measure adequate to the pageantry and ritual of the play, is to be noted, too, in the passages of what the rhetoricians called 'stichomythia', the quick cut and thrust of repartee, when one character, like a duellist, turns a word or phrase used by his opponent against him—as in 1. 3. 258–70, and 2. 1. 87–94.

The substance of the play

The structure of the play, its pageantry, enacts the fall of the king. But this enactment, and the contrast between the demands made of a king and Richard's fulfilment of them, is elicited even more through the poetry than by the events, or the plot, of the play. There is, indeed, a sequence of events in the play: the quarrel between Mowbray and Bolingbroke; their banishment; the death of John of Gaunt and Richard's seizure of his property which by law should be Bolingbroke's; the revolt of some of the nobles who rally to Bolingbroke newly landed in England while Richard is away in Ireland; Richard's return to England; his surrender to Bolingbroke; his deposition; the proclamation of Bolingbroke as king; Richard's murder. But these events are important not on account of what Richard does, but on account of what he does not do. And of this— what he does not do—we are continually reminded by the poetry. There is action in *Richard II* in the sense that there can hardly be a play without some action or movement of its story. But action as an element of *character* seems to be absent from Richard's make-up, and the clear indication of this is furnished in the poetry the dramatist gives him and the images through which the central situation of the play is exhibited.

The only positive action by Richard in the play except for his slaying of two murderers in 5. 5 is his decisive transgression of law in his wrongful seizure of the dead Gaunt's estates. We are told of his complicity in Gloucester's murder, of his shameful conduct with his favourites, of his exactions, and of the reasons for the commons' distrust and dislike of him. The king's character might seem, in the absence of action, to be no more than the sum of his deficiencies according to Tudor belief. The play's man of action is Bolingbroke. But the play's interest is focused on the character of the king, as this is elucidated, not through plot, but by the poetry. The contrast between Bolingbroke and himself is subsidiary to this. The structure of the play shows that Richard is neither impartial justicer, nor physician. He cannot heal the differences between his nobles, and he himself behaves illegally. As gardener he has let his garden run to weeds. As soldier he does not fight. He has no resolution as his rival has; far from soaring at any pitch at all, he sits down on the ground to bewail his fate. He resigns his kingship, and is imprisoned and done to death. What happens in the play happens, not because of any development in the characters of either the king or Bolingbroke, but because the king's character, fixed at the beginning of the play as that of the sovereign unfit to rule, can have no other effect on the events which are to follow except that of bringing the kingdom to the brink of civil disorder and himself to his fall and death.

Everything in the play depends on the way the character of the king is presented. With all the characters in the play he shares in the rich verse necessary to the play's pageantry. He is differentiated from the rest of the persons in the play, first of all by his position as king, which the verse celebrates in the various clusters of images hung round his royalty. The function of these images is both to idealize the figure and also to define it by the contrast evoked between their conventional associations and the actual Richard.

The king is also differentiated from the other persons in the play in the particular blank verse given him in his decline, that is, for the greater part of the play.

The imagery: Biblical allusion. To take the imagery first. The king's pre-eminence is insisted on, first of all, in numerous images from the Bible which parallel his situation with some significant turn in the story of Christ or the biblical history of mankind. The speaker, most often Richard himself, draws attention to the comparison between his situation in the play and the biblical record. Richard, who by Elizabethans would have been regarded as God's deputy, continually thinks of himself as being wronged or made to suffer in the way Christ was. The persistence of these biblical allusions suggests that the dramatist wished his allusion, where it was incomplete, to be filled in by the audience. For instance, in 3. 2. 132 Richard calls his erstwhile favourites 'Judases'. The epithet was so common as a term of abuse for any traitor that it would not definitely follow that Richard here saw himself as the betrayed Christ. Yet it is taken up again in 4. 1. 169 ff. in the assertion that whereas Christ found truth in 'all but one', Richard's plight is worse for he found no one true to him, they were all Judases. Looking on those around him and punning bitterly on the word 'favours'—i.e. their faces, and their false expressions of good-will towards him—Richard's image projects his situation as he understands it. Remembering the words of Christ, he claims that the earth and the stones will be given human senses and will fight on his side (3. 2. 24 ff.); that, as Christ might have summoned legions of angels to fight for him, so God will muster them on his side (3. 2. 60 ff.); that God will strike his foes with pestilence, as he did the enemies of the children of Israel (3. 3. 85 ff.); that his judges seated in authority above him cannot, like Pilate, wash away from themselves the sin of having delivered him to his 'sour cross' (4. 1. 239 ff.). On his entry to London he was scorned and dishonoured by the crowd in much the same way Christ was by the soldiers—York's account of it in 5. 2. 30 'dust was thrown on his sacred head' recalls both the divinity of the king and a frequent subject in religious painting. And Sir Pierce of Exton at the end of the play is thought of as the first murderer Cain.

Religious drama and the Stations of the Cross made the subject of Christ's betrayal and passion both familiar and awe-inspiring to audiences at that time. Imagery of this kind would not only heighten scenes in which the king endures humiliation and suffering, it would also throw light on the king's attitude to himself. Would the most ardent believers in Richard's divinity have been ready at all points to make the straight comparison between him and the figure of Christ? Might not these images suggest an element of self-dramatization in the speaker?

England as Eden. England is regarded as a paradisal Eden where a second fall of man takes place. This scene (3. 4) is one of the most important in the play, for the Tudor garden with its formal design and arrangement is presented as a symbol of the order of the kingdom and of the universe. Medieval and Tudor literature were full of the argument from such analogies. A thesis was supported by the accumulation of parallels which acted as proof. So the principle of order in the heavens was paralleled by the order in every single one of the little worlds or microcosms—of the animals, of vegetables, of fishes, etc.—and by the analogy from music (to which Richard refers in his long soliloquy in Act 5), and from dancing. Here the garden is a symbol of the kingdom. As it cannot flourish unless the plots where plants are to grow are kept in order and the growth of the plants is regulated, so the kingdom cannot prosper unless there is rule and order in it too. Without the head gardener and those who work under his orders, the garden would soon turn into a wilderness overrun with weeds. If we remember that Bacon at about this time or a little later began his well-known essay 'Of Gardens' with the sentence 'God Almighty first planted him a garden', we see how naturally the garden would evoke the religious significances of Eden.

In this scene the Gardener (or the head of the staff of gardeners), explicitly refers to the analogy between the garden and the commonwealth in 3. 4. 33 ff. His words 'All must be even in our government' insist on the order and regularity which have to prevail. Nothing must be too lofty, weeds should not be allowed to spread. These words are echoed by one of the under-gardeners, who makes the analogy plainer, by referring to the garden of England where under its gardener, Richard, everything is disordered. The 'knot' is the ornamental flowerbed, an important part of formal gardens, like that at Hampton Court.

What the gardener says about the king should be noted as sufficient description of his character and of the reason for his fall. He
has been lax in his duties, he has not known how to tend his garden,
so it goes to ruin. The queen, hearing the news of the king's deposition, cannot contain herself and comes out on to the main stage.
She takes up a word spoken by the Gardener: 'depressed' (brought
down), and says, with a pun, 'O I am pressed to death through want
of speaking'—pressed to death being a torture where a man had
heavier and heavier weights placed on his chest in order to force him
to speak. She cannot stand the torture and rates the Gardener,
calling him 'old Adam's likeness', or the counterpart of the first
man who in the garden of Eden committed the sin of disobedience
to God and so brought 'woe' into the world.

In 4. 1. 143–5 the Bishop of Carlisle sees the garden of England
becoming 'the field of Golgotha', where Christ was crucified,
now that the king is going to be judged and deposed. Bolingbroke,
referring to Gloucester's murder as that of Abel, thinks of the blood
of the murdered man calling upon him for vengeance (1. 1. 104 ff.)
which is surely surprising and even sacrilegious, for Abel's blood
called out to God. It was the king, or God's deputy, who had to
judge and punish, as Gaunt in the next scene reminds the Duchess
of Gloucester. Whether Richard realizes the significance of what
Bolingbroke says or not, he is struck by his ambition, and likening
him to a falcon says: 'How high a pitch his resolution soars.'

The king as sun, rose and physician. Another cluster of images
associates the person of the king with the brightness and glory of
the sun. There would be strong emotional significances in this
image, for in ancient belief the sun was god, the source of light and
life. Richard sees himself as the sun (3. 2. 47 ff.). To Bolingbroke
he is the element of fire (3. 3. 58), and a few lines later on the sun
itself (3. 3. 63 ff.). Richard going down to meet Bolingbroke in 'the
base court' thinks of himself as the son of the classical sun-god
Phaethon, who, not knowing how to control the horses of his father's
chariot, fell from the heavens (3. 3. 178); in his hour of agony

standing, deposed, before his rival Bolingbroke whom he sees as the new 'sun', he cries

> O, that I were a mockery king of snow,
> Standing before the sun of Bolingbroke,
> To melt myself away in water-drops!   (4. 1. 260ff.)

Later, looking into the mirror he thinks of himself once more as having been the sun whose radiance made beholders 'wink' (close their eyes), when he says:

> Was this the face
> That, like the sun, did make beholders wink?   (4. 1. 283–4)

The glory that shone and still shines in it he sees as 'brittle', both fragile and unsubstantial. Salisbury, remembering Lucifer, in 2. 4. 18–20 thinks of the king as a shooting-star which falls to the earth.

As the king is sun, or the chief of the planets, so he is the rose, or the most eminent of the flowers. These two images, with those of the lion or the king of the beasts, were conventionally used of royalty. Richard is the lovely rose. The queen calls him 'my fair rose', as if he were some flower she was wearing. Whether this comparison was heightened by a reference to the fresh, ruddy complexion traditionally attributed to this king or not, it adds new force to the figure of the king as the dramatist wishes it to be held in the imaginations of his audience.

Besides, as king, Richard has to be physician. In 1. 1. 153–7 he undertakes this role. In traditional belief in many cultures the role of the king is that of the doctor, whose function is to heal. The great man in many Eastern legends and religions is physician, for he brings medicine for the ills of the world.

The character of Richard

These images give us one picture of Richard. Whether in speaking of himself he is dramatizing himself, or whether those who speak of him recall the divinity with which he should be 'hedged about', these are the associations proper to a king. But the development of the play contrasts all these accompaniments of kingship with the actual holder of the office. Richard falls short of each of the attributes with which these references invest him. He is God's deputy, but he is also the man accused of complicity in the murder of his uncle. In 2. 1. 126 Gaunt in his tirade against him turns inside-out one of the symbols used of Christ in applying it to Richard. In the Christian emblem Christ was the pelican, the bird which fed its young with the blood streaming out of its self-inflicted wounds on its breast. Richard does exactly the opposite. He is accused by Gaunt of 'drunkenly carousing' the blood of his father's brother. Far from shedding his blood for the benefit of his children, he drinks, as in an orgy, the blood of his parents.

We have already seen how the glory bestowed on Richard by other images is dissipated by his failure to live up to the demands of the various roles he has to play. His insufficiency as king culminates in the threat of civil war. Already at the beginning of the play the kingdom is divided against itself and England's peers are at each other's throats. Carlisle's 'prophecy' in 4. 1. 136 ff. is hardly prophecy at all. It is hardly more than inference from the desperate state of a kingdom where the king is unworthy and a rival ascends the throne. If it is 'prophecy', it is fulfilled as soon as it is made, for in 5. 2 we see York in conflict with his son Aumerle, and hear Bolingbroke's complaints about his 'unthrifty' son. The justification for the scenes between Aumerle and his parents and Henry's references to his son are their dramatic sequel to Carlisle's 'prophecy'.

The imagery of the play as a whole defines the contrast between the ideal king and Richard. The verse which Shakespeare gives Richard to speak in his decline expresses his personality. Richard is, in the very words he used of Mowbray in 1. 3. 174, 'compassionate'.

He is, to use a modern expression, full of self-pity. He sees himself continually as an object which moves not only the beholders but also himself to emotionalism. He is a character in a play of his own making, and its intention seems to be that of working himself up to tears about his own unhappy state.

To Gaunt he is an 'unstaid youth' (2. 1. 2); York thinks of him as an untamed colt (2. 1. 70), a young man led astray by flatterers (2. 1. 17 ff.), interested only in vanity. He is too young to be able to see and understand the world around him; as a result he lives in a world of his own imagining. His character is made clear to us by the verse Shakespeare gives him. Through it we are given the young man, not quite grown up, sentimentally attached to the contemplation of his own image of himself. So his rival, Bolingbroke, can tell him in 4. 1. 292 ff., in the very important scene with the mirror:

> The shadow of your sorrow hath destroyed
> The shadow of your face.

Quibbling with the senses of 'shadow' (both that which is unreal, which exists only in Richard's imagination, and what is not the real man, but only his reflection in the mirror), Bolingbroke says of Richard that he lives in a world of unreality in which he mistakes imaginary griefs for real ones, and the reflection of his face in the mirror for the man himself. Whether Richard's griefs were imaginary or not, the verse in which he celebrates his looking into the mirror, his dramatic gesture in dashing the glass to the ground (4. 1. 289 ff.), and his hyperbolic

> Mark, silent king, the moral of this sport,
> How soon my sorrow hath destroyed my face.

fit the dramatic character here given him by Shakespeare. He might be Narcissus in love with his image.

Bolingbroke and Richard. We note the contrast between Bolingbroke and Richard. Bolingbroke is 'silent', he is not free with words, nor prone to speech, except when the occasion demands it. When he speaks, as in 2. 3, to his chief supporters, we see how practical the tenor of his words is:

> I thank thee, gentle Percy, and be sure
> I count myself in nothing else so happy
> As in a soul rememb'ring my good friends,
> And as my fortune ripens with thy love,
> It shall be still thy true love's recompense.
> My heart this covenant makes, my hand thus seals it.

What he promises here is to be as full of rewards to Percy as Percy is full of zeal on his side, and with the demonstrative gesture of giving his hand to Percy he seals a bargain. Percy in 1 *Henry IV* remembering this scene thinks of these promises as Bolingbroke's flattery. Bolingbroke is the 'politician', a word which to Elizabethans was full of sinister suggestions. He knows how to make use of everything which comes his way and of every situation in which he finds himself. In the disgrace of his banishment, he knows how, through his 'courtship' of the common people on which Richard remarks in 1. 4. 23–36, to turn his disadvantage into gain. And when the sentence of banishment is pronounced on him he is not going to soothe himself with imagining that he is not banished, as his father, Gaunt, suggests. To his father's plea that he should not take his sentence so heavily, he replies in 1. 3. 294 ff. that imagining a thing is so does not make it so, which is the opposite of Richard's attitude in the scene with the mirror.

The difference in the attitudes of Bolingbroke and Richard can be seen in the former's concluding words to his father in the scene referred to above:

> Fell sorrow's tooth doth never rankle more
> Than when he bites, but lanceth not the sore.

The meaning of his maxim is: If you are attacked by sorrow, better a deep wound which like the surgeon's knife releases the infection cutting deep, than the superficial bite which infects and causes festering. In other words he tells Gaunt that it is better to accept reality however harsh it is, than to try to solace oneself by pretending the misfortune which depresses one does not exist. Both the sentiment and the verse contrast with Richard's.

The king continually indulges in his sorrow; he is, with his world of make-believe neither facing reality nor curing his grief, but by fingering the tender spot giving himself some perverse satisfaction. He luxuriates in his emotions, even though they are sorrowful.

As Richard's fortunes decline, Bolingbroke's advance. The parallel with Richard should be considered both in the plot of the play and the dramatist's attitude to the two characters. It is clear from 1. 1. 109 where Richard exclaims

How high a pitch his resolution soars!

that Bolingbroke's is an aspiring mind. Like many of Marlowe's heroes he must aspire to the highest position of all. In 1. 4. 35–6 Richard describes Bolingbroke's behaviour as that of the man who already saw himself the heir to the throne:

As were our England in reversion his,
And he our subjects' next degree in hope.

Whatever wrongs Bolingbroke had endured at Richard's hands, however he was aided by Fortune and by Richard's own weaknesses, there was no justification whatsoever for his usurpation of the crown. Not only the Bishop of Carlisle's speech in 4. 1. 114ff. should be remembered, but also the last scene of the play where Bolingbroke, like the pious Christian, vows to do penance for his crime in making a pilgrimage to the Holy Land 'to wash this blood off from my guilty hand' (5. 6. 50). Here, remembering Richard's reference in 4. 1. 239–42, we could say that Bolingbroke thinks of himself as a Pilate, though his form of words expresses his repentance.

Throughout the play Bolingbroke should be considered as one mode through which the dramatist concentrates attention on his main character, Richard.

Richard's verse examined. The verse given to Richard fits the character of the man in love with himself, and so unable to live in a world of reality and be king.

It is of course true that the king uses the language common to all characters in the play—such as in his opening speeches summoning the two challengers to appear before him, or in his attack on Northumberland in 3. 3. 72ff. for not greeting him with bended knees. But we must distinguish between this common tone and language and that given him in his fall. There is little to distinguish the verse of the king in his rage and pride from that of the other characters in the same mood. It has the same strong tones and violent imagery, and fits the speaker in a show where the issues are a kingdom and the participants princes and noblemen. For instance, do we see much difference between Richard speaking of the result of Bolingbroke's invasion of England and Bolingbroke's threat of what would follow Richard's refusal to grant him his demands, both of them in 3. 3? We know from 3. 3. 91 that, as Bolingbroke is referred to, the speaker is Richard; and from 3. 3. 47 that it is Bolingbroke, otherwise the speeches might belong to either, since the staple of language and the references in both are more or less the same. With these two passages should be linked Richard's speech in 1. 3. 125 ff. on the consequences of civil war in the country. It is textually confused, but in its character it belongs to one strand of the play's poetry.

What is more characteristic of the Richard presented to us in this play is the poetry given to him when he is 'compassionate', such as in 3. 2. 6 ff.; 3. 2. 93 ff.; 3. 2. 144 ff.; 3. 3. 143 ff.; 4. 1. 201 ff.; 5. 1. 16–25; 5. 5. 1–66. What in the most general terms is common to all of it? We note first of all that it is softer in its tones than the verse in the rest of the play. This is because Richard is appealing for pity, he sees himself as the king who is wronged, but he assumes the role a bit too readily. In his lines to the queen in 5. 1. 16 the softness of the tones almost contradicts the picture the king paints of himself as 'Sworn brother to grim Necessity'. He begins by addressing his wife as if she were not known to him at all, but someone weeping for him as if she intended to add to his griefs and so bring about his death precipitately. It should be noted that his attention is, first of all, directed to his own grief and not really to hers.

The total effect of some of this 'compassionate' speech seems to run counter to the express intention of the speaker. The rhythm creates an impression of plaintiveness and not at all of the 'sworn brother' to 'grim Necessity'. Similarly, in 3. 3. 143 ff. the intention of the speaker is to suggest his mortification at putting away of all the insignia of royalty, but the effect of the lines is to create the impression that Richard enjoys imaginatively investing himself with the robes belonging to another role—that of the palmer. We feel that he is not giving up anything but taking on something which contents him as much as his royal robes did.

Its lyrical flow. There is, too, in these speeches a lyrical flow which differentiates them from the rest of the play. Richard's tones are plangent and melodious. There is a pleasing tune in them. They do not progress, their thought does not develop. They seem to move forwards and backwards, over and over again, as if with a rocking motion. The pleasant swing which seems to belong to them is given both by their content—the king dwelling on his forlorn state—and their form: their regular repetition and the patterning of the phrases:

> As a long-parted mother with her child
> Plays fondly with her tears and smiles in meeting;
> So, weeping, smiling, greet I thee, my earth,
> And do thee favours with my royal hands.... (3. 2. 8 ff.)

> Say, is my kingdom lost? why, 'twas my care,
> And what loss is it to be rid of care?
> Strives Bolingbroke to be as great as we?
> Greater he shall not be. If he serve God,
> We'll serve him too, and be his fellow so:
> Revolt our subjects? that we cannot mend,
> They break their faith to God as well as us:
> Cry, woe, destruction, ruin, and decay,
> The worst is death, and death will have his day. (3. 2. 95 ff.)

> Let's talk of graves, of worms, and epitaphs...
> Let's choose executors and talk of wills...
> How some have been deposed, some slain in war,
> Some haunted by the ghosts they have deposed,
> Some poisoned by their wives, some sleeping killed....
>   (3. 2. 145 ff.)

> With mine own tears I wash away my balm,
> With mine own hands I give away my crown,
> With mine own tongue deny my sacred state,
> With mine own breath release all duteous oaths:
>   (4. 1. 207 ff.)

'A little little grave, an obscure grave' of 3. 3. 154 is typical of the repetition which shows the self-indulgent way in which the king rocks himself in his grief. In countries where the institution of hired mourners at funerals is still known, it will be remembered that it is customary for the expression of grief to be accompanied by a rhythmical rocking of the body to and fro, the words used to express grief being phrases repeated *ad lib.*

The self-regarding character of Richard. There is something else in these speeches. They leave a clear impression of a speaker who is both regarding himself all the time, and keeping one eye on the beholders. Richard is taken up with his own woes, but not so completely that he does not care whether he is noticed or not. He wants those around him to be equally engaged in them. Richard is aware of himself all the time, and of an audience too. This produces one of two reactions in him: either he is aware that what he is doing, 'wailing his woes', is unworthy of himself and his situation; or he wishes his audience to mark what he does, for only so can he be satisfied that his woes get all the attention he wants them to have.

So he can feel that his words to his country's earth (3. 2. 6 ff.) are being smiled at by those around him and he can say, 'Mock not my senseless conjuration' ('senseless' because he is addressing things which lack human senses); and in 3. 3. 170–1, he knows he is in-dulging in foolish talk and thinks he sees Northumberland and the others laughing at him. Northumberland actually describes him as a man talking wildly because he has been maddened by grief (3. 3. 185–6). Or again he feels that he might as well 'play the wanton' with his woes (that is, not only trifle with them, but give himself up to them in a way unworthy of them and of himself) in his suggestion to Aumerle in 3. 3. 164. To his wife in 5. 1. 101 he uses a similar expression, 'we make woe wanton with this fond delay', in his awareness that all the business of their parting, kisses, and 'witty' words, are a foolish ('fond') dallying, and that they should, without more ado, take leave of each other.

In other cases the king, far from feeling that his exhibition of grief is unworthy of himself, wants his audience to pay special attention to it, and to what he says and does; he must have this satisfaction. He feels, as he says to Aumerle, that he is not really doing justice to the role his woes demand of him:

> 'O, that I were as great
> As is my grief, or lesser than my name!'   (3. 3. 136–7)

Or there is explicit instruction given to the spectators that they should concentrate on him, even as he is giving himself up entirely to his woes. So he turns on them in 3. 2. 177 with the question 'How can you say to me, I am a king?' when it was he, and not they, who had been insisting that he was a king, and that this would be sufficient to dispel his enemies. And in 4. 1. 203 he says: 'Now mark me how I will undo myself', which means not only take off the trappings of royalty, but also destroy ('undo') himself. Then follow the characteristic plaintive lines with which he puts off his kingly array. Again, a few lines later (4. 1. 290) he draws the attention of Bolingbroke to what his action signifies. He has asked the by-standers to listen to his 'reading' of the book (the glass) in which his faults are written and now he wants Bolingbroke to 'mark' the moral he draws from this. There is something similar to this in his last long soliloquy, where, though alone, he instinctively addresses some person imagined on the stage, 'Now, sir, the sound that tells what hour it is. . . .' The 'sir' shows how naturally he provides himself with an audience. He is continually aware of himself, and he assumes that the attention of everybody is turned on him.

How should his character be taken? What then is the character which the play gives Richard? We have seen that as king, tradition and convention made certain demands of him. These he is unable to fulfil. If there is any reason given by the dramatist for his inability, it seems to belong to his youthfulness and his wantonness—his wilful irresponsibility, even in his grief. This was one of the stock attributes in literature of the young man Richard is portrayed as being—the tendency to give himself up to dallying, to frivolity. These, Bolingbroke hints, are part of the character of his young son, the prince Henry: all the qualities Richard lacks as the result of his not yet being a grown man, much less a wise man, or even a king. His is the idleness of youth, its pride in itself, its devotion to itself, and its inattention to the serious duties which manhood and kingship impose. Holinshed, to whom Shakespeare was indebted for the greater part of his material, thought that Richard's fault was 'the frailtie of wanton youth'. *The Mirror for Magistrates* attributed Richard's fate to his 'evil governance' (his bad rule of the state and of himself). When Shakespeare later wrote the two parts of *Henry IV* he gave us a portrait of another young man, in danger of being misled by evil counsellors, but with the saving grace of being able to know reality and to distinguish good from evil. In this play Bolingbroke can say (5. 3. 1–12) that his son is 'unthrifty' (profligate) and dissolute, but yet there are some sparks of better hope in him. Richard, as Shakespeare portrays him, is the young man too much given over to self-indulgence to be able to be either man or king. His story is that of an accumulation of woes on the head of a king who can do no more than bewail them. Richard is aware of his inability to sustain the position to which he was called; his last speech is a beautiful example of his deficiencies as man and king. He knows that he

> for the concord of my state and time
> Had not an ear to hear my true time broke.   (5. 5. 47–8)

and that he 'wasted time' so that now time wastes him, but the speech itself is further illustration of the conduct Richard is engaged in deploring. What is he doing here but being oblivious of the reality? Studying in his grief to equate his prison with the world, he knows he is playing a role all the time. One of the significances of the image from acting in Shakespeare was of the falsity and unreality of actor and stage. When Richard says (5. 5. 31–2):

> Thus play I in one person many people,
> And none contented

we are left with the feeling that he has always been 'play-acting' in the modern sense of the term. In the Elizabethan sense the role he has been playing would be not that of king, but of foolish 'wanton', the young man who gave himself up to the pleasures and satisfactions of the moment without a thought or a care for his responsibilities and duties.

Conclusion. In Shakespeare's portrait of Richard two elements are to be noted: the stress laid on the traditional demands made of the king and the inability of Richard to fulfil them. Bolingbroke has been better able to sustain the role, and it is clear from what we are told of him in 1. 4. 24–36 and in 2. 3 that, like the good politician, he is attentive to what he is doing. In *1 Henry IV* Bolingbroke describes, for the benefit of his son Prince Hal, how he actually played the part.

Both are to be thought of as *actors*, and neither can therefore be a true and proper king. Richard pays for his deficiencies as king and the wrongs he commits. He falls. In his fall he is a pathetic figure. But we are never allowed to forget that he was and is a bad king. Bolingbroke may have been wronged, he may have had abilities which Richard notably lacked, but we are never allowed to forget that he is guilty of usurping the throne and is therefore no rightful king.

When Shakespeare took up the subject of ideal kingship, as he did in *Henry V*, he was confronted with the difficulty of making his ideal figure seem both human and attractive. His task in *Richard II* was easier. The distance from the ideal was so far that both it and its reflection seem to be exaggerated and artificial. Yet to his picture of the king he brought all the resources of his early verse, and within the range of its possibilities Shakespeare provided a well-defined likeness of a tragic figure, whose tragedy lies in his fall and its consequences which are moving.

9. THE MERCHANT OF VENICE

Shakespeare's *The Merchant of Venice* was first printed in quarto form by James Roberts in 1600. It was there described as *The most excellent Historie of the Merchant of Venice with extreame crueltie of Shylocke the Jewe towards the sayd Merchant, in cutting a just pound of his flesh: and the obtayning of Portia by the choyse of three chests.* Whoever was responsible for this account of the play on its title-page, called it a 'historie' (a story). In fact there are several stories in it: of Antonio, the merchant, and the usurer Shylock; of the lady of Belmont, Portia, and the test of the caskets by which alone she could be won, and how the third suitor gains the prize; of Lorenzo and how he eloped with the usurer's daughter, Jessica, and how both of them found refuge at Belmont; of Gobbo, who ran away from his master, the usurer, and, like the others, went to Belmont; and of the two women in disguise who beguiled their husbands of their rings, this too being set right at Belmont. In its most memorable episode Portia comes to the rescue of her husband's friend, and saves him from the usurer; and in the end all the good characters are happily united in Belmont.

More than a fairy tale

The material of this play has often been likened to a fairy tale. Enchanting though it may be, we shall see that the play touches on matters of seriousness, so that there is something to be taken away from it besides the very satisfying impression of romance.

Shakespeare took his story from the Italian. It differs only in its ratio of romance to reality, a reality Elizabethans would understand, from all those stories of love and adventure, which they were eagerly reading in translation—such stories as those of Romeo and Juliet, of Othello, and so on. Whether Shakespeare got his story directly from some Italian source, or from an earlier play, we do not know, nor does it matter greatly. All sorts of fairy-tale material are used in this play, some of it not originally Italian but of very ancient Oriental provenance, as for instance the story of the caskets, and of the pound of flesh. The wealth of story-telling in Eastern, particularly Indian, cultures had given rise to classical Greek, Latin and Islamic analogues, so the story Shakespeare used may have existed in various forms. What is important is the use he made of a well-known tale.

Romance and moral seriousness

The special stamp Shakespeare gave his material is that of the suggestion of something serious, and real, in addition to the romance or the fairy-tale. We shall notice throughout *The Merchant of Venice* how everything in the play has a double character: a connection with the externals of romance, and at the same time an allusion to, or some link with, undoubted moral seriousness. In most of his comedies we find a similar tendency—that of evoking through the gaiety, even the light-heartedness, of its situations the suggestion of something more serious and grave.

In the popular theatre there were no strict rules by which plays had to be written, and Shakespeare's form is often a concoction of various materials. Tragedy could be the story of a great man who came to an unhappy end. Comedy could be a story ('historie') with a happy ending, and it could include something other than, or even opposed to, the pleasurable lightness usually associated with comedy today. We shall see in *Twelfth Night* how the two—the grave and the gay—are blended. There is the same process here. The theatre to Elizabethans was often like the pulpit in the sound morality it preached. And to all people at that time the business of literature and the arts was to teach.

So the romantic story of the extreme situation of Antonio, who is saved from the ogreish Shylock by Portia, the fairy-princess whom Bassanio wins as his bride, and all its other stories have a serious undertone. The impossibility of the 'historie' is based on a moral reality which poses such questions as were the subjects of moral interlude (p. 31).

Structure

The structure of the play depends on a number of situations of trial or test. At various points in the action a character is tested, or a trial takes place. These tests are based on moral criteria such as how should one decide between three offered choices (the casket test), or in the great trial scene which is better: Justice or Mercy? And often everything seems to turn on deciding between appearance and reality.

Looking at the play as a series of tests, we see that it opens with Bassanio's test of his friend Antonio: will Antonio help him in the great exploit of entering for the test to win the hand of Portia? After a scene of exposition which gives us Portia and Belmont, and in which Nerissa very gently tests Portia's reactions both to the suitors so far assembled and to the will of her father, we have Antonio tested again, this time by Shylock. Will he consent to what Shylock calls 'merry sport'? Here we have the situation of man faced by a seeming jest, put to him by another who seems a 'gentle' friend. But we know that behind Shylock and his offer are grim possibilities.

The casket test follows, while Gobbo humorously tests his father, and Jessica, who seems to be a dutiful daughter, leaves her father's house. In the meantime the storm has been gathering and breaks on Antonio's head. In 4. 1 comes the great trial scene, where reality is shown to be superior to appearance and mercy preferable to justice, which can almost ruin the man who puts his trust in it alone. Out of the successful issue of the trial a further test develops —that of the husbands and the rings. They do not recognize their wives, they are deceived by appearance, but in the final scene of resolution in Act 5, the merchant comes to the rescue again, stakes his soul this time for his friend, and everything ends happily.

The characters

Before we examine in detail how this structure is to be seen in the development of the play, we should turn to its persons, for in the way in which they are described and presented we can see how naturally and easily they come to be involved in the situations of trial or test in which they figure.

Antonio. To take Antonio first, the merchant of Venice. He is what the Duke calls a 'royal merchant' (4. 1. 29). This is Gratiano's description of him too (3. 2. 240). He is not only wealthy, but also a person of a royal or kingly disposition. As a man of great wealth Antonio is in a prominent position; in most cultures, certainly in Eastern cultures, the possession of wealth would entitle him to respect, for with it went responsibilities and duties. So in the East the man of wealth is often given an honorific title. Not so long ago in India the wealthy Zamindar was often a Rajah; and in Malaya and China there are special terms of respect to designate the rich man. Such men were expected to be generous, to be spenders of their wealth, and not to be miserly but charitable. Antonio is a man of this kind. He gives all, even his life, to help his friend, the poor man Bassanio, with whom he is, in the way of these romances, linked. That Antonio uses his wealth to help others, we know from 3. 3. 21 ff.

He is also mysteriously and romantically tinged with melancholy. It may be that Shakespeare in shaping his materials interposes a hint of what is to follow. He gives Antonio a premonition of his fate. His melancholy would be due, too, to his loss of Bassanio. That he loves Bassanio so devotedly would not make him specially romantic in Elizabethan eyes, for it was a commonplace that two men could be so devoted to each other. In an early play of Shakespeare's we have Proteus and Valentine who are sworn brothers, and we shall see in *Twelfth Night* how the sea-captain, Antonio, risks his life to follow Sebastian only because of his great attachment to him.

But there is something else. Antonio is not only the fabulous merchant, of an interesting melancholic turn of mind. He is a Christian. This is the first remark made of him by his enemy Shylock. In describing him as a Christian Shylock calls him 'fawning publican', which recalls the type of person Christ preferred to the self-righteous Pharisee. Antonio, in the use of his wealth, comes near to the prescription given to the rich young ruler whom Christ advised to sell everything that he had. The rich young ruler did not do as Christ recommended, but Antonio's pledging of all his wealth to help a friend and his generosity should be contrasted with Shylock's miserliness, and be reckoned part of his 'royal', Christian disposition. In Shylock's own words Antonio was wont to lend money 'for Christian courtesy'. Of him Salerio says (2. 8. 35) 'a kinder gentleman treads not the earth', where 'kind' would mean not only of a kindly disposition, but also full of what should be natural to human beings—feeling for others. ('Kind' is a word with the two senses of which Shakespeare often played.) To Bassanio (3. 2. 293 ff.) he is

> the kindest man
> The best-conditioned and unwearied spirit
> In doing courtesies.

We shall see in the central scene in the play with what Christian virtue Antonio bears himself.

Round this romantic merchant prince of true Christian virtue are a group of characters of whom we can say little, because the dramatist evidently intends them simply as the train to Antonio. As Morocco is attended by a train, as Bassanio goes on his quest similarly attended, so Antonio is given his Solanios and Salerios. If their number was mistakenly increased and a third by name Salerino invented through confusion between Solanio and Salerio, it all goes to show how unimportant they are as persons in the play. They have no function but as frame to Antonio—in his glory and in his distress.

Bassanio. Bassanio is another romantic character—the young man without means beloved by the merchant prince. Shakespeare makes him a figure recognizable to the Londoners of his time—the young

122

man who through extravagance (as Bassanio confesses 'somewhat showing a more swelling port Than my faint means would grant continuance') has no money. But this weakness of the young should not be held against him, since he shows as much by his attitude as by what is reported of him, that though young and foolish in the past, he is in the play the ideal man to attempt to win the fairy princess. We should not think of him as a mercenary fortune hunter, since social institutions then made the desire of a young man for a wealthy bride perfectly regular. Arranged marriages where the dowry of the girl is an important consideration are well known both in the East and the West. Bassanio, when he first speaks of Portia, describes her as a 'lady richly left' (she has inherited wealth from her father), but he goes on to speak of her as 'fair', and

> fairer than that word,
> Of wondrous virtues.

He compares her with Brutus's Portia, and then proclaims her the fabulous object of desperate adventure—the golden fleece after which Jason sailed.

Bassanio is, in Nerissa's words which gain Portia's approval, a 'scholar and a soldier...of all the men that ever my foolish eyes looked upon, the best deserving a fair lady' (1. 2. 107 ff.). And most important of all, we shall see in the first of the great trials with which this play is concerned, how nobly he bears himself, and how rightly he chooses. To Portia in 3. 2. 60 he recalls the demi-god Hercules who rescued the Trojan maiden. Shakespeare gives Bassanio the character of a man of virtue. We should, remembering the test, judge Bassanio not by the outward show but by what lies within.

He is attended by Gratiano, who is, according to his description in the play and in numerous Italian comedies some of which Shakespeare might have seen in London, a comical figure who always will be talking. In the lists of characters in Italian comedy there is often a Dottore Gratiano, a pompous talker.

Shylock. Shylock is the contrast to the good Antonio. Romance likes to work in black and white, and he is black to Antonio's white.

If explanation were needed of his ogreishness, then we should have to say that that he is a Jew is reason enough. Christian Europe reviled the Jew, and portrayed him as a hateful monster. If we are inclined to flatter ourselves that we are better in this respect, we need only pause for a moment to consider our own record in this century, when racial hatreds have involved not only Jews but countless others of all races in shameful treatment from people like our own enlightened selves. Shakespeare's reaction to Shylock as a Jew is likely to have been that of his time. We can understand and condemn it, but we need not consider that it detracts seriously from the quality of *The Merchant of Venice*, for in the play Shakespeare is not concerned with teaching his audience, or ourselves, how Jews should be treated. If this had been his object then we could feel that there is something gravely at fault with the play as a manual of ethics. Shylock's vengefulness, not his Jewishness, is the centre of the play, and it is not written by a dramatist who felt Shylock's wrongs or those of his race deeply.

- If we read the famous lines Shakespeare gave Shylock in 3. 1. 54 ff., we shall see that they do not suggest that a Jew, because he is as much a human being as any Christian, should therefore be treated accordingly. Their intention is to prove that as Jews and Christians are both human beings, it is natural for them both to revenge wrongs done them—a point of view which would seem damnable both to orthodox Christian opinion and Jewish. Shylock is not asking for our tears, he is putting forward the point of view of a detestable ogre.

- The desperateness of Shylock's evil intentions would, to the audience of that time, have been adequately accounted for by his religion. The trial and execution of the Jewish physician Roderigo Lopez in 1594 for plotting to assassinate both Queen Elizabeth and the claimant to the Portuguese throne, would have made audiences the more ready to accept the conventional notion that such dastardly conduct came naturally to his co-religionists. We should not forget, too, that Shylock is a 'stranger'—strange in his religion, his dress, his manner of speech probably (certainly his Old Testament allusions give his language a colour of its own). He could quite easily be taken as that figure in the community who by his difference from the rest has to incur hostility. It is easy to remember how strongly emotions could be stirred against shopkeepers of another race who include moneylending as part of their business activities.

Shylock is presented to us by the dramatist not only as Jew, but more importantly and significantly as 'dog', wild beast and devil. There are several references to him which insist on his 'currish' disposition. In this matter, too, Shakespeare would seem to the humanitarians of our time in need of reprimand, for he always associated with the dog traits which were dangerous and contemptible: dogs always fawned and flattered; they were to be seen in great households licking at sweets—a messy and disgusting habit. It was their nature to snarl and bite, which may seem absolutely contradictory to the fawning, but what seems to be clear is that the image of dog suggested to Shakespeare what was contemptible.

Shylock is time and time again referred to as 'dog'. He himself reports that this is how Antonio had addressed him and treated him. We might ask whether we should think the worse of Antonio on this account. This was the treatment conventionally accorded to Jews, and we shall see, in the most significant scene of the play, how Antonio behaves towards Shylock. His generous attitude to Shylock immediately after he has been saved by Portia is Shakespeare's own invention, and should be taken as characteristic. To the other characters in the play Shylock is 'the villain Jew' (2. 8. 4), 'the dog Jew' (2. 8. 14), an 'impenetrable cur' (3. 3. 18), and Gratiano in execration of him thinks of him as both dog and wolf, with perhaps a reference to Lopez whose name was derived from the Latin *lupus*—wolf. Shylock himself states ironically (3. 3. 7) 'since I am a dog beware my fangs'.

As the opponent of the good Antonio, Shylock is thought of as devil. The conflict of the good man with the devil was a simple Christian fable, and the writer without intending to be explicitly moral can give his work a simple moral point of view.

So we can see Shylock as devil, the natural adversary of Antonio. Indeed he is often pictured as such in the play. Antonio himself, in a warning to Bassanio of which he himself fails to take heed, looking at Shylock on the stage lost in his reckonings and mutterings and remembering his reference to the biblical story of Jacob and Laban, says 'The devil can cite Scripture for his purpose' (1. 3. 95). To Lancelot his master is, 'God bless the mark', as he puts it, because some obscene phrase is to follow, 'a kind of devil' (2. 2. 22 ff.). To Solanio in 3. 1 he is throughout the devil. To Bassanio in 4. 1. 284 he is 'this devil'. And the situation facing Portia, as she sees it in 3. 4. 20 is that of

> Purchasing the semblance of my soul
> From out the state of hellish cruelty.

This we might take as the substance of the serious side of the play seen in miniature. To the Duke in the trial scene Shylock is an 'inhuman wretch', a term which unites both the suggestions of 'dog' (animal and not human) and 'devil' (wretch being the person expelled and driven out as the devil was from heaven).

Portia. Portia in the romance is the fairy-princess, the rich prize for which the heroes contend. To win her they have to undergo a test or trial, a familiar legend both in the East and West. With Portia are associated all the images of rich treasure and fabulous adventure.

Many critics of the play have contrasted Belmont, where she lives, with the mart of Venice, to which she goes only to rescue Antonio. Her house is associated with music and harmony, while the world outside is 'naughty' or full of wickedness.

In the eulogy pronounced by Morocco in 2. 7. 41 ff. she is the world's wonder. To Portia herself her situation, waiting to be won by the champion, resembles that of Hesione saved from the sea-monster by Hercules, the force of classical fable adding its colour to the poet's presentation of her.

On all these scores she is the fairy-princess of romance. The caskets by which she is to be won, the ring she wears and which she presents to the hero who wins her, and what happens to it—all these are its familiar ingredients. Romantic, too, is the mode of her entry into the Duke's court in the disguise of a young lawyer.

But like all the major characters in the play she is associated with things of deeper seriousness. She is not only the princess of romance, she is thought of as divine and a saint. At the very opening of the play Bassanio, in Antonio's words, has sworn 'a secret pilgrimage' to her (1. 1. 120). Her suitors have to swear a solemn oath at a temple or chapel accepting the conditions on which they are permitted to take the test. Morocco thinks of Belmont as a place of pilgrimage where from the four corners of the world the devout come to kiss the shrine of the saint (2. 7. 39–40). To him Portia is an angel, as he puns on the comparison with the English gold coin, the angel (2. 7. 55 ff.). To Bassanio her portrait is like that of a goddess. When she sets out with Nerissa to the rescue of Antonio, she goes and returns to the accompaniment of suggestions of some religious exercise or retreat in which she is taking part. To Jessica in 3. 5. 68 ff. the winning of Portia must be to Bassanio the equivalent of finding the joys of heaven on this earth. And at the very end of the play, to Lorenzo, she is like God who drops manna from heaven on those he pleases to help.

Her role in the main section of the play resembles that of the angel of the Lord who saved Isaac in the nick of time when he was bound on the altar of sacrifice. She comes mysteriously from Belmont to help Antonio, she meets the devil Shylock on his own ground and discomfits him. She departs just as mysteriously, but not without extracting some token by which her miraculous descent into the law-court of Venice is to be made known. Typical of her is the music associated with her home, which she commands at the fateful moment of the test. Music is characteristic of concord, love and the triumph of good over the discordant forces of evil, and it is, on earth, the counterpart of the music of the spheres of which Lorenzo speaks in 5. 1. 61–6. This heavenly music, in popular belief, was produced by the motion of the heavenly bodies as they circled round the earth.

Human ears could not hear it, but immortal souls, like the cherubim, could.

Persons such as these could be involved in situations which are the stock in trade of romantic tale, if we overlooked the serious side in them. The play could be looked at as a series of romantic and impossible tests; it could also be seen to turn on important moral decisions. The latter seems stronger than the former as a mode of approach to the play, for to Elizabethans a comedy which had some moral to enforce would be in a familiar tradition.

The two themes

We shall see two recurrent motives in the tests on which the play rests. One—whether a man prefers the apparent to the real good— has already been touched on. These two aspects, false seeming and true inwardness, a person, a situation, a phenomenon, turn the situations in which they are decisive into a conflict between what appears to be so and what really is so. The other, also expressed in terms of two opposites, is the conflict between discord and the harmony of music. In the intense dramatic excitement of the play the poetry evoked by these themes moulds plot, character and attitudes into one. The play itself gains its life and character from the way these various things are made one.

How Shakespeare works out his play. In the unfolding drama of the first of the tests, the two themes, of discord and concord, and of the difference between the apparent and the real, are sounded quite early. The scene is Venice and Antonio's fortunes are at their height, but all the while in the speeches of Salerio and Solanio the storms which might wreck the ships are suggested, and the 'royal' merchant, though he should be happy, seems unaccountably sad. In Antonio's opening words there is a hint that the inner man is not to be judged by the outward show, by what people think him to be. Later in the scene, in 1. 1.77 ff., he sees the world as a stage on which he must play a 'sad' (serious) part.

Bassanio's declaration of his desire to win Portia brings in some of the music which suggests the world of concord and harmony. Though the lines (1. 1. 161 ff.) are rhetorical, they are flexible and easy, unlike some of the stiff and hard rhetorical passages in *Richard II*. The voice recounting Portia's virtues progresses quite naturally from the least important of her qualities to her great excellence, and then goes on to an exuberant flow of verse in her praise.

The next scene shows Portia to be as unaccountably sad, 'aweary of this great world', as Antonio, the major character in the other plot. She is gently reproved by Nerissa, who pronounces a good Elizabethan maxim, or 'sentence', recommending the great happiness of not having too much of anything, of being in the 'mean'. As Portia takes this up, she herself reiterates another good Elizabethan commonplace on the difference between giving good counsel and following it, between thought or reason (the brain) and passion (blood). This surely has something to do with one of the themes of the play, for when Portia says that 'It is a good divine that follows his own instructions', she remarks in effect that we know the monk not by his robes, but by what he does, not by the outward show but by the inner reality.

We are to take Portia in this scene as the typical heroine of romance, clever and witty in her comments on her suitors, with her bright character-sketches stressing typical satirist's points against them. In this she is like numerous other women in Shakespeare's plays, and the boy players could act this part to perfection. Only incidentally in this scene is the other side of her nature suggested. Her comments on her suitors are reasonable and lively, but she knows 'it is a sin to be a mocker'. There is a reference to Bassanio before this scene closes, with another witty comment at the end from Portia that if the inner man in Morocco is a saint, though outwardly he may look like a devil (he is black), she would rather he were her father confessor than her husband. 'Shrive' and 'wive' come in pat to make her point more neatly.

Shylock's first appearance. We are back in Venice in the next scene, in the world of trade and the merchant, and once again Shakespeare keeps in the background, but not too far away, the suggestion of storms which destroy and cause havoc. He puts Shylock on the stage, and his first appearance is significant. His dark Jewish gaberdine provides a contrast to the rich clothes of the others. He keeps muttering 'well', 'well', and his language, in its references and its fervent asides ('Yes, to smell pork...' 1. 3. 31 ff.), and the clear indication later that he is hatching a plot to catch Antonio on the hip, together with the outburst against the way he is treated by Christians (1. 3. 103 ff.) suggest the storm again.

When Antonio wants to borrow money from him on interest, a well-known practice at that time, but still attacked as against Christian teaching, in order to help a friend, Shylock's justification of interest makes Antonio warn Bassanio against being deceived by the outward show. His lines (1. 3. 94 ff.) are like a text on which a sermon is preached. But ironically the divine cannot follow his own instructions, and Antonio accepts the terms Shylock offers, in spite of Bassanio's protests, as 'kindness' in the Jew. Before they leave the stage, Antonio punning on 'Gentile' addresses Shylock as 'gentle'. But for Bassanio it is difficult to square the outward show ('fair terms') with the inner reality ('a villain's mind'). It was common knowledge at the time that the more specious and innocent seeming the inducement, the more we have to be on our guard, since it might come from the evil one. So in this short scene through the contrasted characters, the language given them, its references, and through the way the two themes are continually being sounded, Shakespeare is giving his play the shape he wishes it to have.

The two plots

Without developing the plots of the two trials in a regular succession, he keeps them before us. As they are built up, they are made to turn on the deliberate choices made by the characters. The importance of the casket test is seen in the three several speeches made by the three competitors who stand before them and have to decide. What each says is important, not only as statement of why he makes his choice, but as lighting up other areas of the play.

When Morocco, 'a tawnie Moor all in white' as the stage direction in the quarto describes him, appears on the stage, a strong visual contrast is being made, and several things are being established about the man and the kind of choice he is likely to make. First of all costume and make-up suggest he is a figure of romance. Secondly, he is romantic in his speech, in its images and its ring, and this suggests the romantic worth of Portia. Then it is made clear that in this test it is not the outward appearance that matters, but the real worth of the competitor. 'Complexion' meaning nature and disposition is important, not 'complexion' meaning hue. Finally, we see a different Portia here, not the gay mocker of her suitors, a little restless at having to submit to a 'dead father's will' (a pun on the legal sense and the sense of wilfulness), but the woman who feels that 'a maiden's eyes' may choose foolishly (the word 'nice' in l. 14 would mean this). She is also a woman who, if she herself had to choose and were not restricted by the way her father had planned it, would look on Morocco no differently from any other rival for her hand. Twice in one speech Portia indicates that more decisive to her than the outward show is the inner being.

A third plot

Before Morocco chooses we are back again in Venice, where in the structure of the play is inserted the subsidiary plot of Jessica's elopement. This is not just a romantic addition which Shakespeare might have picked up from such a play as Marlowe's *The Jew of Malta*. It should be seen as being strongly linked with both tests, for, so far as plot is concerned, the result of the elopement is to inflame Shylock the more against Bassanio and Antonio. Further, the elopement itself, when we consider the theme of the play, stresses both the contrast between Shylock who loves no music and Jessica who steals away dressed as a boy to play the role of a candle-holder in a masque, and the fact that Shylock, seeing only the outward show in Jessica, does not know her at all. He thinks she is his loyal daughter, but she is not. She leaves him, taking away with her what he values more than herself, his ducats and jewellery. We should regard Jessica's 'gilding' of herself with these as good sport, and not as evidence of moral delinquency. Taking them, she exposes Shylock's greed and his avarice. He is entirely devoted to his gold, as we see when he discovers its loss. To him it is his life; in 4. 1. 371 he states unequivocally that his money is his life and the prop of his house.

A comic interlude

Shakespeare runs into her elopement the comic interlude of Lancelot Gobbo, who is himself in a quandary. He has to choose between staying with his master and running away, the conflict being between the devil who advises running away from his master, and his conscience as a good servant which tells him he should not. Unfortunately, if he stays it will be with his master, who is a kind of devil himself. This comic debate, with its allusion to the more serious theme of the play, also contains a humorous allusion to the tricks of the Italian comedians. Their *lazzi*, or their immense repertory of mimicry, ridiculous postures and acrobatic stage business, were well known all over Europe. The talking in different voices, for Gobbo in his debate most probably simulated two different speakers; the rough and tumble on the stage with the old, half-blind father; the way Lancelot plays tricks with the old man, pushing his neck under his hands, and passing the old man's fingers over his fingers spread out on his chest to give the impression that every rib in his chest can be counted, come from Elizabethan popular entertainment. Gobbo is on very good terms with the audience as his 'Mark me now, now will I raise the waters' (2. 2. 45) shows.

The elopement establishes the difference between Shylock and the others. He goes in hate to supper, as he says (2. 5. 14); they go about the business of love. He loathes music; they are the providers of music, and are dressed in masquing attire. There is a further contrast between Jessica and Portia. The one defies her father and runs off with her lover; the other accepts her father's 'will' and is won by the lover of his and her choosing. Jessica, who looks out from the 'upper stage' and then comes down to the main stage dressed as a boy, makes the stock remark that 'love is blind'. Lovers, in other words, cannot see the folly of their conduct.

Her remark is just as conventional as Gratiano's in the same scene (2. 6. 12–13), that there is more pleasure in the anticipation of a thing than in actually attaining it. But both touch more serious chords of the play. Gratiano, with an illustration which adds a serious note to his maxim, compares the finery with which the young man sets out on riotous living to that of a vessel in gay trim, and then contrasts it with the ship with rent sails, a survivor of the storm.

The suitors tested

Morocco. The second of the two plots of the play reaches its climax first, when the suitors choose. In their three speeches we see character, situation, and the underlying themes of the play dramatically and poetically rendered. Morocco, who chooses first, has already been lightly touched in for us in his opening speech. The heraldic language of 'the shadowed livery of the burnished sun', the image of himself as its retainer, the exploits he quotes, and the ring of his verse have prepared us for the man of ambition who must choose gold. The way he describes the caskets, revealed when the curtains separating them from the outer stage have been parted, makes this clearer. The lead is 'dull', and its inscription warns the reader, as bluntly as does the silver casket. Morocco is something like Hotspur in *Henry IV*. It is not strange that he says of himself 'A golden mind stoops not to shows of dross'. For him the outward show is everything. He remembers his exploits, but he is not proud. He can value himself—'Pause there, Morocco', he says—and yet see that his deserving might not extend as far as the lady. Though he pauses long enough to feel that he might deserve Portia, the inscription on the golden casket is too strong for him, for what many men desire is, for him, fame and glory. He places himself in their ranks and chooses the attractive brightness of gold.

The scroll in the skull which he finds there tells him an obvious and important truth: it is not the outward show which matters. It could, in the words of Christ, be the exterior to a filthy sepulchre. Morocco's verse as he chooses is not that of a man who is considering what is before him, it is the rhapsody of the warrior carried away by what appeals to him most. To him bright glory means more than anything else.

Arragon. If Morocco is ambition, a sin close to avarice, then Arragon has to be thought of as Pride, another deadly sin of which sermon, moral tract, woodcut and show warned the Christian. The procession of the Seven Deadly Sins was a theme well known in literature and painting, so in the theatre a reference to them would at once be taken and immediately appreciated.

It would be easy to connect Pride with a Spanish prince. The Elizabethan dealt in stock character features as much as we do, and the pride of the Spaniard was a trait as well known as the drunkenness of the Hollander. Arragon's speech, carefully punctuated as it is, shows how he deliberates and argues. He looks at the caskets, pauses, then in a moment dismisses the lead for the same reason as Morocco. Its appearance is against it. Morocco at least, could, because he set a high value on heroic enterprise, feel that lead was dull, and that the golden mind fired by thoughts of success could not stoop to it. Arragon turns away from it with the comment 'You shall look fairer, ere I give or hazard', in that short line stressing both his acceptance of the outward appearance, and the naturalness of his faith in his own superiority. The 'I' in his 'ere I give or hazard' has a glint of his pride.

So he goes on to argue against the appearance of the gold, which might have attracted him since it certainly looked fairer than lead. But he will not reckon himself one with the many. To him they are the 'fool multitude', with whom he will not agree ('jump'): Shakespeare, interestingly, makes Arragon rightly decide against the gold for the wrong reasons. He declines it because his pride cannot allow him to think of himself as a man like the rest of humanity. It is not only the 'fool multitude' which chooses by show, so when he opens the silver casket he sees himself to be a fool too, worse fool than the others, for in the casket is the portrait of a 'blinking' idiot. But he has not as yet shed his pride, and all he can say is 'how much unlike [this is] from my hopes and deservings'.

In the course of the argument in which he persuades himself to choose the silver casket, we see how once again he starts right but in the end goes wrong, because he assumes that he alone is deserving. It is true that cheats claim honour without the stamp of merit. This was a subject which had long been popular with satirists. But at the end of his ringing sentences on the vice of the times which mistakes the trappings of honour for true merit (2. 9. 39–49), he arrogantly states: 'I will assume desert', the formality of the word 'assume' underlining pride.

Portia's comment on him shows how the dramatist worked the scene. Arragon after careful deliberation has that kind of 'wit' (intelligence) which could only make him lose. This she ironically calls 'wisdom'. More is wanted than intelligence. These two suitors have been, in the Elizabethan phrase, 'hoist with their own petard', or caught in the trap of their own making. This is exactly what happens to Shylock in the great scene of trial. This device gave special pleasure to Elizabethan audiences; they relished such a turn of the plot.

Bassanio. The test Bassanio undergoes is crucial. The circumstances of his choosing, all its accompaniments—the music, the song, the prelude to the choosing, his speech of comment—must all be considered carefully if we are to understand what makes him win. Of course, in fairy tales the third suitor always succeeds, but this is something more than fairy tale, and it is important to see why Shakespeare makes his third suitor successful.

The opening of 3. 2 makes it quite clear that Portia loves Bassanio and would be overjoyed if he won. Her speech, with the caskets once again displayed and the musicians above, is full of hesitation. The punctuation shows how the lines with her falterings of voice and her maidenly desire not to reveal herself must be spoken. She goes far enough though in revealing herself, when she says that his eyes have bewitched her (they have 'o'erlooked' her), and so she could 'beshrew', or put a gentle curse on them. But twice she makes it plain that even if she could help him by telling him which casket to choose, she would not be forsworn. If he loses, if though his by affection she is not his by the result of the contest, then 'Let Fortune go to hell for it, not I'.

The song. These two statements indicate that the song is not Portia's open instruction to him to choose the leaden casket. It repeats what has been said at that time and earlier, and it is dramatically relevant, since from it Bassanio derives that line in his argument which makes him choose right. The music Portia calls for may be, as she says, excellent accompaniment either to his failure, like that of the swan which according to the legend of the time sang sweetest at its death, or to his success.

The stage direction—'the whilst Bassanio comments on the caskets'—makes it clear that Bassanio has already begun reflecting, and he begins to speak when the song reaches the point of ringing Fancy's Knell. As his is a love much more serious than 'Fancy' (fantasy or some imagined passion) he begins with a sentence which shows how his train of thought is linked to the theme of the song— the insubstantiality of that type of love (Fancy) which depends on the pleasure of the eyes. Such love does not last, it dies in the cradle in which it lies.

Outward shows can be far from reality. Yet Bassanio is not sure, and his remark in ll. 81–2 shows how difficult it is to decide, for there is no vice so simple but it wears the badge of some virtue or other. But with examples from his own experience, from the braggart and the painted and bewigged woman made up to deceive the onlooker, he decides not to trust ornament. It could, like a beautiful scarf, hide a dark-complexioned beauty (dark hair and a dark complexion being not in fashion then). He rejects the gold because gold is unnatural, it turns everything nourishing and life-giving into hard metal, as it did for Midas. Silver brings in the thought of money, just as unnatural a bond between man and man. He chooses lead because it threatens; lead being associated with coffins, it reminds man of what he is. Its 'plainness' moves him, he says, more than the 'eloquence' which could be the bright specious tricks of the orator, to be felt in the attractive promises of the gold and silver caskets.

The principle of concord

He wins, but he does not claim his lady until she signifies that she is his. This she does in a speech which in its content shows that, accepting the rule of a husband as 'her lord, governor, her king', she acknowledges the principle of concord and harmony which should direct all things. Her position in the household must now be subordinate to his, and the words in which she says so are part of the Belmont music—harmonious, gracious and modest. For herself she would not be ambitious, as Morocco was, but for Bassanio's sake she would wish to be a greater prize. As for her 'deserving', she sees herself as 'an unlessoned girl, unschooled, unpractised'; very far indeed from what Arragon imagined his own 'deserving' to be. She gives him the ring—a solemn moment coming close upon the kiss with which she seals her acceptance of Bassanio as her husband.

In this way both the plot, or the part played by the ring in concluding the play, and the theme, the perfect concord and harmony at Belmont, natural to those who love each other, are linked.

As master and mistress are now to be one, so Gratiano and Nerissa have decided to make a match of it themselves. The difference between the verse given to Gratiano and that in which Bassanio debates and then expresses his ecstasy at being successful should be noted. As Gratiano puts it: 'My eyes, my lord, can look as swift as yours.' This, in relation to what we have discussed above, would paint the difference between the two of them best of all.

The coarseness of Gratiano's jesting which is second nature to him is cut short by the entrance of Lorenzo, Jessica and Salerio with his letter. Soon Venice, with its discord and 'storms' is brought before us, and we know that the great trial of the play is at hand.

The great test

We arrive at it after we are told once more of Shylock's determination to use his fangs, and of Portia's scheme to go disguised to the court. Shylock is the storm which could destroy a world based on love and concord. He is the fury to which Antonio 'opposes' himself with true Christian patience. In his words (4. 1. 71 ff.) we see Shylock as the force of wind and wave which destroys, the wolf which kills the lamb. What is more, the principle by which his actions are governed is that of 'affection'—mere inclination, the sheer will which must have what it sets its mind upon. This is a principle of chaos and disorder. 'Humour' which in l. 43 is Shylock's justification for his conduct would, in Elizabethan English, range from mere affectation to dangerous passion.

By the time Portia appears on the stage it has been established that nothing can stand against Shylock's passion, and that Antonio, the scapegoat, 'the tainted wether of the flock', will have to be sacrificed. In his self-confidence and assurance Shylock, like Arragon, is sure of his 'deserving', and rises to the pitch of effrontery when he cries to the duke, in l. 89, 'what judgement shall I dread, doing no wrong?' Pride could go no further, but we remember that pride has a fall.

Portia, so different in appearance from the wise doctor of laws commended by Bellario, opposes the storm with her recommendation of mercy as the gentle rain, the natural benison or blessing of the heavens on the earth. She puts to Shylock, quite naturally so far as she is concerned, but ironically so far as the audience is concerned, a possibility which he cannot consider, since he has just said, 'what judgement shall I dread, doing no wrong?' To her mercy is the natural bond between man and man, and man and God. Its specific characteristic ('quality') is that it cannot be forced ('strained'). And she ends her quiet argument—it should not be read as an impassioned piece of oratory, but as sober reproof—that justice may demand one course of action, but mercy would prefer the other. No man can take up an absolute and immitigable point of view.

What follows is a very dramatic conflict in various moves between the two adversaries. Portia has not come there with the mode of settling the case already in her head. If this were so, there could be no great dramatic interest in the scene. It is a wrestling match in which in the end Portia gets Shylock on the hip, he all the while growing more and more confident, she being forced to give way, until she gets him through the opening he himself gives her.

She refuses, as she had refused to make known to Bassanio which casket to choose, to do a little wrong in order to do a great right. If she had done so, the play would lose its force.

The battle between Portia and Shylock

The stages in the encounter between Shylock and Portia are as follows: (1) He refuses to consider the claims of mercy. 'My deeds upon my head!' Whatever the consequences may be, he insists on justice and his bond. (2) He refuses thrice the sum Antonio owes him with the self-satisfied irony 'shall I lay perjury upon my soul?' (3) A second time, he rejects both mercy and the offer of thrice the money. He insists on his bond, and states that it must be paid 'according to the tenour', according to the literal wording of the document. Portia then, with deep meaning, states that the law, justice not mercy, awards Shylock his due on the bond. (4) When she suggests that there should be a surgeon present, he refuses, insisting on the wording of the bond. (5) When once again Portia asks: 'It is not so expressed, but what of that?', must the appearance of the bond, its words, matter so much, would not its spirit mean something different? the sense of what she says stresses the superiority of the reality to the appearance. He refuses to allow 'charity' (human feeling) a place in his world. All he can say is, 'I cannot find it, 'tis not in the bond'.

Before judgement is carried out, Antonio, in what to him is his dying speech, states that he dies for love of his friend, and dies gladly, not repenting for an instant his giving all for love. Bassanio, as he was ready to hazard all for Portia's love, now states that for his friend he would forfeit life, his dearly loved wife, and everything. At which he is taken up by Portia.

As Shylock advances with drawn knife to claim justice, Portia turns on him with 'Tarry a little'. He then sees soon enough what his bond gives him, what the appearance means. He has insisted on the exact wording of the bond, on 'justice', and now he receives it. Three times the sum which Bassanio offers can be his no longer, he shall have 'merely justice and his bond'; not even the principal, only 'justice and his bond'. In Portia's repetition of the words 'justice', we have strongly underlined one part of the play's theme, how insufficient the appearance is, and how it deceives. Shylock, who depended on the 'tenour' of his bond, is destroyed by it.

Justice means in his case the loss of his property and his life, unless the duke is merciful. The duke, showing Christian mercy, reprieves Shylock, but deprives him of all his wealth. Antonio, asked by Portia, 'What mercy can you render him?', shows Christian mercy too. He behaves towards Shylock as the duke in his opening words to Shylock had urged him to act towards Antonio. Antonio will not have the half of Shylock's wealth assigned to him by justice, but insists that half should be held in trust for Lorenzo and Jessica. In keeping with contemporary attitudes is his insistence that Shylock should immediately become a Christian. We at the present day are not likely to see this as a special mark of Antonio's good Christian behaviour, but, as it did reveal the generosity of his spirit then, we should accept it without demur.

The rings

Portia on the stage, which the court has vacated, with Bassanio, Antonio, and Gratiano, asks nothing for herself, but makes the cryptic remark, 'Know me when we meet again'. Pressed to accept some token of reward, she asks for the ring, which Bassanio refuses, and which he is ready to part with only at the express wish of his friend. Bassanio at this stage gives all. His most dearest possession was the ring, since it was solemnly given to him as symbol of his winning Portia. So the situation of Antonio, who gives all for his friend at the opening of the play, is paralleled here.

Music at the close

The play ends to the accompaniment of music and the light of the moon, both evoked by the strong line of Shakespeare's verse. The 'touches', or fingering, of the musicians of the house coming in later, support what the verse with its references and its melody has created. Both music and moonlight are associated with love, and the concord which both suggest is a fitting close to a play which the discord of storms and the blackness of evil threatened to wreck.

Act 5 begins with the lovely duet of Lorenzo and Jessica. Their verse, patterned as it is on repetition, and on the evocation of balmy moonlight and the romantic aura of the classical stories the lovers refer to, has a soft lyrical movement. It tends to cast a sleepy spell, but Shakespeare keeps this in check with the good humour with which the two turn the subject against each other. 'I would out-night you, did no body come', says Jessica.

For them there has been nothing like the experience of the major characters in the play, but, in their celebration of famous lovers of antiquity, they call up for the audience those who hazarded all for love.

With the moonlight and music another note is sounded—an intimation of the serious side of the play—in the reference to Portia with 'the holy hermit' and her kneeling and praying for happy wedlock hours. The previous scene has already told us that the business of the rings is going to be used mischievously by the two women. But it cannot mar the happiness of the end, so all we have to expect is the play's final surprise—the discovery that the lawyer and Portia are one and the same person—and the union of lovers and friends in Belmont after the bitter struggle in the court in Venice.

But before Portia enters there is further preparation which, through its references to music, presents us with a summary of one of the themes of the play. The music which we, like Lorenzo, will hear played by the musicians of the household is the earthly counterpart of what we cannot hear, that of the spheres which only immortal souls like the cherubim can listen to. It is there, though we cannot hear it, though it does not seem to be there.

When they hear the music of the house, from the musicians once more on the upper stage, Lorenzo explains to Jessica why music has such power over her mind that she cannot but be moved when she hears it. 'I am never merry when I hear sweet music' she says, 'merry' being that state of superficial pleasure in which nothing enters the mind to disturb it. So Antonio tells Bassanio in 2. 8. 42–3

> Let it not enter in your mind of love:
> Be merry...

In Lorenzo's lines (5. 1. 71 ff.) which follow we have the power of music celebrated. It transforms and regenerates. 'The hot condition of [the] blood', the unreclaimed nature of human passion, is changed into gentleness and mildness. As the lines go on the discord and the evil of the play are once more suggested. There has been in the play a character too 'stockish, hard, and full of rage' for music to transform. He is conjured up in Lorenzo's lines on 'the man that hath no music in himself'. It is Shylock who was both the tempest which nearly destroyed Antonio, and the evil, 'hellish' force with passions as dark as Erebus (one of the deities of the classical Hades), who was subdued by Portia.

As she enters the stage she likens the light she sees to a 'good deed in a naughty world'. Once more we are reminded of the opposition of evil to good, in a simple biblical image of light which pierces the blackness of night.

The world Portia is entering now is that of Belmont, where order and concord reign, where everything finds its right place. So the greater glory of the moon dims the smaller light of the candles; and the substitute looking like a king, and not a king in reality, when the king appears, as a river slides into the great ocean, occupies a subsidiary place, and loses his importance naturally and rightly.

When she says 'Nothing is good without respect', that nothing is good without reference to other things, she is repeating what she has, in other terms, said already. This is the substance of her plea to Shylock who insisted on the absolute justice of his claim, and refused to consider anything but what was written in his bond. 'Earthly power', she had said (4. 1. 193–4), shows

> likest God's
> When mercy seasons justice.

The absolute of justice is most godlike when mercy tempers it, so, too, when Bassanio has chosen correctly, she wishes for herself (3. 2. 111–14) that her absolute joy (ecstasy) should be 'allayed', or tempered, with some other feelings, or it would make her ill through excess. In these lines she sees how everything is tempered and brought to perfection by 'season'.

The ideal state of order

These lines present us with the ideal state of order in which there is no absolute inflexible rule which overlooks the claims of humanity. The right praise and true perfection of anything depends on the seasoning which human judgement brings to the task of separating the real from what seems to be so.

This is the cue for the final clearing up of the difficulty of the rings which the two men have given away. Portia, as she felt her way with

Shylock in the grim scene in the court, takes on Bassanio now. But it is obvious, in the way she replies to his honest asseverations, that she is playful, and not serious. She repeats his 'If you did know to whom I gave the ring' with lines which could be as serious as his. But as 'nothing is good...without respect', and she knows Bassanio's situation, understanding seasons her judgement. Antonio once again, this time pledging not his body, but his soul, comes to his friend's rescue. As he says in 5. 1. 250ff., he once pledged his body for the sake of his friend's happiness, now he will pledge his soul. But such a serious sacrifice is not necessary, and Portia hands him the ring which he gives Bassanio to keep safe.

With the romantic news of the safe arrival of Antonio's ships which were reported to have been lost in the storm, they leave the stage, and the play is over, but not before Gratiano indulges in a little coarse banter with the audience.

10. HENRY V

2 *Henry IV* ended with an epilogue spoken by a dancer, not unusual as a finale to an Elizabethan play into which song and dance naturally entered. The speaker held out a promise to the audience: 'If you be not too much cloyed with fat meat, our humble author will continue the story, with Sir John in it, and make you merry with fair Katharine of France; where (for any thing I know) Falstaff shall die of a sweat, unless already a' be killed with your hard opinions.'

Whatever Shakespeare's intentions may have been when he wrote this epilogue, *Henry V* does not fulfil them, for Falstaff is not in the play, though his death is reported. It hardly corresponds with its first announcement in the epilogue to 2 *Henry IV*, except as continuation of the story of the newly crowned king.

The national hero

Henry V is Shakespeare's celebration of one of England's national heroes—the warrior prince, Henry of Monmouth, who defeated the French at Agincourt, a battle remembered and honoured nearly 180 years later. In 3. 7. 31–2 the Dauphin speaks of 'varying' (inventing variations on the theme of) the deserved praises of his palfrey. In this play Shakespeare, in dramatic terms, is 'varying' the deserved praise of Henry V. His story was known to Elizabethans, as 5 Prologue states. Henry is Shakespeare's theme, the legendary subject of his panegyric.

We have to consider the play against the background of the meaning of the legend of Henry V to Elizabethans, and not in connection with any promises made in the epilogue to *2 Henry IV*. It is related to that play, and even to *Richard II*, but it exists in its own right independently of them, and we should look at it in the light of its own intentions and achievement.

His legend. The legend of Henry of Monmouth was the familiar story of the young man who appears to be a wastrel and a ne'er-do-well, but who makes a glorious reformation, and becomes a heroic figure. It is like those stories of the ugly duckling who grows into a beautiful swan. For his play Shakespeare used the sober historical material of his time—the chronicles of Hall and Holinshed. In them, and also in contemporary plays, there were popular stories of the hero. The subject would therefore be a combination of fact, and, what is more important, belief in the myth which years of tradition had sanctioned.

Something more comes into Shakespeare's play, and this is his own memory of England at his time. Behind all the histories is a strong nationalist and patriotic feeling, given a new consciousness of itself after the defeat of the Spanish Armada. The England Shakespeare writes of in this play is the England of his time, though the events described are nearly two centuries old. So into this play comes an explicit reference to contemporary events, when Shake-

speare, asking his audience to picture the welcome given to Henry
after Agincourt, thinks of Essex, as 'happily he might', returning
successful from Ireland. But more important than this reference is
the complex of feelings which must have been the attitude of many
men, when they thought of England in 1599, when the play was
written.

This complex of feelings must have been made up of satisfaction
and pride in the past, and confidence in the future if, as Falconbridge
said in *King John*, 'England to itself remained but true'. But there
would also be apprehension and uncertainty about both present and
future. The Queen was as glorious a figure as any past hero. But she
was old. She had reigned for just over forty years, and the end of
her reign was in sight. Yet no successor to the kingdom had been
formally named, and, as Tudor political wisdom had pointed out,
and Shakespeare's own chronicle histories had maintained, the
dangers of a disputed succession were plain for all to see.

So if *Henry V* is the celebration of England's national hero at a
momentous period in the country's history, it should not be forgotten that there are other tones, suggesting the limitations of any
heroic figure, and doubts of the future.

The play is a paean of praise for Henry V. But other things come
into it too—the crime of Henry's father who had usurped the
throne; disloyal nobles; the boon companions of the king's youth;
and the savagery of war. It could be supposed that Shakespeare,
intending the play as tribute to the national hero, found that the
presentation of a man so variously celebrated had its natural dis-
advantages. Inherent in the theme are the difficulties present in any
artistic medium attempting to present the complete hero. The
picture of the good man is usually dull and unattractive. So the hero
'full-fraught and best indued' (the all-round man endowed with all
the graces) would seem wooden and unlifelike, or at any rate less
plausible and human than the less 'complete' man.

We might remember, too, that our attitudes to persons, even those
we admire and revere, are rarely without contradictory impulses of

criticism and even of hostility. There is a human tendency to den.
satisfaction from feelings of aggression to persons whom we honour
and love. If, therefore, as it has so often been held of this play, into
this vehicle for Henry's glory comes in material tending to his hero's
dispraise, it could be put down to Shakespeare's common humanity.
The play must then be regarded as Shakespeare's 'varying' of the
theme of the heroic and ideal stature of Henry V, together with
whatever of a contrary significance becomes naturally attached to
such exercises.

Structure

The play is made up of five prologues or choruses, which enunciate
some part of the theme which the following scenes illustrate. All of
them contribute to the general suggestion made in 1 Prologue that
the great theme is that of the warrior-king. This Prologue states the
general theme: Henry of Monmouth as the hero who, if the medium
used by the dramatist was equal to the task, would 'assume the port
of Mars', that is, formally take on himself as was his right the
bearing of Mars, the god of war. As 1 Prologue is general introduction, we should take 1. 1 as being a further specific prologue to
the scenes illustrating it. The epilogue reiterates the main theme, and
apologizes, as do all the Prologues, for the unworthy treatment of a
subject too great for the dramatist's powers.

We should see the structure of the play as dramatic illustration of
the theme enunciated in the several prologues. The latter provide
the statement, the acts and scenes which follow are their amplification. There is an additional feature in the content of these
illustrative scenes. Quite often there will be found in them material
of another kind, seemingly opposed in its effect to the general
intention of the prologues. The scenes which follow the prologues
should therefore be looked at as both extending the statement of the
prologue, and also contributing something antithetical.

1 Prologue, the general introduction, cites Harry as the god of
war, with Famine, Death and Fire in his control. 1. 1 should, as has
been suggested, be taken as a prologue on its own, or exposition, for

in it are listed the various virtues which belong to the ideal king.
Canterbury's words from 1. 1. 24–59 are the text on which the scene
which follows expands. In this list the king is lover of the church;
scholar; theologian; defender of the commonweal; military
strategist; and statesman who can unravel any of the complications
of statecraft. Above all, as man there is no 'wilfulness' in him; his
tendency to be at the mercy of his passions has been restrained and
controlled.

1. 2, which follows, exhibits his 'grace', his love of the church,
his scholar's skill, his concern for the defence of his people, his
strategy, and his statecraft, when he shows self-control and dignity
to the French ambassador who brings him the scornful message of
the Dauphin. Is there in this scene a suggestion that the king is not
as disinterested as he seems to be, and that the churchmen send him
off to war with France to keep him from dipping his hand too deep
into their coffers?

2. Prologue celebrates the king as 'the mirror of all Christian
kings' and 'this grace of kings'. It is as ruler of the country that he
is placed before us here. It points to the glory that might be
England's if all her children were 'kind and natural', where the two
senses of 'kind' (affectionate, and linked by ties of family) and
'natural', meaning according to that law of nature which stressed the
dependence of human beings one on the other, are used to suggest
the order which should prevail in a kingdom.

2. 1 and 2. 3 show one set of 'unnatural' children—Nym,
Bardolph, and Pistol, who go to war as if it were highway robbery
(a comment on war?).

2. 3, which removes Falstaff from the play, reminds us that,
however justifiable his exclusion from it may be, something which
adds to the play's humanity will be missing in it.

2. 4 puts on the stage yet another unnatural character—the
arrogant French prince. The French have to be 'purged' of their
'humour' of pride, like each of the unnatural English, common
soldiers as well as noble conspirators.

3 Prologue announces as its theme the king in war.

3. 1 and 3. 3 show Henry as warrior. 3. 2 provides the contrast to this mood of stern dedication to duty, and we are given the 'humours' (the personal wilfulness and the specific aberrations) of various soldiers, Fluellen coming in as compensation for the 'unnatural' Nym, Bardolph and Pistol.

3. 5 and 3. 7 give us again the self-willed and proud French. Through this contrast the worth of the English king—his reliance on God, his care for the commonweal (here his army)—is the more strongly established.

3. 6 sandwiched between the pictures of the vaunting French gives us the English king 'and his poor soldiers'. Henry is generous, full of grace, and firm in his direction of the army. Bardolph must be hanged for theft; both justice and statecraft demand it.

4 Prologue announces Agincourt and describes the king as 'royal captain', the stress being now on the plain and simple leader of a company of men. It is Henry as man, as soldier and one of a band of brothers we are invited to see.

4. 1 gives us the sovereign who, like Haroun al Raschid, goes among his people in order to inform himself of their condition. His mind is exercised by the dilemma of kings who are both men and not ordinary persons. The king prepares himself for battle as for a sacrament.

4. 2 contrasts with the poor English the much too lively and confident French.

4. 3—the king as one of a band of brothers.

4. 4 is all we see of the fighting at Agincourt on the English side: the exploit of Pistol who has succeeded in capturing a French knight. The contrast between his demands for ransom from the Frenchman and the king's reply to the French herald in the previous scene should be noted.

4. 5 shows the defeated French resorting to any kind of diversion on the field—'the devil take order'—and its consequence in 4. 6. Following upon the piece of heroic poetry celebrating the deaths of

Suffolk and York comes the order of the king that every soldier should kill his prisoners.

4. 7 and 4. 8 continue with the king as man among his men. Note that there is a further reference here to Falstaff whom the king in 'his good judgements' turned away.

5 Prologue exalts the victorious king as national hero both in war and in peace.

5. 1 gives us the 'purgation' of Pistol by Fluellen. It is impossible that he should be allowed to go unscathed.

5. 2—the king and commonwealth affairs in the settlement of peace, with hopes for the future.

To the hopes expressed here the Epilogue is a counter-scene, for it makes clear that they are all unrealized.

The prologues

Before we examine this structure in greater detail, it is necessary to ask one question: why did Shakespeare use these prologues? Of course they were not unusual on the Elizabethan stage, and in earlier drama there was a 'presenter' whose function was to state to the audience the content of the play, and to draw their attention to any special points made by the dramatist.

The Prologues in this play will be seen to fall into three parts. They are, like all prologues, informative, and announce what has happened in the interim between the scenes just played on the stage and the appearance of the chorus. Secondly they apologize for the inadequate means employed by the dramatist in putting his material on the stage, and acknowledge his 'abuse' of such things as 'time', 'place', and 'numbers'. As 1 Prologue puts it the dramatist has had to 'jump' over 'times'. This 'abuse' of time, according to Renaissance notions of playwriting, was the inclusion in the plot of events covering a greater period of time than that conventionally allowed.

In 2 Prologue the chorus undertakes to make the audience 'digest' another abuse—that of 'distance', or the fact that in the play we are at one time in one place and the next moment in another. This, again, by Renaissance 'rules' was inadmissible.

And both in 1 Prologue and elsewhere the dramatist, unable with the few actors in a stock company to put as many people as would be required on the stage, apologizes for the 'abuse' of 'numbers'.

Finally, the chorus urges the audience to compensate for the stage's deficiencies by using their 'imaginary forces', that is their imaginations are to work, and so 'piece out' or patch up what is wanting in the stage's treatment of its subject.

Why should Shakespeare have felt, in the first place, that he was infringing the 'rules' and, in the second, that his stage was unable to present scenes of battle and a war between two mighty countries? In every single one of his plays up to this time, he had not troubled himself with any 'rules' of time and place, and he was always working with the same slender resources of a stock company. Further, he had never felt, or stated his feelings, that his stage was incapable of giving his audiences scenes of war, or of famous battles. In *Henry VI* the most popular scenes with the London audiences had been those of Talbot in battle. In *Richard III* he had made such a success of the battle of Bosworth that Burbage's cry in his play seemed to be the most memorable thing in it (p. 55). And in the plays yet to come he was to put on the stage momentous conflicts like those between Augustus Caesar and the conspirators, Actium, and the campaigns of Coriolanus.

The most favoured explanation is that Shakespeare taking up the story of England's national hero has a subject on his hands better suited to epic poetry than to drama. Such a subject was hedged about with literary conventions so powerful at that time, that anyone hardy enough to undertake it would neglect the 'rules' only at grave risk to his reputation. Shakespeare's subject, as he seems to see it in 1 Prologue, required epic narration and epic description. There had been plays on these subjects of England's wars and England's heroic figures before, but the dramatist, feeling that his form could scarcely do justice to his material, continually aspires (in his images of fire and air, and in the urgency of his tones with the repeated admonitions to the audience to 'think', to 'look', to 'work with their thoughts') to the height of epic grandeur and excellence.

There is something more. Shakespeare's difficulty, if this account of it is accepted, was not only one of the literary form he chose, but of his medium of presentation. In this play he excuses himself not only for offences against literary canons, but also for the ineptitudes of his stage. This avowal need not be taken too seriously, for he continued to do just what he apologizes for here. What is more, in 3 Prologue, he adds a dramatic touch at the very moment of his admission that dramatic modes are inadequate for his 'task'. His passionate 'work, work your thoughts and therein see a siege' (3 Prol. 25) is followed by the firing of a cannon off stage. The stage direction at 1. 33 'alarum, and chambers go off', proves that imagination, for all its resolution, did not disdain stage effects.

This may seem the unconscious revenge of the theatre on the dramatist a little too prone to slight its resources. The combination in this prologue of the acknowledgement that the medium is inadequate with its efficient use seems typical of other contraries in the play, its material being the celebration of Henry together with a glance at what is unattractive in his character.

Focus on Henry

This is Henry's play. He is the one person on whom attention is continually focused. All the others in the play are there to pay their tribute to him as the ideal king. Numerous persons fill out this long play, but however interesting in their own right—the Dauphin, the typical vaunting knight, or the pedantic and honourable Welshman—their real function is to lend dramatic contrast and illustration to the main character.

Henry—'full of grace'. Two prelates open the play with a scene of exposition which should be taken as the specific prologue to Act 1. They see that the church's best defence is the king's character itself, rather than diverting him, with the offer of a large subsidy, to a war against France. Protestant historians linked the church's offer to the king with its support of Henry's claims to France, but it is clear, in the answer to Ely's question in 1. 1. 21, that the king will not countenance the bill against church properties because he has become the king he is. It is important that in the legend of Henry as the young man addicted to 'courses vain' ('open haunts and popularity' of 1. 1. 59), a less strongly stressed detail should not be overlooked. The king has undergone spiritual conversion.

We should note too how strongly Canterbury opens in 1. 22 with 'the king is full of grace and fair regard'. 'Grace' is a condition which the Christian continually strives after. It is a stronger word than mercy, and should be interpreted as being in a state of reconciliation with God and given power by God to persevere in right action.

The images. The intention of Canterbury's speeches is clear: to present the king as the epitome of kingly excellence. The verse is oratorically full and easy, the images employed—from the service of baptism, from the Bible, and the classical fable of Hercules cleansing the Augean stables—lending their weight to the figure being projected. Is there a feeling, however, that we are being given not a human being, but an unnatural prodigy? The threefold repetition of 'never' in lines 32–5, and the parenthetical 'all at once' in line 36 indicate the determination of the speaker to force into life an unbelievable figure of a man.

When Canterbury goes on in line 38 he indulges in a hyperbolic extension of this superhuman king. Again with a biblical reference —to the wind that bloweth where it listeth—he claims that the air, a 'libertine' because it does exactly what it wishes, is so charmed by the king's excellence of discourse that, dumbfounded and wondering, it hangs about men's ears, just to catch his beautifully expressed maxims. These 'sweet and honeyed sentences' seem to have two tones; of statement which may be sincere and also of crude flattery. Is there anything more in this hyperbole than straightforward praise, or does it, in trying to attain its object, overreach itself, and leave an

153

impression of a kind of person too good to be true, or a speaker too flattering to be sincere?

In this passage and elsewhere in the play it is possible to see that the image, as Shakespeare uses it now, is so embedded in its dramatic context that it is not, as might have been the case in earlier plays, a device of the poetry as distinct from the drama. The image illuminates mental attitudes; it helps us to sense the dramatist's feelings towards the material he is shaping, to its persons and its situations; it reveals the relations of the persons of the play to each other.

Ely notes (1. 1. 60–6), as Canterbury had done, the wonder of the king's character, and, using an illustration from gardening, he points out how the king's study of life had developed and matured under the cover of scapegrace behaviour in his youth. This image is like that of the Constable of France in 2. 4. 39–40, describing the contrast between the wildness of his youth and the nobility of his present character. Ely goes on to remark that the king's powers grew, like summer grass at night, unobserved, because they had the innate ability to do just this. Canterbury agrees. It is no miracle; the king's present perfection must be due to the natural cause ('means') of his inborn goodness of character.

It is therefore clear that what the churchmen say about Henry is to be accepted. He is not so much interested in the offer of church subsidies as in his claim to the French throne, which had seemed to be barred by the Salic law. So in the scene which follows we shall have the archbishop, expert in law, expound it to the king.

The Salic law

In 1. 2 the king comes on the stage. It is obvious that the exposition of the Salic law and its effect on his claims on France are of vital importance. If this were not already clear from 1. 1, the charge that the king gives the archbishop in 1. 2. 13–32 would prevent any possibility that Henry has already made up his mind, or that the prelate duped the king. To treat it, as it is often done on the stage now, as a tiresome irrelevance which has to be dished up with some comic business to make it digestible, is to misunderstand the relation of this scene to the Prologue and the whole of the play.

The gravity of the king's charge to his spiritual counsellor is to be noted. Henry warns the archbishop against any falsification, forcing or perversion of the interpretation of the law, and against endangering his soul by specious legal argument over basically unlawful titles. The archbishop is adjured to address himself to his task of exposition with a conscience like that of the baptized infant, washed pure of original sin. The seriousness of this prelude, in which the king, previously described by the archbishop as a man new made as if in baptismal rite, now asks his counsellor to advise with a conscience like that of any 'christom child', must prevent the long speech which follows from being either perfunctory or useless historical lumber. It is a piece of eloquence which must have been listened to carefully in the theatre.

The archbishop concludes with his opinion that the Salic law is a pretext used by the French to confuse the issue and he exposes ('inbares') the illegitimacy of their position. The king asks again in line 96 'May I with right and conscience make this claim?'.

Henry—defender of the commonweal

On this follows an outburst of patriotism and national pride from churchmen and nobles who cite the glorious precedents of the past— the victories of Edward III and the Black Prince in France. They are all off in their rousing speeches to defeat the French again, but it is the king, with his care for the commonweal, who debates in his mind what will happen in England should the main force of the country be divided with the best part away in France. He has to calculate how his forces should be deployed and how the 'ill neighbourhood'—the hostile feelings of their neighbours the Scots— has to be feared. Could the king be away and the main strength of the country be safely divided?

Nobles and churchmen now reassure the king about the health and sound condition of the kingdom. The substance of what they say is: Do not fear to divide up your forces, setting out with the main body to France, for out of the division of parts comes the full harmony of the whole. Exeter's image in 1. 2. 180–4 was frequently used by Shakespeare to illustrate the concord made up of the voices singing the notes of their various parts.

How order works

Canterbury's is the celebrated illustration of the theorem that out of the diversity of duties, if order or obedience is maintained, comes the perfect functioning of the body politic. The bees provide the analogy. They are creatures who, in the instinctive ordering of their state, are an example to human beings. The archbishop's eloquence knits up a carefully worked out argument. The disposition of human beings in various gradations is the will of heaven, the advantage being the continual stimulus to effort. But all this has to turn on obedience, or the beautiful co-ordination of the whole would be destroyed.

Henry—the Christian king

So the spiritual counsellor calms the king's apprehensions through an argument from parallels. Satisfied that the country will be in no danger, the king asks for the embassy from France. He indicates to the ambassador at once that he is

> a Christian king,
> Unto whose grace our passion is as subject
> As is our wretches fettered in our prisons

—a statement of one of his great virtues. Time and time again— with Montjoy, with his soldiers, with the French—the king shows perfect control of himself and of the impulse to give way to passion. Only once in the play does he say that he has been 'angered' (4. 7. 54).

His reply, therefore, to the insulting message of the Dauphin is a neat and witty rejoinder. Punning on references to tennis as played at that time, he tells the Dauphin that the opponent ('wrangler') he has taken on will undo France and himself. The king speaks as king; of himself he uses the language conventionally used of kings. Like a lion he will 'rouse himself' in his throne of France. Like the sun he will dazzle the eyes of the French.

Twice in his speech which closes the scene, God's help is invoked. The sentiments may be conventional, but the formal occasion demands formal speech. But is there besides the dignity of the speech a sinister touch of grim seriousness in lines 282–99? The destruction of war, its slaughter and devastation are taken by the verse in its stride, but it leaves an impression of hardness and ruthlessness. The 'merry message' has an undertone of grimness.

The second Prologue is off with its description of the preparations for the war. But as soon as the chorus has announced the promise held out to the king and his chivalrous knights, it goes on to state that all is not well with the country. The French, through their spies, have corrupted three important nobles.

Contrast

The next scene, according to the Prologue, is to be at Southampton, where the conspirators will make their attempt on the king. After that we shall be taken over the sea to France. But before the speaker leaves the stage he has another couplet for us, in which we are informed that only when the king appears will the scene be changed to Southampton. And indeed what follows in 2. 1 is a scene in London.

Recent editors of the text have shown that the reason for this change of plan must have been the result of Shakespeare's decision to cut Falstaff out of his play. Immediately after the Prologue he brings on the stage Falstaff's associates—Bardolph, Pistol, the boy, Mrs Quickly—together with a new character Nym. They refer to a Falstaff grievously ill, and in 2. 3 he is reported to have died. In 2 Henry IV Falstaff had been turned away by the king. It would have been difficult to run together the 'grace of kings' with the scapegrace companion of the days when the king was addicted to 'courses vain', and the other evils of his unregenerate past.

That past, however, appears both in 2. 1 and 2. 3 to give us a picture very different from that evoked by the second Prologue of the youth of England all on fire to follow their gracious king. On the stage now is a group of characters all agog to treat the expedition to France as a freebooting raid. But at the same time in 2. 3 Mrs Quickly gives Falstaff, through her combination of honest amiability and her notorious mix-up of words and phrases, as dignified an epitaph as anyone could have wished for him. She is sure that he is in Abraham's bosom, he is in Paradise, not hell. When we remember her account of how death came to him, and how she pays him the tribute of believing that he died in the state of innocence of the child in its baptismal robe, we can feel that if the king in his reformation has reverted to the state of primal innocence, then Falstaff is touched with the same glory.

Its function. Falstaff's boon companions come into the play not to recall the joyousness and the liveliness of the past, but to represent what the king has worked out of his character finally and irrevocably. A new figure is added—Nym. In him Shakespeare is probably parodying Ben Jonson's popular 'humour' character, the man whose words and attitudes illustrated one particular trait. The name Nym in Elizabethan slang meant filcher or thief. He cultivates a pose of cryptic utterance, the repetition of 'that's the humour of it' and a show of valour which is the counterpart of Pistol's. Both of them are impressive in making only the sounds of wrath and courage; they are only too ready, for all their bloodthirsty fervour, to sheathe their swords at the least excuse.

Besides getting Falstaff out of the play these two scenes enable Shakespeare through the slang, the amusingly pretentious language, and the stock types of boastful soldier, to contrive an important dramatic contrast with the youth of England all on fire, with 'honour's thought' reigning 'solely in the breast of every man'. Here we have people whose expectation is not of 'honour', but of profit. Even the boy, as the Hostess looks at him, is marked for the gallows (2. 1. 86).

2. 2 gives us the king's nobles, one of them his 'bedfellow'. They are as 'unnatural' as those we have just seen on the stage. This scene works out the indication given in 2 Prologue. But in its opening lines there is an additional piece of information. The king knows of the plot, by intercepting the letters of the conspirators.

Henry tests them ironically, leading them on to agree with him that there is no one in England but is wholeheartedly with him in his enterprise. The word 'consent' in 2. 2. 22 brings to mind the voices singing together which Exeter in 1. 1. 181 described as keeping in 'one consent'.

Henry—as lawgiver

The king shows Christian mercy in pardoning the man who had abused him when drunk. The conspirators' objection to this, with their distinction between mercy and justice—always a fruitful theme with Shakespeare—is ironically turned aside by the king in 2. 2. 52–60. In seeming to give them their letters of appointment he hands them writs impeaching them for high treason.

The long speech (2. 2. 79–144) places this sudden turn of events in the setting the dramatist intends for it. Dramatic effectiveness and surprise probably account for the king's having played cat and mouse with them. The attitude he takes up shows that their crime makes the conspirators extraordinary creatures, to be pointed at and looked at as queer freaks were at fairs. They are English monsters, just as Caliban could have been thought of as an 'Indian' (or American) monster. For their crime is against 'proportion', the harmony of the well-ordered state. It is more than the disloyalty of a 'bedfellow' to his friend, bad as that might be.

Everything in lines 109 to the end of the speech depends on the enormity of the sin. It is so 'preposterous' (it turns the natural order upside down) that the king rises to a height of eloquence in underlining its illogicality, its combination of treason, murder and inexplicability. Scroop's crime has poisoned the sweet water of trust ('with jealousy infected the sweetness of affiance'). It seems nothing less than a 'second fall of man', as Bolingbroke's crime was to the queen in *Richard II*. Yet when the king says in line 140 'I will weep for thee', are the words sincere, or are they an oratorical device? And the references to God's mercy in lines 166, and 177–81— are they the king's fervent wish, or do they imply that even God would find it hard to forgive such wrongs?

The king's behaviour is obviously in keeping with the traditions of political wisdom. He must tender the safety of the kingdom more than any threat to his person. But does this scene in showing him as wise in his handling of such emergencies leave a trace of dissatisfaction at the sternness of 'this grace of kings'?

The French prince

In 2. 4 the dramatist gives us another unnatural creature—the French prince. He is sure there is nothing in Henry but a trivial, empty, and wayward youth given to the humour of wasting his time with idle companions. We know that this is not so, and so does the Constable of France (2. 4. 29–40).

Exeter adds to this description of the king as wise and sober monarch the picture of the warrior. For this we have been prepared in this very scene by the French king's praise of the English as the soldiers responsible for the defeats inflicted on France. In Exeter's lines Henry is conjured up as a destructive force. Here too the transformation of the king from human being to an elemental force, attended by storm, earthquake, and thunder should be noted. His claim to the French crown is made in the name of God Almighty; it will be enforced through the horrors of war.

Henry—as man of war

The theme of the third Prologue is war. Henry goes to France in pursuance of a claim supported by his spiritual counsellors and by the whole country.

3. 1 opens with the army on the stage with their 'scaling ladders'

before the gate of Harfleur. The whole of the scene is a warrior's call to arms. As usual on the Elizabethan stage war is conveyed most effectively through the speeches of the combatants.

Henry's lines in 3. 1 are the exaltation of the man of war. The human being is turned into an abstraction which combines the animal and the machine. The movement of the tiger, the eye threatening like the cannon as it points at the enemy through its embrasure, the brow in anger hanging like a worn crag over the raging sea greedily devouring its base—these images in the speech are unnatural portents.

It is true that this is the disguise which the warrior must put on. But there is in the organization of the lines such force and strain that we feel doubtful here of the panegyric lavished on Henry as 'this grace of kings'.

Contrast repeated

As for the hand-picked and carefully selected chevaliers who, as the Prologue put it, were followed to France by every young man of spirit, we are given in 3. 2 only the 'horse leeches'. These are not people who can imitate the action of the tiger or put on any of the parts of the warrior. Fluellen, who is contrasted with them, has his own humour—a pedantic devotion to the ancient discipline of war. He drives them off to the breach, leaving the boy on the stage to give us his (and our own) opinion of them. We know they are nothing but swaggerers ('swashers') and common thieves. They are cowards too, and will put up with any insults. Even the boy feels that their baseness turns his stomach, and he leaves the stage with a quibble—to 'cast it up', that is both to vomit out his disgust of his master, and also to have done with them.

The comic business of the three national types is, as it stands, tiresome. The draft we have here must have been so filled out by the players, that without actual stage representation of their touchy humours there seems to be little in this episode but arbitrary pronunciation and Fluellen's 'humour'.

Whatever the ancient 'disciplines' might have been, the king's ch in 3. 3 to the Governor and some citizens who appear on the per stage', shows that war is nothing but an ugly business.

The refusal of the French to agree to the king's just and hallowed claims makes their resistance seem to him 'impious'. They are warring against their rightful sovereign. So for the last time Harry offers them either surrender or the dire consequences of a continuance of the struggle. The details of the speech enforce all the other references to the savagery of war. The soldier 'fleshed' or inured to the taste of blood, with licence to kill the innocent (3. 3. 11 ff.), or blinded by lust (3. 3. 34), cannot surprise us. What is new here is that the king twice takes these for granted as the normal accompaniment of war (in 3. 3. 15, and 3. 3. 19—'what is it...to me?'). But it should be noted that once Harfleur surrenders, his word is 'Use mercy to them all'.

Preparation for Agincourt

Almost immediately after, Shakespeare begins to prepare for the next movement of his play—the surprising English victory at Agincourt—with the king's announcement of the toll taken of his troops by sickness and the withdrawal of the army to Calais.

3. 4 'Makes merry' with Katharine of France who is given an English lesson. This is stock comedy fun, where a great deal depends on the coarse suggestions of the words, mangled as they are learnt.

From 3. 5 until their defeat at Agincourt the attitude of the French is stabilized; a combination of arrogance and surprise that the contemptible English are capable of so much. To the Dauphin, Britaine, the Constable (who had a different tale to tell of the king in 2. 4), the English are little better than the dregs of the lust of the Norman forefathers of the French. Their country is a wretched island deeply indented by the sea—'that nook-shotten isle of Albion'. It seems impossible that their climate or their ale could have made them fiery of spirit. The conclusion is that if the owners of a country like France, rich in its wine and its fields, cannot beat the English, then it will have to be called poor in its lords.

The French king's roll-call of the famous names of France is one part of Shakespeare's preparation, through the potency of the audience's response to these titles, for the battle to follow. We know that before the actual battle we shall see the French herald Montjoy with the boastful message that Henry should pay ransom to get out of the predicament in which he finds himself.

But before he appears in 3. 6 the first of the 'horse leeches' is pulled off. Bardolph is sentenced to death for his theft of a pax. Pistol, whom Fluellen mistakenly takes for a hero, blusters in vain, and is shrewdly summed up by Gower who predicts the fate awaiting him. When the king appears on the stage his summary dismissal of the case of Bardolph is further proof of his skill in statesmanship. Bardolph's death is decided not only by justice, but also by expediency. For, as Henry says in 3. 6. 109–10, when 'lenity and cruelty play for a kingdom, the gentler gamester is the soonest winner'. That the law of court-martial would have cut off Bardolph's nose is understandable, but what are we to make of the king's prudential morality?

Montjoy enters and speaks with calculated offensiveness. He curtly remarks, without any courteous preamble, 'You know who I am by the costume I wear'—his herald's tabard. The king, full of modesty and dignity, sends him back with the reply that his ransom is his body, let the French take it if they can. The contrast between French and English is pointed both by the king's

> Yet forgive me, God,
> That I do brag thus! (3. 6. 148–9)

and his calm reply to his brother Gloucester in 3. 6. 167, 'We are in God's hand, brother, not in theirs'.

3. 7 is an extension of the scenes painting the pride of the French. It is the night before Agincourt, and on the stage are the French lords impatient for the morning and for the battle they never doubt they will win. The Dauphin composes variations upon the theme of his horse. The characters on the stage go off into witty quibbles on horse and mistress, getting most of their fun out of the indelicacy in the references.

Henry—the man

Of all the Prologues the fourth is the most interesting, because it creates a scene free from the extravagance and the hyperboles of the earlier prologues, and places squarely in it neither a 'grace of kings', nor a god of war, but the man Harry. If the earlier prologues are busy with a hero soon to 'assume the port of Mars', or a statesman unravelling the Gordian knot of policy, here the 'touch of Harry in the night' makes us conscious that Shakespeare's hero was a human being too.

In this Prologue the poet's sensitiveness to the great event of which he is writing enables him to provide a strong impression of expectancy, movement, and life. The references to darkness which strains the eyes, to the fires which are springing up all over the field, to darkened faces caught up in their dull light, have dramatic reality.

In this setting he gives us the French army 'secure' (an intensification of the Latin sense of '*securus*', free from care) and the English as victims destined for the sacrifice on the morrow. The hero of his play is treated not as king, but as the captain of a band of soldiers. To him now his men are not the horrid engines he had urged them to become at the gates of Harfleur, but 'brothers, friends and countrymen'. The 'touch of Harry in the night' is a 'little touch' only because the dramatist is conventionally doubtful of his ability to put the man on the stage. 'As may unworthiness define' shows us this. But we may be grateful for this little 'touch', or account of the king, for it does much to humanize the idealized figure the play has been putting before us.

The great difference is that for the first time we have a king who speaks in natural tones. In the bluff humour of the scenes in Act 4 which follow we are made aware of a man, and not a hero. The king is capable now of seeing the reality of his situation. In both his prose and verse in 4. 1 we note tones of liveliness and criticism which have not entered his speech till now. His remark in 4. 1. 4–7 on the 'soul of goodness in things evil' is not a solemn moral tag, it is the rueful joke of a man who in the worst position of all resolves that the best thing to do is to turn off most things with a laugh. To dwell on the uncomfortable reality would be to discountenance his men, so he continues with a good jest on 'dressing fairly for our end', and drops the light-hearted remark that even the devil himself, if need be, could be put to good moralistic use.

In the same strain are his remarks to Erpingham that if an analogy (an 'example') helps a man to endure distress, why should it not be used, for if the mind is revived, then the physical frame is once more active, like the snake which has sloughed off its skin. The dramatist is exhibiting here another facet of the character of the ideal monarch —his ability to keep up the spirits of his men.

The king and his men

The king himself, who asks to be left alone because he has a matter of conscience he must examine (4. 1. 30 ff.), is aware of the contradiction between the warrior-king and the human being, and feels the difference more keenly when he meets his common soldiers ignorant of his identity.

First of all, he is confronted by a picture of himself as he used to be in the days of his wild youth. Pistol talks of him as 'the imp of fame', and a 'bawcock', terms that Falstaff might have used of him in *Henry IV*.

Then Fluellen passes with his idealized picture of wars according to the ancient discipline. This little sketch points both backwards to the 'horse-leech' Pistol, and forwards to Williams, who gives us not the idealized picture of wars, but the reality which Henry himself had invoked in his threats to the Dauphin and at Harfleur.

In his conversation with Bates, Court and Williams, the king is confronted with his own image of war. In the discussion which follows we see that both Williams and the king are caught in a dilemma. The king, to Williams, bears the responsibility for leading his soldiers to a death in battle, which they cannot refuse because of their loyalty as subjects. When the king replies that 'every subject's duty is the king's, but every subject's soul is his own', he may be effective in argument, but he does not really answer Williams. There are occasions like the present when the subject forced into war endangers his soul by committing just those enormities which the king had described to the citizens of Harfleur.

His soliloquy. Alone once more, Henry reflects with some bitterness on the hard condition or state of being a king. Royalty is subject, he says, to the criticism of every fool who is incapable of feeling anything but the gripe in his own belly. The colloquial flavour of that line sets the key for the king's ironical satire of the 'Ceremony' which alone distinguishes king from commoner. The man who answers his own question in 4. 1. 241 on the real nature of the adulation of the royal state, finds, like all monarchs in Shakespeare, that the wretched slave who stuffs himself with the bread he earns with his toil is in a better case than any king. The sentiments are conventional, but the fervour of line 255 and those following shows that the king comes to the solemn conclusion that this disadvantage of kings is the defect of the disposition of the world. As things are, kings have to rule and subjects benefit from it.

This is the furthest point the king can reach in his consideration as man of his responsibility. We would be wrong to expect anything more. That he is troubled, and that there is this debate with Williams prove how strongly Shakespeare must have been exercised in his mind about the problems of war and human responsibility for them.

The king's prayer which follows (4. 1. 285–301) is spoken out of a heart oppressed by guilt. This is accounted for by the Tudor philosophy of the heinousness of the sin of usurpation, and by the weight of dissatisfaction with his recent argument on his soul. The prayer is not an unsatisfactory bargain struck with God. It is in keeping with the whole of the play to see it as Henry's acknowledgement of the stern justice of history. It is also his admission that heroic and hyperbolical though his talk of war had been, as man he feels his responsibility for endangering his subjects' lives by it.

4. 2 repeats the strong contrast between the two armies. This time, in addition to giving us the pride of the French, the dramatist provides an account of the wretched English army. Grandpre's words (4. 2. 39–55) dramatically combine both.

Henry—captain of the band of brothers. The king's speech in 4. 3. 18–67 should be taken as the best rejoinder to the arrogance of the French. It arises so naturally out of his quick reply to Westmoreland's wish for just two thousand of those who would at that moment in England be enjoying the holiday commemorating the two saints Crispin and Crispian, that it cannot be thought of as a carefully prepared set-piece of oratory. Harry warms to his subject. He is racy, full of good humour and high spirits. He speaks as a man speaking to men. He acknowledges that if it be a sin to covet honour, he is the most offending soul alive. Throughout, the king speaks with a sense of occasion and also of the persons for whom he speaks. The humour of his 'with advantages' in line 50, and 'familiar in his mouth as household words' followed immediately by 'Harry the king', show the liveliness of the mind at work. 'We few, we happy few, we band of brothers' is the resolute transformation of loss into gain. It would not be going too far to see in the freshness of the language and the easy movement of the lines the superiority of the English to the French.

Montjoy appears for the second time, and again the difference between his frigid utterance and the king's lively rebuttal of his supercilious demand that Henry should come to terms about his ransom should be noted. We are conscious through the king's speech (4. 3. 90–125) of the army behind him, the way they laugh at his jest, support his boldness, and take every quibble he makes, even the suggestion in 'fresher robes' that death will be the lot of some of them.

The battle

From 4. 4. to 4. 7. 85 the dramatist gives us the battle of Agincourt, through scenes which throw an ironical light on war, through straight dramatization of the defeated French, and through epic description. Of the fighting we see nothing at all, not even the several duels into which a battle was often broken up on the Elizabethan stage. Even the episode of 4. 4 follows upon fighting which, if it took place at all, must have been off stage. Pistol is in luck and the French knight compounds with him for ransom. As for the French in 4. 4 all they can do in their rout is to hope that the confusion in which they have been put to flight may be useful to them. The Constable's 'Disorder, that hath spoiled us, friend us now' (4. 5. 17) is the clue to their 'honourable' exploit of killing whomever they chance upon—in this case the boys left in charge of the baggage in the English camp.

4. 6 gives us a piece of epic description. Exeter's speech on the beautiful manner of the deaths of York and Suffolk is in keeping with the scene he pictures. The chivalrous gesture of these two friends belongs to the idealized war of 'culled and choice drawn cavaliers'.

The necessity for the killing of the prisoners is explained both by Fluellen's opening words in 4. 6 and the king's anger in 4. 7. 54 ff. Either the French must give up their disorderly attacks, or the king will command his men to cut the throats of the prisoners just taken (Bourbon among them).

The picture nearly complete

With the third and final appearance of Montjoy (4. 7. 64), now purged of his humour of vanity, the battle is over. The king's first reaction: 'Praised be God', is taken up again when he makes the formal announcement of the victory of Agincourt in solemn lines, full of biblical undertones. The dramatist, in this way, completes his picture of the Christian king and warrior, which he has contrasted throughout with the French full of self-confidence.

The episode of the glove he had exchanged with Williams is worked out in characteristic folk-tale style. The king is generous; the soldier who had reproved him is rewarded with a glove full of gold coins. The portrait of the king as man, and captain of a band of soldiers, is thus completed.

Elizabethan England

Shakespeare does not put Henry's triumphal return to London on the stage. Instead the fifth Prologue describes such a scene as must have been familiar to Londoners accustomed to royal processions and the ceremonial welcome given to visiting notables: the crowds, their noise, the 'whifflers' at the head of the procession in its solemn state. In order to actualize the scene, he permitted himself a topical reference and a prophecy, comparing London's welcome of the warrior-king to what would be Essex's reception. Was this really a 'lower likehood' to Shakespeare? 'The general of our gracious empress' as Shakespeare calls him, must then have been in the minds of many men as the hope of the age. When he wrote the lines Shakespeare did not know that these visions were to be as illusory as the hope of Henry V in the son he looked forward to.

Henry—as peacemaker

The fifth Prologue, having established Henry as national hero and Christian prince, goes on to complete the study of Henry as the ideal king. He is first in peace as he was first in war. His character, both as statesman and the architect of peace, will be filled in. So 5. 2 will show how the warrior sets about making peace and restoring order to both countries, in the only way in which peace was then secured—by a dynastic marriage. Henry will be exhibited to us, not as lover, but as statesman.

Pistol 'purged'

But before this Pistol has to be dismissed, 'purged' as the others have been. Bardolph and Nym have been executed; Pistol gets a sound drubbing, escaping a severer fate probably because, as his last lines suggest, he took the place of a more important character who had to be let off more lightly than either Bardolph or Nym. Pistol is made to eat a leek, swallowing it and swearing revenge to the accompaniment of Fluellen's cudgel about his back. Since he has lost everything—'my Doll is dead'—he has no option but to swell the ranks of the impostors in London. As the Hostess who was his wife was Nell Quickly, his reference to Doll, who could be none other than Doll Tearsheet, Falstaff's love in *Henry IV*, would indicate that the speaker of these lines must have been, at some early stage in the play's writing, Falstaff himself.

Henry as statesman

5. 2 for the first time brings the two mighty monarchs, France and England, on the stage together for the purpose of discussing the terms of peace. The English king is not the engine of war of the earlier acts, nor is he yet a romantic squire who will look 'greenly' or love-sick. Henry in this scene is the statesman who keeps the affairs of the commonwealth very clearly in front of him. He has certain justified claims on France, and he does not abate a jot of them. The marriage proposal is item no. 1 in his list, as he says in 5. 2. 96–8. The peace he is interested in has to be 'bought' from him, as he has won it through his victory over the French. We should not read this scene therefore only as an amusing sketch of the warrior unskilful in love wooing his princess. It is a demonstration of one of the qualities of the ideal king. Here Henry unlooses the Gordian knot of policy. How skilful he is in the role of suitor, though with conventional modesty he depreciates his abilities, the scene will show.

That peace is necessary to the French is shown in Burgundy's speech in 5. 2. 31–67. His is a picture of the waste of civil war, the fair garden ruined and turning to wildness because war has upset the natural order. The image of the country as a garden which it is the duty of the king to tend, and which cannot flourish unless order prevails, is already familiar through *Richard II*. What Burgundy says of France would come home to the imaginations of the English, to whom the threat of civil war was always a fearful possibility. The comparison of France to a garden, the symbol of the state, sets the level at which the scene of courtship should be taken. It is no real love-scene. Wise forethought which must benefit both states is its main impulse.

Henry as 'lover'

In the scene with Katharine, Henry is the blunt soldier who though, he says, he lacks skill in words, yet has a good sense of the occasion and an impressive readiness of speech. Two details in the make-up of an ideal king are stressed in it: his devotion to his country and his honesty of purpose as man. As lover he is, like the best of Shakespeare's lovers, not romantic but full of good sense: 'To say to thee that I shall die is true; but for thy love, by the Lord, no: yet I love thee too.' Comedy enters into it too, both in its breezy references to the physical and in the contrast between the soldier and the man.

So the match is made; Henry gets all he specified, even to the details of his royal titles; and the French king hails a union which will plant 'neighbourhood' and Christian-like accord between two kingdoms.

A grand procession crowns the play, and the chorus enters for the last time as epilogue. The actor apologizes, as usual, for the short-comings of the dramatic medium. He is also careful to point out that none of the fine hopes raised by the last scene was ever fulfilled. Though no reason is given for this, there is in the words 'whose state so many had the managing', an eloquent hint, that England was divided and there was lack of unity in the country. So France was lost and England bled. Shakespeare has dramatically 'varied' the praises of England's ideal king at a time when the wonderful reign of a monarch her people idealized was drawing to its close. The connection between England at the beginning of the fifteenth century and at the end of the sixteenth was clear. This play, like the other histories, was a 'mirror' for England.

11. JULIUS CAESAR

Though Julius Caesar, written in 1599–1600, was not printed during Shakespeare's lifetime, it must have been an extremely popular play, to judge from the numerous references to it in Elizabethan plays. Leonard Digges, in lines apparently written to be printed in the First Folio edition of Shakespeare's plays, referred to one scene in the play (4. 3) which must have stirred the audience.

That it was performed in 1599 at the Globe, a new theatre at the time, we know from a reference to a performance there in the account of the travels of Thomas Platter. He says nothing of the play itself, but was delighted with the jig for four dancers performed after it. The play must have been as new as the theatre, but its form probably differed a little from its 1623 Folio printing. The most likely explanation of a mystifying repetition of Portia's death in 4. 3 is author's, or editor's, revision which the printer failed to notice. This habit of revision was regular in the theatre of the time and is just as familiar now.

History with special significance

In this play Shakespeare was not only taking up again a historical subject, he was also dealing with a specially significant part of the historical past—that of classical Rome. English plays on Roman history, written both in Latin and in English, were well known. The history of Rome was very rich in emotional associations, and special value was attached to contemporary notions of the ancient Roman character. There were two words particularly associated with it—*gravitas* and *virtus*. They embodied the admiration felt for qualities of philosophic strength (*gravitas*) and zeal for the public good (*virtus*), which were supposed to be the reason for the success and might of Rome and its civilization.

If all history was a mirror which Renaissance man could use to help himself in the problems confronting him in public affairs, then Roman history was a mirror with stronger powers of magnification, for the Romans were regarded as the upholders of values which later ages had scarcely equalled or approached.

The source of this play was Plutarch, a Greek who lived in the first century after Christ and wrote the biographies of a number of prominent Romans, with just the same intention of providing a useful guide to public men. Shakespeare used his *Lives* of Caesar, Brutus and Antony, as they were to be found in North's translation of Amyot's French translation of Plutarch, for his play of *Julius Caesar*. North's translation was an English full of vigour and dignity.

Both history and tragedy. Shakespeare's play was not listed among his Histories in the First Folio. It must have been taken, on account of its subject-matter, as being a mixture of both tragedy and history, for its theme was the fall and death of Caesar, a prince or great man if ever there was one, for Caesar was a historical figure of legendary reputation in England, which he had conquered. In popular fable he was supposed to have been the builder of the original Tower of London.

As moral edification and history *Julius Caesar* does not differ very much from *Henry V*, but as tragedy it is a development on that play, also written in 1599.

Julius Caesar marks Shakespeare's greater involvement with profound questions that had been exercising his mind in the plays already examined. The conflict in this play is not the fairly simple and clearly defined struggle between the generous good-hearted man and the evil usurer which we saw in *The Merchant of Venice*. Nor does *Julius Caesar*, which also deals with the murder of the ruler of a state, pose quite the same questions as are raised by *Richard II*. Though Shakespeare's general attitude to the world may be the same in both plays, *Julius Caesar* brings in its train other issues, concerned with forms of government and difficulties of moral choice, quite out of the range of possibilities in *Richard II*. And if there is some similarity between *Julius Caesar* and *Henry V* in the seemingly ambiguous nature of the central character, much clearer in this play are the contradictions between the avowed motive and its consequences. This is to be seen in the ironical result of actions undertaken for what seem to be the noblest considerations, and in the play's background of images and allusions. Just as Henry, the mirror of a Christian king, sometimes appears to be the unlovely figure of a war machine, so Brutus, the embodiment of Roman *virtus*, discovers that the nobility of his motives brings not freedom, but civil strife and sordid struggle for power, and, as far as he himself is concerned, sickness at heart and the loss of what is dearest to him.

The issues of Shakespeare's time

This play of Rome and Romans, really of London and Englishmen, throws light on Shakespeare's world of contemporary England and Europe. Throughout *Julius Caesar* places, institutions, and even costume seem to belong much more definitely to Elizabethan times than to anything connected with the classical: craftsmen on the street on holidays; lions in the Tower of London; its suburbs with their houses of ill-fame; doublets; the kerchiefs worn by the sick, which would recall not Rome but their own life and times.

As in *Richard II*, Shakespeare's mind is exercised by the issues of his own time. His attention is directed to contemporary interest in the state, its defence and well-being, at a time when conspiracy threatened its head. In Shakespeare's mind were such assumptions and prejudices as belonged to supporters of the Tudor monarchy and the political philosophy based on such beliefs as we have examined in the general introduction and in nearly every one of the plays studied so far. His attitude to Caesar has various elements composed of the extraordinary hold of that figure on the popular imagination; notions of Roman character; the feeling that such power as he wielded could be used tyrannously; and also the belief that as accepted ruler of the state he was in a position resembling that of a contemporary monarch.

If this was Shakespeare's attitude to the events in Plutarch which he transformed into his play, then we shall notice throughout it a strong distrust of subversion and conspiracy. These were, in the knowledge and experience of all Elizabethans, the greatest disruptions of the state. The *Homilies*, appointed to be read in churches throughout the realm, have already been mentioned. Shakespeare not only knew these; he apparently accepted their instruction. In them he would have found the lesson driven home that conspiracy is dangerous, that it is never to be trusted, and that directed against the king or ruler it is both against God's commandment and doomed to create confusion involving both conspirators and the country. It could be nothing but evil. As the writer of *Certain Sermons and Homilies* put it: 'He that nameth Rebellion, nameth not a singular or one only sin, as is theft, robbery, murther and such like; but he nameth the whole puddle, and sink of all sins against God, and man...all sins, I say, against God, and all men heaped together nameth he, that nameth Rebellion.' If conspiracy against the head of the state was looked at in this way, how could it be possible that the good man or hero could be drawn into committing this most grievous of all sins?

It is probably with a mind made up on these points that Shakespeare read Plutarch and wrote his play. Yet what we find in *Julius Caesar* is no straightforward statement of what the *Homilies* had satisfactorily proved. If it had been only that, then it would have been plain moral lesson with none of the complexity of Shakespeare's play. What marks the plays is the tension between Shakespeare's attitudes to the subject he was handling and the eventual shape it took.

Structure

As the subject of this play is a conspiracy against a ruler and its issue, in which the hero is involved, there are likely to be three points of dominant plot and character interest in it. First of all, the conspiracy and its consequences. Secondly, the fall of the great man. Lastly, the subject intertwined with both these—the position of the hero, drawn into a course of action which transforms him into a conspirator against the ruler of the state and his slayer.

These are presented in a structure which could be grasped as a series of situations in which we are shown men being worked upon, or 'fashioned', by others. Through their own faulty reasoning or through their predisposition that they are in the right, they become the instruments of conspiracy. Mr John Crow has drawn attention to its numerous images in which 'the characters are seen in terms of metals'. The Elizabethan word 'mettle' was used to describe not only 'the stuff or life force of which man or beast is made', but also metal literally, the substance of which numerous articles were worked.

'Fashioning' human 'metal'. Before we examine the play in greater detail we should see how characteristic is this pattern of scenes of 'fashioning' or working upon human 'metal'. It opens with the two tribunes who work upon the crowd assembled to celebrate Caesar's triumph. This opening scene has the economy and significance of Shakespeare's best expositions, for here we are given not only its typical action, but also a decisive element in the play: the crowd who make up the state. Besides, the scene marks the first 'motion' or impulse of opposition to the head of the state.

The rest of Act 1 brings all the characters of the play, except Octavius and Portia, on the stage. It demonstrates how Cassius sets about working upon the 'metal', not only of Brutus but also of Casca. His soliloquy which ends 1. 2 is of particular interest because it is a clear statement of his role as arch-conspirator or artificer.

2. 1 is a demonstration of how Brutus works upon himself and moulds his own attitude towards Caesar and the conspiracy. It brings conspiracy on the stage—at night, hidden, and in deceitful guise. Further, it shows how Brutus, on every important issue, after he has 'fashioned' the situation on which decision is taken, works on the rest to accept his presentation of the case.

2. 2 presents us with the great man, the ruler of the state, being fashioned, first by his wife, and then by the conspirators.

3. 1 ironically shows how Caesar, refusing to be worked upon by the petitions of the conspirators, at the moment of his greatest pride

in the resistance of his 'metal', is struck down and falls. The conspirators are now supreme, Caesar lies on the ground. Their symbolic action of 'stooping' to wash their hands in Caesar's blood marks the beginning of the active transformation of high principle into sordid reality.

Antony enters and begins to 'fashion' the conspirators, notably Brutus, who once again decides on a course of action which ruins them.

3. 2 is the central scene of the play in so far as the results of conspiracy are dramatically represented on the stage. Both Brutus and Antony 'fashion' the crowd, and the chaos which must inevitably follow conspiracy is enacted in 3. 3.

In 4. 1 the new rulers of the Roman world are shown to be 'fashioners' as unprincipled as those who had conspired against Caesar.

4. 2 and 4. 3 extend through repetition the fate of conspiracy as it has been shown to us so far: there is disagreement between the two chief conspirators. Their quarrel is composed, and Brutus again decides, working upon Cassius to accept his decision, how events are to be tackled. Before the scene is over Brutus's depressed thoughts, the lateness of the hour, his confused sight and the music 'fashion' the apparition which appears to him.

Act 5 works out the end of the conspiracy in confusion. Its leaders are at cross-purposes. In the end Cassius kills himself, wrongly crediting what his weak sight made him believe he saw, and Brutus, against the rule of his philosophy which forbade suicide, kills himself with the sword which ran through Caesar.

Two strains of verse

In dealing with the play, we should keep the following points in mind: first, the presence of two strains of verse, one persuasive and rhetorical, intending to produce its maximum effect on its hearers through emotional means. Antony's great speech in 3. 2 is a potent appeal to passion. The other kind of verse is the cold, almost dispassionate examination by the speaker of the issue confronting him. If it makes any appeal, it is to judgement and reason. It is well worth considering specially, as examples of this kind, Brutus's soliloquy in 2. 1. 10–34 and his speeches in the same scene. His prose address to the Roman crowd in 3. 2. is in the same mode, which appears to eschew the tricks of deliberate demagogy. But can it not lead to just as wayward and false a conclusion as that the specious orator is concerned with producing?

Play—more than tragedy of an individual

One should also note the importance of repetition in the situations of the play, particularly the stress laid very early on the crowd as actor, and the ominous supernatural happenings which are related to the action. Through allusion and image the world of Rome is revealed as one of strange, unnatural happenings and prodigies of all kinds. Contradictions follow from generous impulse, deceit cloaks friendliness, and the main character in the play is heartsick throughout.

The result is the growing feeling, as we study the play, that its subject is not only the 'tragedy' of an individual, but the large theme of the state and its functioning. This is a characteristic of the tragedies which follow *Julius Caesar*. They are more than the story of the central figure, they involve the whole world in which he is placed.

Its opening

Julius Caesar opens with a scene which could be taken as illustrative of the whole play in miniature. Its 79 lines sketch the course of the action: the way in which human beings are worked upon by those who have the power to move them. 1. 1 may be taken as anticipation of 3. 2. One line of this scene 'You blocks, you stones, you worse than senseless things!' seems to be echoed in Antony's veiled instruction to the crowd at the moment he knows he has moved it as he wanted to

...move
The stones of Rome to rise and mutiny.

The scene brings on the stage an important actor in the play—the Roman crowd—never absent for long throughout its first part. More importantly, it establishes two highly significant points about it. The crowd is basically well-intentioned and likeable. This can be seen in the humour of the replies of the commoners to their questioners. It is also raw material in the hands of its betters, as this scene proves. Assembled to honour Caesar's triumph, it is sent home tamely as a result of the emotional appeal of Marullus, who, like Antony, plays with its passion, its memories of the glory of Rome, its share in that glory, and its feelings of gratitude. The language which carries the appeal is regular, impassioned, repetitive. It works on the single idea slowly and gathers fire and speed as it moves. Rhetorical question and balance in construction and phrase weight the speech and make its conclusion inescapable. When Marullus turns on the crowd the final question with its simple contrast between strewing flowers and Pompey's 'blood' (both his progeny and his blood literally), he can, as the next step, majestically order it about its business with his 'Be gone!' That the crowd vanishes 'tongue-tied' in its guiltiness shows that it had been made to feel ashamed of its lack of loyalty to Pompey's memory. It may be, as Cassius described it in 1. 3. 108–11, 'trash', 'offal', the shavings and rubbish with which fires were kindled, but it will be noted that it has to be set on fire by some external agent.

When Flavius notes: 'See, whe'r their basest mettle be not moved', in his pride he makes a direct comment on their malleability. They are responsive to the fire of eloquence as iron is to heat. Flavius at least knows that Marullus and himself have acted indefensibly. To Marullus's question, 'May we do so?', he replies 'It is no matter'. This, as the development of the play's action and the reflections of its characters on their share in it show, provides the keynote to the attitude of the conspirator. What determines his actions is expediency, and most often his envy of the power of a rival or opponent. So the metaphor from hawking—of feathers plucked from Caesar's wing —is going to be taken up in other forms by other characters.

Finally, this scene shows how readily the interest of the super-natural powers—'the gods'—in the Roman scene could be evoked. Throughout the play the attitude of practically all its persons is that the heavenly powers, or nature, are sympathetic to events on earth, and either comment on them or, reflecting them, warn humanity.

The crowd leaves the stage at 1. 1. 65 only to return fourteen lines later in Caesar's procession! It is never far away. Even if it is not seen, it is heard and its shouts off-stage work on characters on the stage. They make Brutus reveal himself the more quickly to Cassius. Note, too, how Casca's attitude to the crowd resembles that of Flavius. He is contemptuous of it, because he feels superior to it. Like Flavius, he thinks he can control it, but it is this same crowd which drives him and the other conspirators out of Rome.

How Caesar is presented

Caesar enters twice during the scene, his first entry coming straight after the words of Flavius which describe him as the bird of prey whose wings have to be clipped. He is on the stage for a few moments, goes out, and in a short while Cassius talks of him with irony and envy as a man of feeble temperament raised through the unworthiness of the Romans to the stature of greatness. When Caesar comes back, Shakespeare takes care to point to his anger (which the actor would clearly have shown in his bearing and gesture), his arrogance and his physical infirmity. It would seem that, what-ever Caesar's legendary reputation might have been, Shakespeare wishes to present him as a human being with a fair share of human weaknesses. However this might be, we do see that Cassius is animated by personal grievance. There is, to take one example, a world of difference between Brutus's simple statement that Caesar suffered from epileptic fits in 1. 2. 255 and the way Cassius works on it in order to press his point. Shakespeare's portrait of Caesar may have owed something to contemporary plays on him. As he is presented in this scene and later, we can see that something of his seeming arrogance may be due both to a difference between Elizabethan manners and ours (for we are likely to think of a person who speaks about himself as boastful), and to the necessity of Caesar's quite plainly speaking about himself. If he did not tell us about himself how should we know?

A parallel to the opening scene

The scene between Brutus and Cassius is important. It is a very much more subtle repetition of the substance of 1. 1. It establishes Cassius as arch-conspirator and Brutus as the honourable man who, if he had not been worked upon, might have remained 'at war with himself' but uninvolved in conspiracy. Brutus is frank, he speaks plainly, and what he says is free of the ironical overtones of every one of Cassius's speeches.

The latter in a bitter parenthetical reference to Caesar whom he calls 'immortal' (1. 2. 60), therefore a god, and to the servitude of the times in which they live ('the age's yoke'), makes his drift clear to Brutus. 'Into what dangers would you lead me, Cassius?' and the two lines which follow show both Brutus's knowledge that he is being tempted and his disinclination to be moved.

It is the crowd with their shout off-stage which gives Cassius the first opportunity. But again Brutus is perfectly candid: he cannot think of Caesar as king, yet he loves him. However, if what Cassius has to say concerns the public good and is honourable, then he is prepared to listen. 1. 2. 82–9 are interesting because they mark the extent of Brutus's initial dilemma. The sense of the lines is that to him honour is an absolute value, where it is in question he can even look at death unconcernedly. Is there a hint of danger here? That the devotion to honour should be linked automatically with death seems significant. There is some desperation in Brutus's lines: he repeats the words 'honour' and 'death' after his questions to Cassius as if he had to work himself up to seeing the alternatives in the way he puts them. What he states about himself, that he loves honour more than he fears death, points to his particular difficulty— that of convincing himself that it would be honourable to kill Caesar.

Brutus's conception of honour as an absolute determining principle forces him to exercises of reasoning in which life and its claims seem to be forgotten.

All the help Cassius can give is of little consequence. He launches into personal attack (1. 2. 90–131): it is intolerable that Caesar, who lacks Brutus's physical powers, should be a great man. When on the second shout off-stage Cassius turns to Brutus, all he can do is to try to prompt similar feelings in the latter with his 'Brutus will start a spirit as soon as Caesar'.

Brutus's reply (1. 2. 162–75) is a temperate and clear statement that he knows Cassius is a friend of his, and that he can guess what Cassius 'would work' him to, but he refuses to be urged any more. So far, Brutus's metal has been as hard and intractable as flint, as Cassius's words (1. 2. 176–7) show.

Casca's account of the offer of a crown to Caesar and his remark that the people would not mind Caesar's being either king or tyrant, apparently change Brutus's attitude. This, together with Caesar's angry entry, decides Brutus to hear Cassius again, for in 1. 2. 305 ff. he goes back on his earlier statement.

Alone on the stage Cassius can now reflect with some satisfaction on how even 'honourable metal' can be wrought from its true character. He acknowledges the difference between his motives and Brutus's when he remarks that honourable men, if they wish to prevent themselves from being perverted, should always consort with people like themselves, and that had he been in Brutus's position he would not have been 'humoured' (influenced) as Brutus had been by him. He resorts to a trick—letters in disguised handwriting will be thrown in Brutus's windows.

On the evidence of this soliloquy we see how well Caesar's description of Cassius fits the man represented on the stage. He is dangerous, for hearing no music he is, in the words of Lorenzo in *The Merchant of Venice*, fit for 'treasons, spoils and strategems'. We have seen him trafficking with them throughout the scene.

Heightened dramatic interest—the storm

Shakespeare, moving now to the climax of the Ides of March (15 March), runs together the events of the previous scene and what follows across the interval of time which must necessarily have elapsed between the Lupercalia (15 February) and the murder of Caesar. The heightened dramatic interest of the storm and the references to the supernatural portents which accompany it distract attention from the implausibility of the speed of the action. The storm, pointing to some catastrophic event, both makes good any seeming lapse on the dramatist's part and provides the dramatic background for more scenes of 'fashioning'.

The storm is just as much an actor as the crowd. As the crowd is worked upon, so the storm is used to influence the course of action. Up to 2. 2 we shall see various interpretations of it and its significance for human beings. Casca is ready to be influenced by any interpretation of it which accepts it as a warning from the gods to Rome. Cicero regards it as a natural phenomenon, extraordinary weather and nothing else, for which men can, if they are so minded, provide explanations absolutely at variance with each other.

The 'fashioning' of Casca

This is what Cassius proceeds to do. He suggests that his personal courage and daring in the storm give him the right to expound its meaning. As he puts it, only Casca's dullness prevents him from seeing what it means. He therefore works on Casca in order to strike from him the sparks of life which should be in him. The 'fashioning' of Casca (1. 3. 57–78) is a piece of emotional oratory, deliberately aimed at recounting once more all those 'prodigies' which had reduced Casca to fright in order to make him the more pliable. The repetitions of the word 'why' disguise the emotionalism of Cassius's argument. With the phrase 'Unto some monstrous state' (1. 71), where he pauses for effect, Cassius provides little else but typical envy of Caesar whose personal prowess is no greater than his, he says.

Cassius's deliberate apostrophe to the evil times in which he lives (ll. 80–4) is good demagogy, as is the scornful reference to the 'womanish' acceptance of servitude by the Romans. His broad hint in line 89 at suicide ('I know where I will wear this dagger then') is really a demagogue's trick too. It recalls Caesar's similar trick when, in Casca's account of what followed the offer of the crown (1. 2. 264–7), with a dramatic gesture he asked anyone who wished to cut his throat. Cassius's threat is as effective a piece of attitudinizing as his pretence in lines 111 ff. that he has been so moved by his sense of Rome's grievances ('grief') as to have risked revealing himself to 'a willing bondman'. 'Faction' (conspiracy) is now brought to birth. Its aims are likened by Cassius to the storm-wrecked sky: 'most bloody-fiery and most terrible'. Casca's remark as they begin to leave the stage that Brutus's countenancing or supporting what they do will, like alchemy, transform any baseness of motive or action into pure gold, recalls the image of the artificer working upon metals. As the Arden editor points out, there is a significant irony in this remark, for this transformation of base metals to gold was exactly what alchemy had failed to do.

Brutus 'fashioning it'

Brutus in his 'orchard' under the same storm-laden sky, debates what he should do, and shows again how men are 'fashioned' by themselves or by others. The key to his soliloquy (2. 1. 10–34) is 'fashion it thus'. This word 'fashion' could be innocent of all suggestions of fabrication in our sense of 'fabricating evidence', yet there are too many similarities between what happens here and earlier and later scenes for us to neglect the connection between this scene and the others. The soliloquy ends on just as specious a note as any of the previous scenes of working upon 'the metal' of a character, yet there are great differences between the way in which Brutus addresses himself to his task and the procedure of Cassius. There is a difference, too, in the impulse. Is Brutus honest with himself when he says to himself 'Fashion it thus', or does he intend to provide his case ('quarrel') against Caesar with a pretext?

The mode is different from Cassius's. The verse is almost cold as Brutus goes reasonably over the grounds of discussion. Personal reasons do not weigh with him; it is only the fact that the state ('the general') is involved that moves him. What has to be discussed— 'There's the question'—is just this: How would Caesar act as king? The argument proceeds by analogies which are on the face of it objective, barely revealing the emotion which lurks behind them. The adder (l. 14) and 'the climber-upward' (l. 23) prejudge the issue against Caesar, but the voice of reason says what has to be said of Caesar: that neither his will nor his desires ('his affections') seemed to sway his judgement. Yet the push given by the analogy decides. From it comes the logical inference: 'So Caesar may' (He can, it is possible). From this follows, after a slight pause: 'Then, lest he may, prevent' (Lest he should, forestall it). As a consequence the case is 'fashioned' thus: not the Caesar we know, but 'what he is, augmented' would be guilty of such and such acts of tyranny. So the third analogy which follows repeats the first, and Caesar becomes the serpent's egg (l. 32), which it is the duty of any man of good-will to destroy.

The argument is that of a man in a state of distraction. 2. 1. 61–9 repeat Brutus's earlier remark to Cassius in 1. 2. 56 ('poor Brutus with himself at war'), and are a convincing picture of the analogy between the human frame caught in the toils of such a desperate act as conspiracy and a kingdom torn by civil war. The image Brutus uses of his meeting with Cassius repeats many which have previously been used. He speaks of himself as a knife whetted by Cassius—the blade worked upon by the human being who gives an edge to it. Cassius had worked on Casca in just the same way.

Brutus in the conspiracy. Brutus has no illusions about 'faction'. Its 'monstrous visage' can scarcely be masked in the darkest cavern by day. Here and later in 2. 1. 224 ff. he is forced into advising dissimulation and disguising one's true intent in smiles and affability.

From the moment Cassius has apprised him of the conspiracy—in an aside while the characters on the stage debate where the east, from which the sun will soon light up the fatal day to follow, really lies—Brutus takes charge. He decides that no oath is necessary among men of high principle; that Cicero should not be told; and when Cassius puts against Antony much the same case Brutus himself had put against Caesar (he may be dangerous, so he should be prevented) this time he does not accept it.

His refusal to agree (2. 1. 162–83, 185–9) is interesting on several counts. First of all, the verse is kept going on a high level of discourse; then, the comparison of Antony to a limb of Caesar's once made, the rest follows naturally and logically. Further, it should be noted that Brutus, in keeping with the character given him here, sees himself well able to differentiate between the 'spirit' (the principle) of Caesar and the human being. For all his acceptance of Caesar's murder as a priestly rite of sacrifice, he is forced into acknowledging that it is impossible to 'come by' or get possession of Caesar's spirit without dismembering him. So in the end all it comes to, with another image of 'purgers' (physicians or surgeons) not 'murderers', is a disingenuous recommendation of dissimulation. The noble deed of striking Caesar down has to be given the right 'colour'.

Brutus himself has arrived at such a stage in his development as conspirator that he undertakes to 'fashion' Ligarius. This, he says, will be done by giving him reasons. Yet when he appears, Ligarius ironically enough decides only out of his affection for Brutus, quite unconcerned about any of the reasons proposed. This should be remembered both as ironical comment on Brutus's knowledge of the world and the way the crowd is moved later.

Brutus and Portia. The scene with Portia immediately tests Brutus's ability to behave as he had just advised his friends to conduct themselves, disguising their real feelings. But he is worked upon by a person who is at first reasonable, then turns on him the strongest emotional means in order to gain her point. When with a mixture of affection and irony Portia taxes Brutus with treating her

not as his wife, but as his 'harlot', she forces him from an acknowledgement that she is as dear to him as his life's blood. This image,
the liveliest and most memorable in the play—'the ruddy drops that
visit my sad heart'—strikes a disturbing note. It would have suggested not only the warm and breathing human being, but also the
person anatomized. It would seem to belong to all those references
to blood of which the play is full. Furthermore, as Brutus uses the
figure to convey his depth of affection for his wife, his identification
with her, there is a strange note of foreboding in it. The reference
to his sadness of heart, and the drops which 'visit' it imply that he is,
so to speak, outside himself viewing a physiological process in
himself.

Shakespeare took the main points in this scene from Plutarch.
Besides accentuating the high seriousness of the Roman character,
it focuses our attention on Brutus, sick and disturbed at the problem
he has been debating. If dramatic presentation of 2. 1. 61–9 had been
required, it would have been provided by this scene.

Caesar 'fashioned'

2. 2 should be placed beside all the preceding scenes of 'fashioning'.
As in all previous scenes it is the personal appeal which is most
successful. Calphurnia kneels to Caesar and he decides not to go
only to give way to her mood. He is, however, too confident, as
Calphurnia notes. His self-interest and the thought that it would be
ridiculous for him to be kept at home by his wife made him ready to
fall in with Decius Brutus's suggestion. Decius Brutus's avowal of
his 'dear dear love' to Caesar's 'proceeding' (his advancement) is
the 'glass' with which the 'bear' is betrayed (2. 1. 205).

So Caesar goes, surrounded, as he thinks, by his friends, leaving
Brutus on the stage to confess his guilt in an aside to the audience.
There is a straight irony in the line (2. 2. 128). There is also a
reference to Brutus's own mode of arguing through analogies ('likes').

First climax—the murder

The first climax of the play follows quickly after a short scene of suspense and a few moments of anxiety for the conspirators. Caesar is struck down at the very moment when he claims for himself qualities verging on the preternatural. He compares himself to the 'northern star'; he is unique among men, the only one who cannot be worked upon. His is the hardness of ice which cannot be thawed. Only the foolish ('fond') could believe that he could be melted.

Soon after this he is struck down. He accepts his fate when he sees that Brutus strikes too. His words, 'Then fall, Caesar', dramatically call attention to the position of the great man now. At the beginning of the play, in image after image, he stood above all others—he was the falcon aloft in the upper air; the Colossus; the monarch seated on his throne; a lion, etc. He was the imperial glory of Rome; now, like Richard II, he lies stretched out on the ground. His fall is acted out on the stage, and its physical reality insisted on by both Brutus and Antony. The body of Caesar has always to be kept clear in our vision, together with the blood streaming from it (realistically presented on the Elizabethan stage through the use of sheep's or pig's blood concealed in a bladder and pierced at need). Both body and blood are important because they give a concrete reality to numerous images and references in the play, and are part of the dramatic action. For instance, when Antony says, 'My credit now stands on such slippery ground' he is using the adjective 'slippery' both metaphorically and in grim literal earnest, for if the ground is slippery, it has been made so by Caesar's blood.

Counter-movement

If the first movement of the play begins with Caesar triumphant and 'immortal', it is over as soon as he falls. The counter-movement begins immediately—when those who brought him down themselves stoop to his body. It is almost over when Brutus sees the figure of Caesar standing before him in 4. 3. 272, and it works itself out to its fulfilment when both Cassius and Brutus lie low in death. Moulton stresses the entry of Antony's servant as sign of the 'reaction' which follows upon the highest point of the tide. This would certainly be so if we took the subject of the play as Caesar's murder and its revenge, but if we considered it as the paradoxical evolution of Brutus's noble purpose then the symbolic and extravagant action he would have the conspirators perform is proof that he has deceived himself. He had taken up arms against 'the spirit' of Caesar, and now he, and they, are to bathe themselves in Caesar's blood, as evidence of the truth of the slogans 'Peace, freedom and liberty'. This peace needs the brandishing of blood-stained swords, and the Romans who are called upon to rejoice in freedom and liberty disappear in fright that they, too, are to suffer. The high-minded wish to be sacrificers, not murderers, has had an unexpected consequence.

With the entry of Antony's servant a piece of fantasticality on Brutus's part is over. The servant falls prostrate before Brutus (3. 1. 123). This must be seen as Antony's position too. It is from this position that he has to raise himself. That he can do so is due to his power of 'fashioning' Brutus and the others. The servant's message is couched in terms curiously like Brutus's later speech to the crowd. As it is addressed to Brutus, it uses measured tones and intellectual reasoning which he would appreciate. When Antony himself appears, he goes down on his knees before Caesar's body, his words 'O mighty Caesar, dost thou lie so low?' (3. 1. 149) giving us in a single sentence the essence of the narrative sequence of the first part of the play.

Antony and the conspirators

Antony's meeting with the conspirators is a masterly piece of writing, for Shakespeare makes him begin with a true dramatic gesture. His words 'Who else must be let blood?' (3. 1. 153) implies that they are the physicians they claim to be. His offering of himself to their swords is as good a demagogic piece of business as any other in the play. While Brutus is quick to assure him that they do not intend his death, it is Cassius who makes the pertinent comment that it would be advantageous for him to cast his lot with them.

When Antony goes on later to liken Caesar to a deer hunted by the conspirators, who, according to the traditional custom, have daubed themselves with the blood of their quarry (3. 1. 206–10), the image has, we note, changed. The conspirators are hunters now, not physicians. Antony's answer to Cassius's plain question, 'Will you be pricked in the number of our friends?', is a request for reasons, for these he knows Brutus will be ready to provide. Upon that he insinuates his own request to be allowed to speak in the 'order' of Caesar's funeral—that is, in the customary arrangements which included a funeral oration. Once again Brutus decides against Cassius.

Antony's soliloquy (3. 1. 255–76) makes his attitude plain. He has in fact been a better actor than any of his enemies. They are now 'butchers', and his invocations of the chaos and war which are to follow Caesar's murder are the words of a man determined on revenge. How far this is from Brutus's picture of the man who, on Caesar's death, was to fall into a melancholy and pine to death (2. 1. 186–7). Caesar's death, to Antony, can result only in civil strife and confusion. Only Ate, the goddess of mischief and revenge, can fittingly preside over what follows.

Octavius's servant by his weeping surely anticipates the course of Antony's speech. 'Passion' (sorrow), as Antony sees, is catching. He will remember this when, as his own words make it clear, he 'tries' or tests—as metal was tried or tested—the reaction of the crowd to Caesar's murder.

Second climax—the 'fashioning' of the crowd

The second climax of the play follows the two 'fashionings' of the crowd by Brutus and Antony. What Cassius says to 'satisfy' the crowd we are not told, nor is it important, since Shakespeare's interest is focused on Brutus. The speech Shakespeare gives him (3. 2. 13–47) is his own invention; it owes nothing to Plutarch, except perhaps the reference to Brutus's skill in the plain Spartan style of speech.

The difference between Brutus's speech and Antony's should be noted. Brutus speaks in prose, effectively sustaining an argument because he has to provide a satisfactory reason for the assassination. He begins by addressing the crowd in much the same way as Antony does later, but we notice that his first word to them is 'Romans', since it is as Romans they have to consider the 'cause', or the matter in hand. Antony starts by placing the crowd on the same level as himself: he calls them 'friends', but apparently they will not, or do not, hear, and he has to go on calling for their attention. Brutus's is an appeal to reason and judgement, Antony's is a gradual feeling of his way until he can appeal to the passions of his audience—their grief, and later their self-interest. Brutus invokes Rome and the principle of freedom; Antony appeals to the crowd's memory of the man, he shows them Caesar's blood-stained mantle and concludes with reading his will.

When Antony begins he has the crowd against him, and has to overcome their hostility. His tones are quiet and slow after he has succeeded in making himself heard against the noise. The commas following each of the words, 'Friends, Romans, countrymen' (3. 2. 74) are an indication of the way he has had to strive for attention.

The speech is a clever piece of construction, improvised as the speaker feels the crowd responding to him. At every stage in its quiet opening he inserts praise of Brutus and the rest, and at every repetition we see the speaker feeling the pulse of his audience. Antony's speech is not pitched on the level of judgement and intellect, he is there not to refute Brutus, but only 'to speak what I do know'. Quite early he tries out a straight appeal for tears, and weeps himself to give his hearers their cue.

The slight pause, lines 109–18, in which it is plain that the crowd has been wrought upon, not so much by anything he has said as by his tears, should be compared with what Casca felt about this same crowd in 1. 2. 264ff. How far Antony has worked upon it can be seen by comparing line 70: 'This Caesar was a tyrant' with line 117: 'There's not a nobler man in Rome than Antony.'

When he resumes in line 119 we see his greater confidence in his expansive verse, his strong contrasts, the quickening of the pace of the poetry, the deliberate playing with his audience: the conditional clause 'if I were disposed to stir'; the showing of the parchment followed by 'which, pardon me, I do not mean to read', and the exaggeration which turns Caesar into the counterpart of a Christian saint.

The third stage of the speech (lines 141 ff.) is punctuated by repeated calls for patience. Once he had to plead for a hearing from the crowd, now he has to restrain it. By 3. 2. 152 when he says, 'I fear I wrong the honourable men', he has the crowd on his side. He then works upon it passionately till he has made it hysterical. Having shown them the mantle, worked in the pathos of Caesar's situation—the conqueror of the Gallic wars, killed by his dearest friend—he accentuates the situation with the extravagant image of Caesar's blood rushing to see whether it was Brutus who had 'knocked' (3. 2. 179–81). When the mantle is whipped off Caesar's face the cry is 'Revenge'.

What follows is excellent mob oratory. We know that each one of the formidable list of attributes of the orator in 3. 2. 222–4: 'wit', 'words', 'worth', 'action', 'utterance', has been amply manifested. Even if he lacked all these, Antony has certainly proved that he has 'the power of speech to stir men's blood'. When the crowd streams out with shouts of 'mutiny', 'fire', 'revenge', Antony can say to himself 'Mischief thou art afoot'. He has brought his own prophecy to fulfilment.

The results of conspiracy: riot and civil war

The tearing to pieces of Cinna the poet (3. 3) is all Shakespeare need show of the riot which follows, and completes the fulfilment of the ominous signs and wonders seen the previous night. The crowd to

whom Brutus appealed to 'censure' (judge) him in their wisdom sets
upon the unfortunate poet, only because his name happens to be
Cinna. This is the last we see of the crowd as the Roman populace,
but the persons who made it up appear in the scenes that follow.
They are the armies accompanying the two sides struggling for
control of the Roman world. The scene now shifts to the civil war into
which faction and conspiracy have plunged the country and its people.

4. 1 should be taken as index of how the troubled state of the
country is reflected in the deliberations of one side in the coming
war. When Plutarch referred to the meeting of the self-appointed
committee of three, or Triumvirate, he used it to point to the
meanness and scandal of the revenge taken by the three on those
whose nearness in kin to them should have guaranteed them better
treatment. In addition Shakespeare underlines the further meanness
of Antony, who intends to prune the legacies of which he made so
much play in his funeral oration.

Besides all this, the scene repeats the motive of working or
'fashioning' a man. With the immense stakes of the world before
them, why, according to Antony, should Lepidus be a sharer with
them? His two statements to Octavius (4. 1. 18–27, 4. 1. 29–40),
a man just as keen presumably on his own advancement as Antony
is, give us Antony's attitude of mind. Lepidus is to be treated as a
beast of burden, 'as *we* point the way', the stress falling quite
decisively on the pronoun (4. 1. 23). Octavius's reply betrays something of the clear-sightedness which makes him difficult for Antony
to control. To Antony Lepidus is like a horse to be trained to do
exactly as his master wishes. The image is not that of fashioning
metal, but is taken from the 'manage' or riding school, where horses
were trained and put through their paces.

The quarrel between Brutus and Cassius

In the next scene we return to the conspirators, but see only two of
the numbers who formed the 'faction'. Things are not well between
Brutus and Cassius. The scene which follows their meeting must be,

as Brutus will not let it be in front of the two armies, a 'wrangle'. This is the famous scene of the Romans 'at half-sword parley'.

The very terms of its description as a quarrel scene should convey the real importance of 4. 3 in the structure of the play. This scene shows the Roman world divided against itself; it underlines the fate which dogs conspiracy; and it shows how sick at heart the chief character is. Throughout the scene the verse keeps crackling with the sparks of hot anger, and Cassius's hand must have at times been fingering his sword.

Besides, the man whom both the friends now quarrelling helped to strike down is seen once again. His ghost appears and stands before Brutus, another portent like those which 'blazed forth the deaths of princes'.

Furthermore, it illustrates the paradoxical quality of Brutus's character. For all the 'honesty' with which he is armed, he does nothing but what lays himself and his friends open to attack. Despite his claim that he cannot be moved, in the end he is moved not by threats but by an appeal from his friend. There is some similarity between Caesar's self-regarding pride in his constancy and Brutus's notions about himself, his strong stand on honour.

Finally, the scene which brings the news of Portia's death not only recalls her, but also the occasion of Brutus's disquiet when the two were shown together on the stage. Then he was in his own words 'suffering the nature of an insurrection'. Now he is 'sick of many griefs'. His state of mind is in keeping with the sick state of the world.

In discussing the actual quarrel between the two friends we should note that Cassius takes up the position that in such a time it is not proper that every trivial affair should come in for comment (4. 3. 7–8). Against this Brutus counters with the uncompromising position of honour and integrity. In his reference to the assassination of Caesar he asks a rhetorical question: who would be such a scoundrel as to stab Caesar but for the sake of Justice? The use of this particular word for the first time as one of the reasons for

Caesar's death, together with the business of 'supporting robbers', should not be cavilled at. Justice, freedom, liberty, peace, they are all one. They are the high principles which moved Brutus to strike the 'foremost man of all the world', and what have they come to now?

Confident of his own strength, Brutus proceeds to treat Cassius as if he were a sick man in need of a homoeopathic cure ('You shall digest the venom of your spleen'), and a person whom he, Brutus, will use as an object of laughter. For the second time Cassius must have been close to drawing his sword, as we see in his angry remark: 'I may do that I shall be sorry for' in line 64. Only Brutus's reference to Cassius as a friend gives Cassius the line he is to take. As Roman, and a soldier, Brutus can face Cassius, but appealed to as friend (l. 85) he cannot hold out. The extravagance with which Cassius offers his dagger and his breast to Brutus should be taken as parallel to the attitudinizing of Caesar when, in Casca's description, he 'plucked ope his doublet' to the crowd, and of Antony when he asked the conspirators to 'fulfil their pleasure' on him. Brutus's acknowledgement that his friend may in future 'dishonour' (insult) him if he wishes (108), and he will take it as mere 'humour' (a whim), shows how he has capitulated, since to him honour was an absolute value. And though he is ready to stomach Cassius's 'humour', he gives short shrift to the luckless poet's exhibition of his 'humour' (4. 3. 127–36).

Portia remembered. Alone with his friend, Brutus confesses that he is unable to stand the strain of the grief oppressing his mind. Reminded by Cassius that his philosophy should keep him from giving way to misfortune ('accidental evils'), he tells Cassius of Portia's death. The mention of Portia recalls her own strength of mind and seriousness of purpose, both of which were part of the excellence of the Roman character as Elizabethans imagined it. Yet she was unable to stand the strain herself, nor can the two now on the stage.

The second reference to Portia's death should be taken as an earlier stage of the text of the play, later cancelled out. There seems to be no good reason why Brutus should pretend to Messala that he did not know of it. Besides, his words in line 194, 'Well, to our work alive' should be taken as referring to Cicero, dead, in line 178, which it should follow.

Caesar's ghost. Music, the reference to the advanced hour of the night and the sleepiness of Lucius to whom Brutus is characteristically tender, prepare us for the entry of the ghost. It must have been recognized as Caesar's, for the Folio stage direction ('Enter the Ghost of Caesar') makes this plain. When it speaks, it says that it is Brutus's evil spirit. It is also the same sort of premonition of evil as the signs and wonders of the first movement of the play. Now, in its second movement, Caesar who was struck down is seen to be stalking the land. In spite of its promise it does not reappear at Philippi, but Brutus's suicide could be taken, in a double sense, as his keeping his tryst with the ghost, for he both takes his own life and expiates the wrong he had done.

The two armies meet

The battle brings on the stage the supers who also made up the Roman crowd. It ends what the Ides of March began, in cross purposes and confusion. First, Antony is proved wrong in his estimate that the enemy would not come down to an encounter. Then, it becomes plain that Octavius is a man who does what he decides. He tells Antony in 5. 1. 20, 'I do not cross you, but I will do so', that is, I am not thwarting you, but I mean to do what I have just said. It is he, too, who stops Brutus, Cassius and Antony entering into a scolding match, by drawing their attention to the 'cause', the business at hand. The other three are their old selves: Brutus confident of his honourable reputation; Cassius scornful of the abilities of his rivals; Antony adroit in bandying words. It is Octavius who is really in command here. He states the 'cause'—the fight of the state against 'conspirators' and traitors—against whom he draws his sword (l. 51).

The previous scene showed the two friends almost falling to blows. Here both of them are so much shaken by the turn of events that they have no philosophical supports on which to depend. Cassius can 'partly' believe that the stars presage events on the earth. Brutus is confused; suicide is 'cowardly and vile', yet he will not be taken captive.

In the battle which follows Brutus gives the signal too early and fails to second Cassius, surrounded by Antony's forces. Cassius misinterprets everything and commits suicide with the sword that ran through Caesar. In the two tributes paid to him by Titinius (5. 3. 80–90) and Brutus (5. 3. 99–106), the line 'Alas, thou hast misconstrued everything!' should be remembered. Titinius's speech, with its succession of questions to which the answers are self-evident, is almost a text illustrating Cassius's course of action throughout the play. Still, like a true Roman, he has chosen death rather than captivity, and Brutus's lines (5. 3. 99–106) emphasize his heroic Roman spirit.

Shakespeare fuses the two battles of Philippi into two encounters on the same day, the play ending with the failure of Brutus's second attempt. Having failed to persuade his friends to help him kill himself, Brutus commands his bondman, 'a fellow of a good respect'...whose 'life had some snatch of honour in it'—considerations which are important to him—to hold his sword while he runs upon it. Like Cassius he remembers Caesar in the moment of death. It is characteristic of Brutus that he is confident of the honour and glory of an action which marks both his defeat and the denial of his philosophy.

'Brutus only overcame himself'

The alarums, the trumpets sounding throughout the battle, have ceased, the 'retreat' is heard, and nothing remains but the discovery of Brutus's suicide. In the epitaphs composed over his body should be noted the stress laid on 'honour' and 'nobility'; Strato's proud claim, which could be taken ironically as description of the whole course of Brutus's part in the play, 'Brutus only overcame himself' (5. 5. 54–7); and Antony's assertion that of all the 'conspirators' (he does not hesitate to use the word) Brutus's motives were the noblest (5. 5. 68–75). As it is put in Antony's measured statement with its oratorical close, only through the pressure of his concern for the public good ('in a general honest thought') did Brutus work upon himself to become a conspirator. The significance of the play may well lie there—in the tragic way in which the good can sometimes be worked upon to become the bad. The 'noblest Roman of them all', the most excellent combination of everything that makes a man was yet a 'conspirator' and killed his greatest friend. The good in Brutus did not save him. He was worked upon by others and also seduced himself into taking part in a conspiracy against the ruler of the state. However inadequate the ruler might have been, conspiracy and murder could result in nothing but ruin for the conspirators and civil strife in the state.

This is a simple statement of the thought of the play. Its poetry shows how much more there is in it than these forthright outlines.

12. TWELFTH NIGHT

The alternative titles of this play, *Twelfth Night* or *What You Will*, will probably provide no clue at all to many of its readers. But when the particular significance of *Twelfth Night* is known, its alternative, *What You Will*, is easier to understand. Though the traditional festival which used to mark the end of the twelve days of the feast of Christmas is no longer celebrated as it used to be in English-speaking countries, the reader who knows the church calendar will connect the play with feasting and merriment.

Traditional revelry

It is necessary to relate Shakespeare's play in very general terms with the traditional revelry of the feast of Twelfth Night, or the Epiphany. Such traditional revelry, associated with the great winter festival in temperate climates and with the spring festival in warmer regions, celebrated the promise of the return of life and warmth after the winter's cold. As held in Western Europe, the festival encouraged the abandonment of restrictions and social barriers, and the parodying or mocking of figures and institutions which the community at other times accepted and honoured. Disguising, and a certain amount of hoaxing and practical joking would also be common. The satisfaction to be derived from these activities will easily be apparent to anyone living in a strictly organized community, even at the present time when Twelfth Night has ceased to be a feast. Boys and girls at school will appreciate the pleasure in mimicking the figure of authority in the school community—the teacher. The more authoritarian he is, the more the fun will be relished.

At such times of festival in the community the conventional figures of authority and the ordinary code are turned upside down. In medieval communities the Lord of Misrule was a well-known figure at some of these festivals. He held court on Twelfth Night, and for the duration of the feast the strict formalities of the group were turned upside down.

Crude fun, a certain amount of horseplay, practical joking and even obscenity would be typical of these bouts of revelry. Where such festivals are known in other parts of the world they might be used as illustration. In India during the spring festival of Holi even the most serious and important persons are made to unbend, and people let themselves go, flinging coloured powders and streams of water on each other. This is not dignified fun, and it may be that the present-day participants in it feel it a nuisance and a bore, but as it is traditional revelry it did, and still does, provide a useful outlet for those who look forward to it.

We could then say that a festival like Holi does combine the gay and the amusing with some vestiges of the serious. The drenching and the bespatterings of people's clothes have nothing to do with seriousness. But the popular feeling which goes into the festival is serious, and the opportunity it provides for the expression of feeling is both necessary and good.

Gaiety and seriousness

Through its title *Twelfth Night* suggests this mixture of gaiety and seriousness belonging to a popular festival. Whether the reader knows anything of the traditional revelry of medieval and Tudor times or not, he ought not to have any great difficulty in seeing the hilarity of the play. This is surely as plain as can be: the complications caused by Viola's disguise, and by her twin brother; the drunken 'humours' (in both the Elizabethan and the modern sense) of Sir Toby and his crony; the fooling of Feste; the practical joke played on Malvolio; the way in which practically everybody in the play is fooled.

Of the gaiety there could be no doubt. But what of the seriousness which lies in the background of traditional revelry and which, we might suppose, enters this play too? To stress it at the very start of work on the play is probably inadvisable, although any examination of how the play works will show that what happens in it is the result of various kinds of delusion. But the play is so well poised that the seriousness which is there all the time, notably in the verse of its opening as it presents situation and attitudes, is so thoroughly well worked into its fabric that it might, at first sight, pass unnoticed.

There is a further difficulty: Comedy at the present time seems to be so concentrated on the purely amusing and entertaining that it is difficult for most people to see that it could include any seriousness at all. Most young people certainly would believe the word 'comedy' means only that which is 'comic'—laughter-provoking and nothing else.

The serious joke. Yet it is easy to accept the possibility that there is seriousness in the play, if we remember that the practical joke, which turns out to be its major business, could be a very serious thing. The play of *Othello* is, if we consider its action, a grim and terrifying practical joke in which four or five people are 'gulled' or fooled, as four or five people are fooled here. And, besides the practical joke, there are in *Twelfth Night* two sets of people who are involved in a delusion. The self-delusions of the lovers, as well as the practical joke played on Malvolio, are facets of a theme which is serious, however entertaining its presentation on the stage may be.

Having read the play for the first time, we might ask ourselves what is common to all its people. Are they not—to use the word Shakespeare apparently invented for this play—'fantastical'? That he coined the word does not mean that the attitudes for which he used it did not exist before his time. But his word seems to provide the right suggestion of the absurdity of self-delusion to which numerous people in the play are prone. Such attitudes could be a symptom of, or lead to, grave moral deficiencies. But the level on which Shakespeare keeps his play going, from the suggestions of the verse to the very turns of the plot, shows that he does not extend his judgement of his creations beyond criticism which is for the most part good-natured.

The play in its time

This is apparently how the play was taken when it was first produced in 1601–2. As we have seen, contemporary references to Shakespeare's plays do not tell us much, and the two to *Twelfth Night* quoted in the Appendix are useful only as indications of what their writers picked out for comment.

The first is from the diary of John Manningham, a Middle Temple lawyer, who writes on Candlemas Day, 2 February 1602. The second reference, though much later—from Digges's verses prefaced to an edition of Shakespeare's *Poems* in 1640—gives the popular reaction to the play. (It will be remembered that from the same writer came the reference to the quarrel scene in *Julius Caesar*.) Both select the practical joke for special comment. Would this mean that for Elizabethans there was nothing in the play but the 'gulling' of Malvolio? Manningham's comments show that the fun of the proceeding was thought of as specially attractive, and the right kind of fare for the occasion. Digges's reference speaks of the audience's special enjoyment of the fooling of Malvolio, the 'cross-gartered gull'. This should act as a useful preventive against the tendency to turn him into an ill-used tragic figure. If we are prone to think of Malvolio as a character of tragic potentiality, we should realize that this is to disregard the contemporary Elizabethan attitude to him. When Manningham comments on the suitability of the device used for 'gulling' Malvolio, we notice that he regards it as 'a good practise', or an apt piece of plotting. Malvolio, like Rosencrantz and Guildenstern in Hamlet's eyes, was 'hoist with his own petard'. The punishment, as we might put it, fitted the crime.

First reactions now. To read the play for the first time is to be made aware of its range of persons and situations, from the high-fantastical to the crassly absurd. There is a difference in the way they are treated, though all of them are taken up into material which is composed in the main of gaiety and revel. If the playwright had worked a heavier strand into his fabric, he might have subjected it to too severe a strain. At the end of the play Olivia calls Malvolio a 'poor fool', and the word 'fool' expresses both amusement and also tenderness for her servant who had been roughly treated, however much he deserved it. Malvolio himself is all for 'revenges' at the end of the play, the rancour of his reaction showing how much he merited his punishment.

In the play Shakespeare's language achieves easily and smoothly all the various demands he puts upon it, most notably in the natural-ness with which image and the turn of the verse embody his attitudes to his persons and the situations into which he manipulates them. The old skills of verse and prose—the speed with which the ball of wit is tossed about, the fine rhetoric, the ingenuity of the references—are all there. The play in addition provides rich opportunities for the actor: the conventional characters are all sharply presented; it has a number of gay and amusing situations which call for a high degree of technical skill; song runs through it, and as usual has dramatic point. *Twelfth Night* is, by comparison with the plays we have studied so far, mature in its handling of its medium.

The structure

In structure the play is based on a sequence of declarations of love. In practically every case the love is based on some delusion, or misunderstanding, so the result is confusion and complication. It would be interesting to work out the series of situations in which a declaration of love is made, either through an emissary or in a letter. The lovers themselves are not genuinely in love, and either deceive themselves or are duped. The suddenness with which some of them are attacked by love would show that, in most of these cases, love is a sickness of which its sufferers have to be cured. What, for instance, do we make of Orsino as a lover? Or of Olivia? One of the images which run through the play leaves the impression that love is a dish which has affected the digestions of all who partake of it.

The complications caused by these declarations of love transform the lover. Two of the transformations are so complete that the result would be in keeping with the topsy-turvy world of traditional revelry. As for the pattern of the complications produced, it is the well-known one of *A* in love with *B*, who falls in love with *C*, who turns out to be in love with *A*, and so on, until the resultant tangle is all at once unravelled by the revelation of a fraud or a mistake.

The confusions arising out of tangled love-intrigues were well known in Italian comedy, and Shakespeare had used a plot device like that in *Twelfth Night* in *The Merry Wives of Windsor* and in *A Midsummer Night's Dream*. In Italian comedy the stock situation was that of the girl for whose hand there are several suitors, one being her father's choice, another the mother's, while the third is her own. Out of the attempts of all three, aided by one or other of the characters in the play, the complications of the intrigue are produced.

Several suitors—self-deluded

In this play there are several suitors for the hand of Olivia. Orsino fancies himself to be desperately in love with her, while she is so completely in love with the memory of her dead brother that she cannot love anyone else, and must therefore withdraw from the world as if into a nunnery. For Olivia's hand there turns out to be another suitor—the absurd knight Sir Andrew. He is pushed into the position of lover by Sir Toby, Olivia's kinsman, who is cheating him. A third suitor for the hand of Olivia is produced by craft— Malvolio, deceived into believing that he is the specially favoured lover.

For the second declaration of love, his first having been turned down, Orsino employs Viola who is disguised as a boy. Viola carries Orsino's declaration to Olivia, but meets with an unexpected response. She is loved by Olivia, but unfortunately (and quite properly) she loves not Olivia, but Orsino. The list of lovers so far includes the self-deluded (Orsino and Olivia and Malvolio), the absurd (Sir Andrew), the unfortunately and ironically placed (Viola), and the manifestly impossible (the steward Malvolio). The fantasticality of the world of this play is seen in its reaction to love. All the lovers have to be fooled, the world has to be turned upside down before there can be a return to the normal. Malvolio's declaration of love for Olivia is as complete a symbol of the reversal of the normal as any one could wish. The only treatment for him is the madhouse.

Into this world turned upside down comes Sebastian, the exact twin of Viola. So to the complications of the cross-purposes of love is added another physical complication. Olivia, mistaking Sebastian for 'Cesario' (Viola), marries him incontinently, and the absurd lover, Sir Andrew, is forced into challenging 'Cesario' only to find that he encounters not 'him', but Sebastian. The complications are all untied when Orsino himself, for the first time in the play, visits Olivia with his Cesario. When there is no more need for the embassage of love, love's hazards are finally settled in marriage. For the absurd knight and the upstart Puritan steward there can be no partners. But the fat Sir Toby, we are told, has married the diminutive Maria: another indication of topsy-turvydom on the physical, though not the social, plane.

The major characters of the play suffer from a tendency to give themselves up to a false notion of themselves. What happens to them in the situations developed by the dramatist may be regarded as their purgation, or cure. No one is exempted from the necessity of being purged except Feste, the fool, who is no lover. He is wiser than his betters, and, as in all folk stories, is no fool, but the wisest of them all.

Orsino

i. i gives us Orsino's mood of love and the return of the first embassage to Olivia. His extravagance of attitude and the richness of atmosphere in the play are at once put across by the music and by the words of the duke as he comes on the stage, beautifully costumed. Dukes with Italian names, in a country which we learn in the next scene to be Illyria, would require such accessories as Shakespeare provides in his costuming and the music. Orsino speaks his lines to the accompaniment of music which Shakespeare intends us to hear, the words vibrating with an excess of feeling which calls attention to itself. What the lines are saying is of the greatest importance, for they provide a clue to one attitude to love in this play which is made up of declarations of love. Lines 1–15, with which the play opens, celebrate not only the potency of music which is the 'food' of love, but the much greater power of love itself which outlasts music, and can turn everything into its opposite. So the music which Orsino wished to have in excess, in order that he could sate his appetite on love's food, in a trice becomes 'not so sweet' as it was before. Yet the spirit of love, with its vigorous and hungry power to absorb and transmute everything, is invoked by a speaker who knows that, if he gives himself to it, its only result can be the awkward predicament of providing new material on which love must feed. The full, grand movement of the lines is intended to celebrate love, but their sense makes us aware of just the opposite feeling: that this love ('fancy') is an insatiable appetite for novelty, and that it alone can produce figments of the imagination which delude.

The words are those of a speaker who affects to think of himself as so devoted a lover that he cannot have too much of love. Yet he will, as the image shows, so feed himself on love's food (music) that he will make his digestion sick, have some more of it, and then cry 'Enough'. The image from food on which the eater sates himself, or from drink for which the person is 'dry', runs through the play. One set of characters is occupied with the food of love; another is concerned only with physical food and drink; while yet another character is so extreme in his objection to such things as 'cakes and ale' that he is just as badly in need of a cure as those who cram themselves with music, or love, or drink. For sick or 'distempered' people there must be a cure, and the play works out, through the development of its declarations of love, the appropriate cure for all who are distempered.

The plain sense of the concluding lines of Orsino's first speech is interesting. He draws a moral, or a 'saw' which reveals that if he were truly aware of what he was saying, he would have known himself to be both over-pleased with himself, and obviously self-deluded. From the song in *The Merchant of Venice* we know that the word 'fancy' most often suggested the dangerous propensity of the lover to be led by the unsatisfactory evidence of the eyes alone. The 'shapes' fancy produces are the result of an over-heated imagination which too often confounds the imaginary with the real. There is, therefore, an undertone in Orsino's lines which he perhaps does not notice. It warns the audience, but Orsino goes on, in verse as rich and affecting as before, chasing the very trite pun of 'heart' and 'hart', in a hyperbole which makes Olivia out to be some divine power which cleanses the air of plague, while he, poor devil, has suffered like the hunter in the classical story of Actaeon. By the time we have reached this stage, we can see that Orsino is transported, his fancy is producing fantastic 'shapes'.

When Valentine enters—how appropriate to the god of love his name is—he brings Olivia's declaration of love. Orsino's embassage has not been fortunate, the lady declares that all her love feeds on is the 'shape' of her dead brother.

Olivia

How should we take Valentine's description of Olivia's attitude? Is it a straightforward picture of a person's grief, or do we feel that Shakespeare is criticizing the attitude of another lover? It is difficult to avoid the conclusion that Shakespeare gives this rhetorical account of Olivia's grief and love for her brother the same kind of extravagant frame Orsino has just been placing round himself and his 'fancy'. The verse is just as full and regular as Orsino's. It, too, advances through hyperbole to the amazing figure of 'seasoning' a brother's dead love, which she would keep fresh and lasting, in her sad remembrance. The suggestion in the image is of food, 'seasoned' with salt (and spices) to prevent it from going bad. We note that Valentine calls it 'a brother's dead love'. Basically this means, as often in Shakespeare, love of a brother who happens to be dead. But the position of the adjective 'dead' suggests that the love is over and done with, and that all this attempt to keep it 'fresh' is fantastic. The image of feeding is linked again with the reference to love.

To the duke, however, it is obvious that no critical reflection on Olivia's conduct is possible. So he is off again: if she loves her brother so dearly, think what will happen when all those places supposed at that time to be the centres of passion, judgement and sentiment (liver, brains and heart) are occupied by the image or 'shape' of the one and only man who is going to rule over her. Of course he hopes it is going to be himself. The thought of such happiness leads him now to want, not music, but another conventional accompaniment of love—'sweet beds of flowers'. He is going to lie in some pleasant bower and dream his thoughts of love.

This gratification of sensuous desires comes readily to the duke's mind. Malvolio, we shall see in 2. 5. 48, in his 'love-thoughts' imagines himself on a 'day-bed' with Lady Olivia.

First twist to plot

As the duke leaves the stage, Viola enters with the Captain and now we are given an exposition of the play: we are told where we are and who the main characters are, and the plot of the two fantastical lovers is given its first twist when Viola, undecided which of them she is to serve under, makes up her mind to disguise herself as a boy and seek employment under Orsino. This is a frequent device in Elizabethan plays; we have already met it in *The Merchant of Venice*, where Jessica, Portia and Nerissa disguise themselves as young men. Viola the boy player is going to present herself to Orsino as a page who can sing and is skilled in music. We must expect then that she will be the emissary of love.

Viola

There are two points in this scene which should be noted. The people in it are eminently practical. Viola may have lost a brother in the shipwreck, but, unlike Olivia, who is in the same situation, she is not absorbed in the contemplation of lost love and decides to make her living by working. The contrast with Olivia should be noted. And the captain is praised for the rare virtue of the perfect harmony between his outward form and his inner character (1. 2. 46–50). This, according to Viola, is not usual. We have seen in *The Merchant of Venice* that the fair wall can often hide the mouldering skeleton. Yet Viola, who praises the captain for the truth of his character, is going to disguise herself, so that there can be no correspondence between what she appears to be and what she really is. In the previous scene we have already met one character who deludes himself; another is referred to in the same scene. Now we have a third character whose disguise is going to delude everybody in the play. Viola's disguise is not only part of the play's jesting; it helps to sketch in addition the play's background of seriousness.

Second twist: sub-plot

1. 3 brings on the stage the second suitor for the hand of Olivia, lover no. 3—Sir Andrew Aguecheek. Shakespeare here works another strand into the plot, twisting into the main action of the two lovers another which has to do with a third lover. The subplot repeats the main plot with a great difference. The two lovers in the main plot are extravagant and fantastical. What sort of a lover is Sir Andrew? Sir Toby describes what he looks like—a very thin man with light-coloured hair (1. 3. 105-7)—and by his side on the stage his own bulk is an effective contrast to his crony's excessive thinness. Here we have the good stock joke of the two comedians distinguished by their opposite physical characteristics. To the fat Sir Toby, whose name 'Belch' tells us all there is to know about him—he is a drunkard and glutton—Sir Andrew is a figure of fun.

Lover no. 3 is really being 'gulled'. He is in love because he has been deluded by Sir Toby into believing that he can win Olivia's hand. 1. 3. 108-14 show how Sir Toby leads him on. Sir Andrew is as much a deluded lover as the other two, but in his case he is being made a fool of by Sir Toby for his own advantage. 2. 3. 190-2 show the kind of lover Sir Andrew is, and how he is being cheated. Orsino and Olivia deceive themselves with their 'shapes' and 'fancy', Sir Andrew is a fool who sets out to win an heiress, and is being egregiously duped.

Its comedy. Beside the two knights is Maria, Olivia's gentle-woman—the very small boy player whose smallness is insisted on by the others. She is witty, she can play with words as well as any of them. A great deal of the banter in 1. 3 depends on the pun, the double meanings of some words, and on topical references which are now obscure. At the time of the play's writing they must have been appreciated as shrewd hits at people and institutions, or they would scarcely have appeared in it. What can we do with 'Castiliano vulgo' or with 'Mistress Mall's picture'? What must once have been a winged jest is now a heavy lump holding up the pace of the word-play. But by contrast the fun which depends on mime and action comes across probably as strongly as it used to, as we can see in the stage business accompanying 'Accost' in 1. 3. 50 ff. Of this type of humour the scene is full. Sir Andrew leaping in the dance is meant to be absurd, and into this play the absurd, even the physically laughable, must enter.

First complication

With 1. 4 the main plot is not only under way, but has sailed into its first complication, for at the end of the scene Viola, before she convey's Orsino's declaration of love to Olivia, confesses that her situation is one of conflict, for 'Whoe'er I woo, myself would be his wife'. The duke, who forecasts the success of his new page, does not realize what a strong irony there is in his recommendation of Cesario, and how much he is deceived by the evidence of his eyes. Cesario's advantage over all other messengers (1. 4. 29–34) is that 'he' does not yet look a man, but seems to be a young girl (which in fact she is). Besides, it is clear from the short exchange between the former 'nuncio' Valentine and Viola (Cesario) that the duke has been impressed by her and taken up with her so remarkably quickly that Viola has to ask 'Is he inconstant, sir, in his favours?'

We shall see in 1. 5, when Cesario and Olivia meet, how unexpectedly the duke's prophecy is fulfilled, in a sense he had never imagined. Not only is Olivia responsive to Cesario's declaration on the duke's behalf, but far from reacting to the messenger as if 'he' were not man, but young boy, or even girl, she falls precipitately in love with the exterior of a man. The outward show takes her in, and she is in love with the figure of a boy-actor-pretending-to-be-a-girl-pretending-to-be-a-boy. This was a device very pleasing to Elizabethans, to judge from its recurrence in their plays.

Feste

1. 5 then, gives us Cesario's first embassage, but before 'he' appears on the stage, the clown Feste enters. It is clear that he is in some trouble from which he must extricate himself by the use of his

wits. This he proceeds to do in his demonstration that the outward show proves nothing of the inner reality. The argument, besides underlining one of the play's themes—the tendency of human beings to be deluded by the outward show and by the shapes of fancy— shows that Olivia's love for her brother, which makes her mourn for him, is as great a delusion as any we can think of. As Feste says, he is no fool ('I wear not motley in my brain'); it is the lady who is the fool.

Malvolio

When Olivia, pleased with the jest, turns to Malvolio, her steward, for approval of the fool's wit, he breaks his silence with such bitter words (1. 5. 73–5) that they stand out in the context of the play's mixture of light-heartedness and pointed criticism. Their harshness is frightening: 'Yes, and shall do, till the pangs of death shake him.' When Malvolio persists in his hostility to the fool, Olivia has to reprove him. The image in her words: 'O, you are sick of self-love, Malvolio, and taste with a distempered appetite', recalls the suggestion already made in the play that if a person gives himself up to 'feeding' on some imagined excellence, then the consequences are likely to be harmful. Orsino who wants to feed himself to satiety on the food of love; Olivia who is 'seasoning a brother's dead love', could be thought of as being self-deluded. Now there is a third to be added to the list: Malvolio, who feeds on his own pleasing image of himself, and who, as a result, cannot taste anything aright, his appetite being distempered or unhealthy.

Olivia, as she appears here, is not entirely the veiled lady given over to mourning her dead brother. She is ready to be amused at the fool, and she can see what is wrong with Malvolio. Is there something ironical in her accusing Malvolio of suffering from a delusion strangely like her own?

However we interpret the lines in reference to Olivia, it is clear that Malvolio is 'sick'; he is in need of a cure. The practical joke which follows later performs this cure for him. Does not this scene show that if ever a butt for such a joke existed it is Malvolio? He sets himself against any kind of fooling, so will have to be made a fool. And he will have to be attacked through his good opinion of himself, his 'self-love'. The scene between Malvolio and Feste provides us with a clue to the development of the plot. If Malvolio is to be fooled, then it will be Feste who will take the fooling to its height.

When Cesario is introduced by Malvolio in a speech which very ambiguously refers to the difficulty of deciding whether he is boy or man, are we not made aware of another of the play's themes, the difficulty of deciding between what seems and what is? Malvolio, who is very superior to Cesario in his description of him, makes this new messenger of Orsino's the more interesting to his mistress. She decides to see him, and Cesario's first embassage of love begins.

Is there anything in this embassage of Viola's (Cesario's) which is noteworthy? There is a suggestion that her attitude to the declaration she is making, not for herself but for someone else, is not completely serious. She is, as Orsino had advised her to do in 1. 4. 26, 'acting' his woes. So in her lines to the two ladies, before she knows which is Olivia (1. 5. 171–7) it is clear that she has a set piece to recite, and she wishes to know to whom the recitation, with appropriate modulations of voice and gesture, should be addressed. When Olivia asks her whether she is a 'comedian' or stage-player, it is clear that Cesario is performing the role of Orsino in love, making his love-suit to his lady.

Having got the better of Maria and held her own with Olivia, Viola is alone with the latter. She again plays the role of Orsino's messenger, with such success that Olivia unveils. In her wit, her conventional description of the lover (1. 5. 259–60), in the stock Elizabethan commonplace that the beautiful woman should marry and bear children, and not lead her

> graces to the grave,
> And leave the world no copy,

Viola is an accomplished performer of the role of lover. When in lines 272–80 she goes on to exaggerate wilfully her pose of constant lover, we see at once how Olivia is affected. Viola's lines are surely not to be taken seriously; they are an excess of imaginative power; but Olivia is carried away by them. It is obvious that she has fallen in love with Orsino's ambassador; so when Viola, again in conventional exaggeration, says before she goes out: 'Love make his heart of flint that you shall love', she is forecasting the development of the main plot.

Second complication

Olivia alone on the stage feels that she has caught the plague: she whom Orsino thought of as 'purging the air of pestilence'. And worst of all she feels Viola's perfections creeping in at her 'eyes'. Once she has despatched Malvolio with a ring for the ambassador of love, she all but acknowledges what is wrong with her: her eye is 'too great a flatterer' for her mind.

The main plot with its conventional pattern of *A* who is in love with *B* who is in love with *C* who is in love with *A* is now quite plainly drawn. Viola in 2. 2. 33-41 sees its difficulties as too hard for her to untie. In her description of the scene which has just passed between her and Olivia, do we not see the clear marks of the person 'charmed' by love?

In the meantime her twin brother Sebastian, saved from the wreck, has appeared and stated his intention of going to Orsino's court. Another 'lover', his devoted admirer the sea-captain Antonio, is added to the list of those on whom love takes strong hold. These two have not been introduced except for the purpose of making the complications worse complicated. When Viola therefore in the next scene, to which we have already referred, asks: 'How will this fadge?', those of us who see the play for the first time can only ask 'How indeed?'

Third twist—second subplot

2. 3 shows how Malvolio comes to be suitor no. 3 for the hand of Olivia. His Puritanical objection to song and drink, his interruption of the revelry of the two knights, and his resentment at being mocked by Feste, make him a suitable object for the practical joke which is

now planned. To him revelry is 'this uncivil rule'. He may be right in objecting to the drunkenness of the two knights, but he thinks because he is virtuous that there should be no more cakes and ale (revelry). It is his 'distempered appetite' which is responsible for his attitude.

Sir Andrew can think of nothing better than to make a fool of him by challenging him to a duel, and then backing out of it. But Maria, the ingenious boy player, has something much better up her sleeve. He is to be gulled, and as 2. 3. 155–9 make clear, for the very reason that his good opinion of himself lays him open to the delusion that 'all that look on him love him'. As Maria plans it, Malvolio is to be deceived by a declaration of love which will seem to come from Olivia herself. When she says in line 178 'I know my physic will work with him' (another metaphor of purging), she means that he will greedily swallow her decoction, which, if he hadn't been deluded, he would not have touched as too strong a potion for him. To Malvolio, as to the others, the experience of 'fancy' is like food or drink, to be lapped up without consideration. In the scene of his gulling Fabian remarks (2. 5. 116) 'What dish o' poison has she dressed him?'

Viola's declaration

2. 4 is important, for in it Viola declares her love for Orsino. She speaks as Cesario, and tells the duke how her father

> 'had a daughter loved a man,
> As it might be, perhaps, were I a woman,
> I should your lordship.'

Her words have to be ambiguous, and it is one of the play's ironies that this love of Viola's, which seems more genuine than the passion of any of the other lovers, has to be stated in such indirect terms. Orsino, who looks upon himself as the ideal lover, is, as he has to acknowledge in this very scene, in his love 'more giddy and unfirm', 'more longing, wavering' than any woman. Though in 2. 4. 18 he states that his impulses ('motions') are skittish and unstaid except in so far as his constancy to Olivia is concerned, his changeableness, already hinted at earlier, is quite plainly put to him by Feste in 2. 4. 73–7. So that his talk of the strength of his love as compared with any woman's love, expressed as it is in images of feeding, of the palate, of hunger as keen as the sea's, and of digestion, seems to be nothing more than an exaggeration of what we have already felt about such unnatural descriptions of love.

The concealed love which Viola attributes to 'her father's daughter' has its exaggerated and romantic side too. As she kept it to herself, like the canker in the bud, it fed on her smooth and beautiful cheek. It is not a natural or healthy love. The lines are generally accepted as the perfect type of the silent lover, but they picture a sick, and even a dead state of immobility. The love which sits like a painted statue on a monument is not natural. Besides there is the difference between the outward show, 'smiling', and the inner reality, 'grief'. If in this scene the duke is, as usual, romantic, Viola has the advantage over him. At least she has a real, if unrequited, love. Before she goes off on her second embassage, she has the good sense to see that man, or any human being, always ('still') proves to be a much greater protester of love than a true lover. The show, in other words, is more important than the inner reality (2. 4. 116–18).

Feste's role

Feste in this scene establishes himself as the fool who sees more than any character in the play. Shakespeare has several 'fools' in his plays, but is there not a difference between such well-known figures as Touchstone, and the fool in *King Lear*, and Feste? There is something common to all three of them; they share certain characteristics of the type: they are witty, they speak incisively, they dare say more than most people in the situations in which they appear are allowed to say, and they have the satirist's power of seeing through the illusion to the real.

Feste has all the skill and the plausibility of the stage type of the time. He is there to divert the audience, with his singing, his miming, his speaking in different voices, and his parody. But through the diversion he affords, he is able to make a few serious points. In this scene he sees through the duke's pretensions to be the constant lover, as we have noticed, and in his song he takes to its highest pitch, as it were, the sentimentality of the love-sick Orsino. It may be that the song Orsino describes as 'silly sooth' is not quite what Feste provides, and that what we have in the Folio of 1623, 'Come away, come away death', did not belong to the play as it was originally performed. But in its accumulation of the sentimental stock-in-trade of unrequited love, it would be appropriate to Orsino, and also critical of his pose as lover.

Recent editors of the play have pointed out that Viola (Cesario), who should have sung the song, as she was skilled in singing according to her own description of herself in 1. 2. 56 ff., does not sing it. But Feste, according to Curio, is the person who 'should sing it'. Whether the boy player (Viola) at the time this text was used in the theatre could not sing, or whether all the songs in the play were given to Armin, who was well known as singer and composer, is difficult to say. It is plain, however, that Feste is the singing fool, and from what we know of Shakespeare's use of song, we must expect that the words and the music of his songs would have had some special point.

The gulling of Malvolio

2. 5 contains a double declaration of love—the faked message from Olivia, and Malvolio's confession and transformation from Puritan to lover as a result of Maria's device, the dropping in his way of 'some obscure epistles of love'. This frankly unrealistic and absurd scene on the fore-stage, with the conspirators hiding behind some piece of property suggesting a hedge or tree, follows the established pattern of scenes of the declaration of love in the play. There is exaggeration, the character is transformed by the love of which he partakes, as if it were either food or drink. So transformed, the character lays itself open to criticism, as Orsino, Olivia, Sir Andrew, and even Viola are meant to be judged.

The lovers we have come across so far have been either extravagant romantics, or absurd. In Malvolio we have a lover, who, because he was so determined a Puritan before, is changed by love into a laughable, but also an unpleasant figure. Love makes a 'contemplative idiot' of Malvolio. 'He says nothing, but gazes into vacancy.' But when the 'dish of poison' which Maria has dressed for him really works, we see that there is a strong sensual side to his love-thoughts. Some of the difficulties in understanding the references in his comments on the letter he picks up are certainly due to their coarseness, and to their topicality. Malvolio is being cheated, and it is clear from the allusions to game of all kinds by the conspirators, who watch him being fooled, that like any animal he is being trapped. Once caught in the trap, he reveals an unpleasant and frightening side. As Sir Toby puts it in 2. 5. 199, love has worked on him like strong drink—'like aqua-vitae with a midwife'. In his earlier remark Sir Toby suggests what the only treatment for Malvolio can be. If, as it is suggested, he is to be thought of as having 'run mad' (2. 5. 196–7), then he will have to be treated like a madman, or as someone possessed with the devil, which is exactly how he is handled in 3. 4 and 4. 2.

Olivia's declaration

Now that the three suitors for Olivia's hand have been produced, and the cross-purposes of the wooing have been made quite clear, all that is left to provide is the final twist by which Sebastian, as soon as he appears, is mistaken by Olivia for Cesario. By the time this happens in 4. 1, Olivia has already made an indirect declaration of her love for Cesario in 3. 1. 109ff., soon to be followed by a plain statement:

> I love thee so, that, maugre all thy pride,
> Nor wit nor reason can my passion hide.

The couplets in their jingle are well suited to a declaration of love which is an impulse amenable neither to the understanding nor to reason. If Olivia is, as Viola tells her in 3. 1. 141, quite transformed by love: 'You do think you are not what you are', this is a temporary aberration which the meeting with Sebastian will cure. She is in love with a face and a figure, and in Sebastian she will have them both.

Depressed with the ill-success of her suit, Olivia in 3. 4 sends for Malvolio to advise her. Ironically enough he appears physically transformed into a 'smiling' lover in a costume which must have had a strong dramatic liveliness for Elizabethans. He is left to Sir Toby and Maria, who treat him as if he were possessed of the devil. His cure is already beginning.

Third complication

Before Feste undertakes the cure in 4. 2—a scene which immediately proves how skilled the performer must have been to have satisfied the demands made of him in this ceremony of exorcism—Olivia, mistaking Sebastian for Cesario to whom she had already made a declaration of love, makes it quite clear to him what her feelings towards him are. All he can say, in an aside to the audience, is, 'What relish is this?' To him, too, the declaration of love offers a dish which is very strange to the taste. And as he goes on we see that the only conclusion he can come to is that he is either mad or dreaming. He is ready to allow 'fancy' love to keep drugging his understanding ('still my sense in Lethe steep') so that he can forget reality. Like all the other lovers, Sebastian, who accidentally becomes one of their number, is ready to give himself up to it.

Malvolio purged

In 4. 2 the conspirators Maria and Sir Toby hand over to Feste the business of purging Malvolio of his love-sickness. Feste does it, disguising himself as a priest, making the remark as he dons his disguise, that he is not the first to 'dissemble' in such a gown. Malvolio is treated by Feste as if he were both mad, and possessed of a devil who torments with thoughts of women.

However, Malvolio is on his way to being cured, for he is ready to talk sweetly and gently to the fool against whom he was so severe in 1. 5. As Feste goes out to do Malvolio's bidding he sings a tag which recalls the Vice of the old play. In the old Morality and Interlude the Vice rode on the devil's back to Hell, all the while tormenting him. Surely there is more than a hint here that if we want the devil we should look for him in Malvolio, for, to the anti-Puritan of that time, saintly Puritanism was often the disguise of the sensualist.

Denouement: the end to the delusion of false appearances

Shakespeare ends his play in a mood which shows how the fun and the seriousness are mixed. Cesario finds himself confronted by Orsino and Olivia, who both accuse him of lack of faith, after 'he' has been attacked for the same defect of character by Antonio. 'He' can do nothing but protest when faced by the priest. The deliberate solemnity of the priest's enunciation of the marriage contract between Olivia and the young man for whom Cesario is mistaken trembles on the edge of parody. It is so dignified in its vocabulary and movement that the speaker can hardly say 'two hours ago' without transforming it into:

> Since when, my watch hath told me, towards my grave
> I have travelled but two hours.

Pat upon this with its passion, and the high seriousness of 'dissembling' and the bandying about of 'protest', 'faith', 'swear' and 'fear' enters Sir Andrew, his head bandaged and his 'For the love of God, a surgeon!' The effect of this is to bring us down to earth. The plot cannot be complicated any longer, for now the twins are side by side, and the cause of one set of delusions is removed. The duke with his quibble

> One face, one voice, one habit, and two persons,
> A natural perspective, that is and is not

makes the reason for all the confusion not a weakness of attitude, but a material cause. As in *Richard II* a 'perspective' could be a picture so painted that what it looked like depended on the angle of vision or a stereoscope.

So the play comes to an end, with more fooling from Feste. As Fabian points out, the gulling of Malvolio was carried out with 'sportful malice' (5. 1. 365) which should produce laughter not 'revenge'. That Malvolio should harbour 'revenges' in his mind is just his 'humour'.

Olivia has confessed (5. 1. 280) that a highly concentrated ('extracting') madness of her own, her love for the Cesario figure, had driven out of her mind all remembrance of Malvolio's distraction. This is her last reference to her 'fancy'. Orsino, as he goes out, has now another object for his—Viola, who is assured of being 'Orsino's mistress and his fancy's queen'.

The end of the play

Feste alone on the stage sings a variation of a traditional song, the meaning of which seems to be 'Make the best of things anyhow, it's all one, whatever you do from boyhood to old age, you can't escape the reality of the wind and the rain'. If there is any philosophical tinge in the doggerel of the song's words, it might be coloured with the reflection, appropriate to this play, that, however diverting revelry may be, reality cannot for long be evaded.

The play began with one kind of music; it ends with another. It started off with a sophisticated air, as the accompaniment to Orsino's affectation of passion, it ends with a traditional song to the accompaniment of the tabor. Two couples have been married, another will shortly go to the altar, and there is a promise of the marriage feast to come. The love-stories have followed the usual course of true love—they have not run smooth. But nothing mars the gaiety of the close, and when Feste goes out singing

> But that's all one, our play is done,
> And we'll strive to please you every day

whatever the philosophical import of his song may be, at the end he is an actor, enunciating the most important principle of the actor's code.

13. MACBETH

The earliest account of a performance of *Macbeth* was given by Simon Forman, who saw the play at the Globe Theatre in 1611. Unfortunately, he tells us very little of what we should like to know. He remembered an illustration from Holinshed's *Chronicles* as clearly as anything he saw on the stage.

From his account of *Macbeth* and of other plays of Shakespeare's he had seen, it would appear that he was interested only in such details of the plot as were morally improving. *Macbeth* presumably affected him as a warning to prospective criminals on the retribution which always attends crime.

The play and its first audiences

It would be useful to try to recollect what the play must have given its first audiences. That it must have been exciting seems clear. Shakespeare puts on the stage material which must have appealed to the common interest in the supernatural and the abnormal. Both King James I, who had written on the subject of witchcraft, and the populace would know of and accept the reality of the powers of evil and the consequences of trafficking with them.

Its first audiences would have found these things in the play: three witches with a gift of prophecy and ambiguously worded utterance; a woman who solemnly invokes evil spirits to take possession of her; the state of hallucination of a man who sees a dagger drawing him to the room of his victim; the appearance of a ghost at a banquet given by his murderer; the materialization of a show on the stage at the express injunction of a man who orders witches to call up their masters; a guilty woman walking in her sleep and recounting some of the details of the crime which weighs upon her mind.

Besides all this the play begins and ends with warfare; there are references to unnatural prodigies; and the rule and order of a kingly court are insisted on throughout, both by contrast and by actual example.

Its staging

Furthermore, *Macbeth* must have been presented on the stage with all the ingenuity and attention to detail of which the Jacobean stage was capable. By the end of the first decade of the seventeenth century there was much greater attention paid to stage illusion than before, and the influence of the staging of court masques was beginning to be felt in the popular theatre. In this play, for instance, there is the cauldron which in 4. 1 disappears through a trap-door; a 'show of eight kings'; a royal visit to the castle of a nobleman; two banquets; the advance of an 'army' with branches from a wood in its hands. Finally, the play ends with the acclamation of the rightful king and the usurper's head brought in on a pole.

On the stage today *Macbeth* may lack some of these excitements. To contemporaries sceptical of, and even amused at, a belief in ghosts and in the powers of darkness, it may seem childish. To use all the technical resources available on the modern stage to make it plausible may, however, obscure the great strength of the play Shakespeare wrote. On his stage the ghost of Banquo, 'blood-boltered' (with his hair clotted with blood), did appear and sit on the stool reserved for Macbeth. If, in order to make this implausible proceeding acceptable to a contemporary audience, the scene has to be played in barbaric darkness with a figure projected by the camera in the background, then the ironical significance of the entry of the bloodstained ghost into the atmosphere of light and brightness necessarily associated with a solemn royal feast must be lost. We should continually think of *Macbeth* as a play, but not as a play which has to be squared with present-day points of view.

Stage performance, as always, lessens various difficulties, making what is doubtful to the reader clear and self-evident to the spectator. Audiences are not likely to be greatly troubled as to whether it is a real dagger which Macbeth sees in 2. 1. 33: whether Lady Macbeth's fainting in 2. 3 is genuine or feigned; whether the Third Murderer was Macbeth himself; and so on.

The source of the play

For the material of his play Shakespeare was again indebted to Holinshed's *Chronicle*. He used three separate stories, and we see in the appendix dealing with his sources that he altered some details in Holinshed's account and invented new material, like the knocking at the gate, the appearance of Banquo's ghost, and the sleep-walking scene.

Its date of composition. The play was first printed in the Folio of 1623. It was certainly not a new play when Forman saw it in 1611, and references in earlier plays to the well-known scene of the appearance of the ghost and in the Porter Scene (2. 3. 8–11) to 'equivocation', a subject much discussed during and after the trial of the Jesuit Father Garnett for complicity in the Gunpowder Plot in 1606, make it possible that *Macbeth* was written in that year. A subject from the history of the Scots, in which one of the major characters was Banquo, the mythical founder of the reigning house of Stuart, would have made the play interesting to James I, who came to the English throne in 1603.

The text. The text of the play is short, one of the shortest of all Shakespeare's plays. This, it has been suggested, is due to abridgement, the work of a later writer. As the extent of probable corruption of the text of the play is still in dispute, the only reasonable course is to accept the judgement of recent editors that the scenes in which Hecate appears (3. 5 and 4. 1. 38–43) are interpolations by another writer and to regard the rest as Shakespeare's. The two scenes contain directions for songs known to be by Middleton and taken from his play *The Witch*. The text as we have it includes at least these two pieces of un-Shakespearean material.

Structure

The play presents us with two worlds of reality, both recognizable by the audience and actualized for it through the speech of persons and through stage presentation. One world of reality is that of the normal as we and Shakespeare's audience know it. This is the world of royalty and the well-knit state; the world of Duncan, his two sons, Banquo, Macbeth and the whole of Scotland and England. This world must have been recreated on Shakespeare's stage. It is seen; it is always present, and even when some parts of it are repudiated it is there by implication.

The other world of reality, just as carefully recreated on the stage, is that of the reality of the evil of witchcraft, or spirits. This becomes the world of the two main characters, who are drawn into it from the other. To most of us at the present time the actuality of this world might be questionable. But to Shakespeare's audience it was a valid world, strongly presented on the stage. If neither Shakespeare's poetry nor our imaginative apprehension can realize it for us, then an important part of the play must be taken on trust.

These two worlds exist together and at times seem to fade into one another; as in the cinematic process called the 'dissolve' the images projected on the screen seem to merge from one to another picture, so that two different things seem to run together and we are doubtful whether one scene is before us or another. In these two different and co-existing worlds of *Macbeth* move two characters influenced by both. Their actions throw the sharpness of the reality and the difference between the two into confusion.

In structure *Macbeth* gives us a dominant impression of an uncertain and unstable state where one world appears to 'dissolve' into the other. It is, of course, possible to describe the structure of *Macbeth* as a series of situations exemplifying the conflict between good and evil, or the story of the fall of a great man. It could even be described as a parable illustrating how man can be gulled by the forces of evil into accepting what seems to be true as the truth. But structure abstracted in this way would not include the dominant impression left by the play. This impression is not simply the effect of its plot, though plot contributes to it.

The quality of the whole play is, more than in any of the plays studied previously, conveyed by the *poetry*, which reinforces the situations and their representation on the stage. Structure in *Macbeth* can be best apprehended from the way the poetry fills up and fills out everything given by plot, situations, persons and ideas.

What the poetry gives us is this impression of an equivocal and ambiguous world, where what is seen appears to be different from what is, and what is naturally expected is confounded by what unnaturally intervenes. One world appears to superimpose itself on the other. In the very opening scenes of the play are numerous references to the difficulty of distinguishing one thing from another. The riddling phrases of 1. 1 are capped with 'Fair is foul, and foul is fair'. If these words, taken up by Macbeth in 1. 3. 38, state anything plainly, they call our attention to the similarity between opposites. The world of the play is one in which the established differences between the two worlds we have mentioned do not seem to count.

Four main images

If the bare statement of some of the lines provides this impression, the play's images tend to deepen this and give the equivocal greater definition. Miss Spurgeon has noted 'at least four main ideas in the images and many subsidiary ones'. These are 'interwoven the one with the other, recurring and repeating'. They are: clothes which are too big for the wearer; echoing sound; light contrasted with darkness; sickness. In all can be seen the contrast between what is supposedly there and what in reality is there. We expect clothes to fit a man, to be his and not someone else's. But in *Macbeth* this is not so; there is disproportion between what ought to be and what is.

The images of echoing sound also fit a background where the deeds of men cause sound to reverberate through the emptinesses of space. When Macbeth in 1. 7. 18 ff. imagines angels pleading 'trumpet-tongued' and Heaven's cherubim blowing the horrid deed in every eye, we are being given a picture of the appalling consequences of his crime, as he apprehends them imaginatively. The normal course of time is overturned and the murder of Duncan converts the now of today into the last judgement.

So too the images of darkness suggest that the light of normal day is forced to give way to the darkness of night, or that the darkness has an abnormal obscurity to match the dire deeds committed in it.

The images of sickness stress the undermining of the natural state of the human body, particularly by that type of disease whose cause and cure are difficult to discover.

Their effect. The function of these images is substantially the same as that of one of the 'other subsidiary motives in the imagery which ...insensibly and deeply affect the reader's imagination'. This is 'the idea of the *unnaturalness* of Macbeth's crime, that it is a convulsion of nature'. All these images should be regarded as facets of the unifying insight into the nightmare world which results from the confusion of the two worlds of reality. *Macbeth* deals with the offence done to the natural order—to one world of reality—by characters who yield to the promptings of another world of reality which should have been rejected. The effect of the images is to create and define this dominant impression of the play.

Structure in the play is here the creation by the poetry of a monstrous world in which what should not be is. This is reflected in its situations and its characters, until the world of nightmare ceases to exist when its world of reality is destroyed. An unnatural state gives way to its opposite and things show as what they are. Though the movement from the ambiguous to the clear is articulated, the whole of the play seems to subsist on the interest of the dramatist in the equivocal world of its two chief characters.

The opening

The play opens in some undefined and indeterminate place. The Folio stage direction says nothing of place, but calls for thunder and lightning. The three persons on the stage refer momentarily to the place of their future meeting with Macbeth, but where they are at the moment of speaking is uncertain. This ambiguousness of locality, the details of the stage presentation, thunder, lightning, the disappearance of the speakers in resinous fumes, the rhymes of the speakers, their references to their familiars, surely envelop the scene in an aura of the other-worldly—out of time and also of place. 'Fair is foul, and foul is fair' provides the key to the world called up here and throughout the play.

I. 2 with its 'bleeding captain' as he is described in the Folio stage direction, or 'sergeant' in the text, on top of the references to 'hurlyburly', or uproar, in the previous scene, brings in suggestions of destruction and blood in a play made up of murder and war. Blood, as it is spilt, stands for both the vitality of life and its un-natural destruction. Its colour, its viscosity, its warmth are grisly reminders of a motif which runs through the play.

The sergeant's extravagant account of the battle has its special point. In addition to his picture of two exhausted swimmers dragging each other down, the two contestants are described in almost similar terms. Macdonwald is aided by Fortune, an unreli-able mistress; Macbeth is the minion or darling of Valour. Fortune, like the whore she is, deceives Macdonwald, while Macbeth rages like a spoilt child, for he behaves most ruthlessly and unceremon-iously towards his foe. The reference, 'ne'er shook hands, nor bade farewell to him' followed by the savage 'till he unseamed him from the nave to th' chops', seems to stress the difference between noble courtesy, such as is expected of a host, and Macbeth's actual treat-ment of the person he met. Of course, it describes the logical code of conduct in war, but the violent image and the praise of Macbeth by Duncan which immediately follows should be noted.

This rhetorical account of the battle gives a necessary prelude to the action which soon follows. Once again, in the sergeant's words, there is the sharp contrast between expectation and the event: from the east, the traditional source of light, life and comfort, 'discomfort swells'. With references to blood and the greatest crime of all crimes in the Christian calendar ('memorize another Golgotha') the sergeant's piece of narration is over. Ross reports victory for Duncan's forces, and the scene closes with Duncan's solemn pronouncement that no more shall Cawdor prove false to the confidence and affection reposed in him. Cawdor has not proved to be what he seemed to be. So when Duncan says 'What he hath lost, noble Macbeth hath won', are we not left with a twofold impression: both of the king's generosity and the foreboding that the position just vacated by a traitor is to be occupied by a person whose ruthless deeds seem to be at variance with his description as 'brave' and valorous.

The first appearance of Macbeth on the stage is preceded by the entry of the Weird Sisters to the accompaniment of thunder. Their short lines of rhymed verse, with its popular verse rhythms, and the references to activities connected with witchcraft, give a special significance to what follows on the stage. Not only the verse with its references but also the action—the spell, in the form of nine sweeping movements enacted as soon as the drum announcing Macbeth is heard—must heighten this significance.

That they are ambiguous figures, in keeping with the equivocal world of the play, we are told by Banquo (41 ff.). They do not seem to be humans at all, yet they are on the earth; they do not seem living, yet he wonders whether they will speak; they seem to be women, yet their beards deny this. Later they disappear, and seem to Banquo an illusion; to Macbeth what seemed to have a body has melted like breath in wind.

What they are is plain to Banquo. They must be 'instruments of darkness', the agents of evil. Their riddling speeches, the threefold greeting addressed to both Macbeth and Banquo, the promises held out, are a true-seeming falsehood. Such beings could delude a man with 'honest trifles', which might be correct in a matter of no consequence, but must unfailingly trap him and ruin him in matters of the greatest importance. Banquo's words (1. 3. 123–7) which Macbeth perhaps does not hear or attend to, present the balance of opposites in the play.

To both of them the greeting would perhaps have been no more than an interesting event, had not in Macbeth's case one of the promises been already fulfilled. He knows that he is thane of Glamis. This is the 'honest trifle' which sets him on his way.

Macbeth caught

But the 'addition' (title) of Thane of Cawdor, with which he is greeted by Ross in 1. 3. 105–6, catches Macbeth, and from that moment he feels that 'the greatest is behind', that is, it is there in the background, soon to take its place on the full stage. 'The prologues to the swelling act of the imperial theme', with the image from the stage, suggest that 'behind' is what is 'upstage', as we would call it now, ready to advance and take up the focal position in the centre.

The soliloquy of 1. 3. 127–42 makes it clear that Macbeth has been caught by the 'honest trifle', and is now proceeding to the affair of 'deepest consequence'. His state of mind, poetically rendered by his words, quivers in an uncertain and uneasy balance between good and evil. His speech begins with a grandiloquent ushering in of what seems to be good—'the imperial theme'—but which is really evil, since the words refer to the kingship which cannot be his except through evil means. So throughout the lines the mind is faced by a situation which "cannot be ill; cannot be good". What could the 'horrid image' be but the temptation to realize 'the imperial theme'? As Macbeth goes on it seems clear that 'the imperial theme' (129), transformed in his imagination to the vagueness of 'horrid image' (135), has changed yet again, to be named now as the imagined 'murder' (139). In the confusion of his mind these 'fantastical' (imaginary) shapes lose their identity and he can feel that his imagination has altered the world of reality and upset the course of nature. As a result his little world of man ('single state of man') is in such a state of internal war that what should direct his mind ('function') is smothered by imaginings. Throughout the speech the difficulty of distinguishing between two opposites and the suggestion that the good is being choked by the bad are prominent. Macbeth's state is expressed in words which echo the Weird Sisters: 'Nothing is but what is not.'

The weighing motion of the balanced rhythms of the speech as it opens, then its growing complexity, and the speed with which the fluctuations of the mind are pictured, are expressive—that is, they seem to enact the very condition the words describe. If anything is clear to Macbeth's disordered mind it is the suggestion of a world in unnatural revolt against itself, the counterpart of his own state. 'Single' in 'single state of man' would seem to mean not 'feeble', but 'retaining its integrity', the little world of man so often at this time likened to the great world or universe.

Macbeth's mind is disturbed and he cannot distinguish good from evil, what is from what is not. His imagination has taken him out of the bounds of time and place. Banquo, looking at him, can think of him as a man 'rapt' or in a trance. He puts it down to the new honour he has received, apparently as strange to him as new clothes are to a man unaccustomed to them. The image from clothing suggests the disparity between what should be and what is.

The Macbeth who leaves the stage at the end of 1. 3 is a man whose world is, according to his own words, in a state of imbalance. His two asides continue this impression in the indecision they reveal. 'If chance will have me king, why, chance may crown me' (1. 3.143) suggests the dismissal of the 'horrid image' and a decision to take no action; but the aside to Banquo that they should, when they have time, talk quite frankly about the meeting with the Weird Sisters, contradicts this.

When in 1. 4 Macbeth enters pat upon the king's words, which remind us of the difference between appearance and reality, the irony is very forcefully pointed. The king now greets with honour and gracious favour a man who has seen him in his mind's eye as already murdered.

The world of Nature

The exchanges between king and subject in 1. 4. 22–9, conveyed through the images of natural growth, insist on one sense of the word 'nature' of which the play makes use. Behind Duncan's speech in 1. 4. 34–43 lies the world of the natural order planned by God, maintained in the succession of kingdoms and in the duties of subjects and nobles to their sovereign. Shakespeare deliberately avoids any suggestion that Macbeth's legitimate hopes of the succession were frustrated, as Holinshed had observed, in Duncan's naming of Malcolm as heir to the throne. What is more, in this context, with the poetry to enhance it and stage show to actualize it, what could be more natural now that rebels and invaders have been vanquished and the king is surrounded by his faithful lords than that he should think of the future of the kingdom? The references to his tears like rain, to the investiture of Malcolm as Prince of Cumberland, followed by the image of the hierarchy of nobles like stars or orbs fixed in their courses, provide the background of natural order and royal ceremony which offset the world we have just seen taking shape in Macbeth's mind.

Its opposite. Yet that world returns in an instant; ironically it follows the king's farewell 'My worthy Cawdor!', in Macbeth's aside in 1. 4. 48–53. There is a further stage reached here. The thought of murder which was 'fantastical' has now become that kind of evil reality which a man seeks to dispel by refusing to see it. The stars which Duncan had just seen as shining 'on all deservers' are bidden to 'hide' their fires. The sense of the lines in which darkness is contrasted with light is 'Let the horrid deed be done, so long as it is not seen'. Macbeth quite clearly wishes to deceive himself with the specious comfort that if it cannot be seen it is not there. The eye will 'wink', or be closed, so that it does not see what the hand does, yet he insists that what the hand does should be done, even though the eye may fear to contemplate it. The play will go on to show how deluded he is. As for Duncan, he is deluded too. So is Banquo, who has been commending Macbeth to his king, while the dreadful aside has been spoken. 'It is a banquet to me' is the greatest irony of all; for Macbeth whose praise is thus called a source of life by Duncan is thinking of murdering him, and a banquet is to follow at which the host contemplates bearing the knife against his royal guest.

The entry of Lady Macbeth

When Lady Macbeth enters, we are made more strongly aware of the equivocal position in which Macbeth now stands. Though he does not enter until 1. 5. 53, he is there on the stage in the letter and in his wife's two soliloquies. These are important, not so much because they throw light on the sort of person he is or on her, but because they precipitate a deeper atmosphere of evil which seems to be gathering over them and the whole action.

Lady Macbeth sees Macbeth in a state of imbalance, one who knows what he wants and yet will not acknowledge to himself what has to be done to get it. His nature may be 'too full o' th' milk of human kindness' yet he is not without ambition. He will not 'play false', but yet would 'wrongly win' (1. 5. 20–1). She sees her determination to push him towards an unnatural crime as pouring poison in his ear ('pouring my spirits in thine ear'), and chastising or whipping with the valour of her tongue 'all that impedes thee from the golden round' (the crown). What might these impediments be? His better nature, or evil proclivities in him still irresolute and in need of the incentive of persuasion? It is interesting that later, in 1. 7, when Macbeth applies the goad to himself, he can talk of his having no spur to 'prick the sides of (his) intent' but ambition. As he has this, he has the seeds of evil in him.

The invocation of evil. Lady Macbeth's forcible and strained images reveal the pressure she puts upon herself. It continues in her invocation of the spirit world (1. 5. 39–53), which at that time could not have been anything but an appalling shock to the audience. As prelude to it she imagines, since she is already in a kind of trance, that she hears the raven, the bird of ill-omen, croaking under the battlements. The real world withdraws and a world of unreality takes its place. The invocation is solemn; it categorically asks for a transformation of her human nature—her blood thickened, her milk changed to gall—into the inhuman, the distortion of nature ('nature's mischief').

Her accents are slow and solemn, the imperative 'Come' thrice repeated has a magical effect and imaginatively actualizes the transformation. Yet it is ironical that imagining herself as the perpetrator of the murder she too asks for that darkness Macbeth had urged in the previous scene, as if the inability to see the deed in the darkness she conjures up could mitigate its horror or prevent it from being damned by heaven.

When she meets her husband she behaves as if her refusal to use the plain word for what is in her mind does alter its character. She really greets him, with her 'all-hail hereafter!', as king (her greeting recalls the Weird Sisters). To Lady Macbeth the reality could be veiled by a form of words. The murder is 'this night's great business' which is to be put into 'her dispatch' (l. 67). The deliberate understatement with the pun on 'dispatch' is sufficiently grim to strike the audience. It also reminds us that for all her forcing of herself she cannot say the word on which her mind dwells.

Both Macbeth and Lady Macbeth have reached the point of deluding themselves that not to see evil for what it is and not to mention it by its proper name is to transform it into something that is not evil. They are indulging in a form of magic, as potent as that of the Weird Sisters. With noises off, the 'hautboys', announcing the arrival of Duncan at Macbeth's castle, a further stage of the play is reached.

The world of order

The contrast with this delusory world of evil is emphasized in 1. 6, immediately after Macbeth and his wife decide to dissimulate, to 'beguile the time', that is, to cheat the world by pretending to be what they are not. The scene of the welcoming of the king by his hostess very strongly presents the world of order and allegiance, and this is reinforced by the poetry as it conjures up life, light, religion and the tenderness of humanity in both Duncan's words and Banquo's. The sweet and gentle air which 'nimbly' (briskly) recommends itself to the senses; the suggestion of the freshness of the height at which the birds built in distinction to the depths of evil glimpsed before; the temple-haunting martlet which builds in churches; the sacredness of home in 'pendent bed and procreant cradle'; the suggestions of the tenderness of the tie which binds humanity to children and home; 'the heaven's breath' which smells wooingly, all of it should be noted as a strong contrast with the darkness and un-naturalness of the previous scenes and the pretended welcome of Lady Macbeth.

Every word she speaks (1. 6. 14–20) adds to the impression of what is expected and required in a world sanctified by order and to which she pretends to belong: the service owed by subjects to the king; the honours which flow from him, in grateful thanks for which they are in duty bound to pray as 'hermits' (beadsmen). And when Duncan speaks, he speaks not as king, but as gracious guest of his hostess. When he leaves the stage, he goes to seek out Macbeth, to whom, as he says, his 'graces' will continue.

In the scene that follows, stage business immediately accentuates the primary relationship of Duncan to Macbeth and his wife. The 'Sewer' who crosses the stage, the 'divers servants', are a visual reminder of the simplest of all ties, hospitality, which should bind Macbeth and Lady Macbeth to the man they are entertaining. It is against this background that Macbeth's soliloquy and the scene between host and hostess should be seen.

Macbeth's soliloquy

The soliloquy reveals the real against the false show of the banquet behind. The turbulent flow of the verse with its ambiguous first line, followed by the explicit 'assassination' and the conspiratorial hissing of the sibilants flood the blank verse line and almost disrupt its regularity. The disorder of the mind is revealed. The plain sense of the lines seems to say that provided he could escape the consequences of his crime in this life, he would not mind risking the life to come. Yet what is most vivid in his mind is his vision of doomsday. He is trying to delude himself, but his strong imagination does not let him escape. The repeated stress on 'here', on which the Folio punctuation insists, almost steadies the torrent of the whispering on the stage and a calmer movement follows: 'But in these cases...to our own lips.' He knows what happens in the real world, he can see further what his position is. He is kinsman, subject and host. But the words 'murderer' and 'knife' bewitch his imagination, and he is away from the world of the present into a magnificent picture of the last day. That the images are confused is surely in keeping with the violent cataclysm pictured. Its general sense is clear: such a deed can only make a doomsday of present time, when angels will trumpet Macbeth's crime, and pity is thought of as a tender, new-born babe astride the winds of indignation aroused by the murder.

After this violent burst, the voice settles down to an ironical contemplation of his own position: he is like the man who attempting an exploit beyond his abilities ('vaulting') makes himself a pitiable spectacle.

To Lady Macbeth who enters he can then try to state that he will wear the honourable clothes and decorations he has just earned and which are still fresh and new; and not throw them away. She turns this aside by another image from clothing in which she derides him for 'dressing' himself with hope like a drunkard boasting in his cups (ll. 35–6). From his undecided state letting 'I dare not' wait upon 'I would', she rouses him by a speciously logical argument, which derives its force from the interpretation she puts upon the word 'man'. He dares 'do all that may become a man'. To her, to be more than what he is would mean that he would be 'so much more the man'.

Natural ties rejected

What it can mean to her is revealed in the very violence with which she denies and rejects everything which the common meaning of the word 'man' or 'woman' includes. She knows the horror of her statement, and in 1. 7. 54–9 she declares that she would violate the most natural of all ties, that between the helpless babe at the breast and mother. This visualization of what could be acts upon Macbeth as a spell. He is won over, and his only concern is with the prospect of failure. Against this too she has a potent charm—he is to wrench his whole frame to the point of violent action, screwing his courage, like a crossbow or a musical instrument, to the sticking place. So in a state of trance he is ready to accept any possibility she offers him. The words in which she describes what she will do read like an incantation which dispels his fears. The reality of the murder is dissolved by her words into 'our great quell' (l. 72), as if their objective had been ridding themselves of noxious vermin. Macbeth's words in 1. 7. 79–82 confess the strain to which he subjects himself. He is settled, as the couplet which ends the scene shows. It is calm acceptance of the fact that in his world nothing is but what is not. 'The time' is to be 'mocked with fairest show'.

The prelude to the murder

Before the crime, which is not represented directly on the stage, is committed, the dramatist carefully builds up the atmosphere of darkness and the heavy sense of the presence of evil, contrasting with it touches from the world of light and graciousness. Banquo himself is affected with the premonition of evil, and in 2. 1. 7 invokes the 'powers', or the order of angels who strove against the legions of the devil, to keep his mind from the horrible dreams to which 'nature' (both the physical frame and humanity) is prone to in sleep.

If anything could have recalled Macbeth to the world of order to which he should have belonged, the gift of the diamond from the king should. It was peerless among stones, and it protected its possessor. We should remember that he has this on him when he goes to kill the kinsman and king who sent it to him. Macbeth's ambiguous words about the Weird Sisters are met by Banquo's frank statement that so long as his mind is 'free' and his loyalty without stain, he is ready to discuss any suggestion made by his friend. These words cannot recall Macbeth to reality. His duty to the king, the honours done him, his position as host, have to give way to what he has willed—the murder to which he is to be summoned by the bell.

The hallucination

The interim between the exit of the servant and the sound of the bell off-stage (2. 1. 32–61) is a period of suspense. We know that the bell must ring, and here is Macbeth on the stage, having failed twice to return to the world of reality to which Banquo's words should have recalled him. In the soliloquy which follows Banquo's exit it is the world of unreality which is present, the world of the Weird Sisters and of his wife's incantation. The world of fantasy takes over and he is in a state of hallucination. He sees a dagger which is both there and not there.

It is in this condition that in his imagination he enacts the murder he is to perform. It 'informs', or takes shape, before his eyes. The excitement of the poetry, with its contrasts between what seems to be and what is, lays bare the tranced mind. In lines 33–43 he is actually living in his own disordered world, for which he can provide no other explanation but his strong imagination of the murder which makes the dagger take shape before his eyes.

From line 49 till the sound of the bell breaks the hallucinatory atmosphere, Macbeth creates the murder which he wishes to thrust from his imagination. It is as if he is outside himself, watching himself at the dead hour of the night when over one hemisphere nature (both the world of human beings and the kindly world) is dead, and he like Murder creeps towards his victim with Tarquin's strides. The first representation of the murder is in the poetry of this world of witchcraft, the 'offerings' (rituals) of the underworld, and the invocation to the earth not to hear the steps of the criminal. It is dramatically rendered for the second time in the dialogue of the next scene, and, for the third time, it is given grimmer significance in the Porter's grotesque make-believe that it is hell-gate over which he presides.

The equivalent of the murder is provided in 2. 2, in Lady Macbeth's words which break the stillness with their references to noises off—the owl, Macbeth's cry offstage in 2. 2. 8—and to the grooms, drugged and neither living nor dead. The ominous atmosphere is heightened by the pauses in the dialogue, the short sentences and the monosyllabic words. We should note that when in 2. 2. 12 Lady Macbeth says, 'Had he not resembled my father as he slept, I had done't', she intends to make light of the crime, to point to the easiness with which even she, a woman, could have done it. In her world of evil such a deed is a triviality; but in the other world which is yet faintly felt it would have destroyed the strongest tie which binds man to man, parenthood. And indeed for that reason she could not do it—a kind of proof of her own humanity.

Macbeth is again contemplating himself from outside himself. His hands, stained with blood which he and the audience see, are not his hands but a portentous force which will turn red all the seas of the world. Lady Macbeth and himself develop what resembles a musical figure: the one, Macbeth, descanting on the fantastical or imagined world which evil has brought into being; the other, with a ground bass of practical, commonsense short lines trying to recall him to the world of reality. In every case each of these 'sensible' remarks has ironic overtones which she cannot at this stage realize: 'a little water clears us of this deed'; 'how easy is it then'.

Macbeth's obsession

Beside these interjections of hers his strong speeches, with their obsessed repetition of words like 'Amen' and 'sleep', show that he is a man possessed. The beat of the lines, their compulsive rhythm, insists on the superior reality of the world which his imagination unfolds to him to that which she tries to make him grasp. The pulsation of his speech is taken up by the knocking, and this sets him off on his last frenzied utterance as he looks at his hands again. As he leaves the stage he is already in the state of torture; he cannot 'know his deed' and he cannot know himself. There is no difference between them, both are states of horror.

The knocking

The knocking which begins at 2. 2. 57 continues right up to 2. 3. 19. It is like a supernatural intervention, Macbeth feels the knocking is an attempt to wake the dead. Literally it is a knocking at the south entry, and De Quincey claimed that it also represented the world of normality returning, and asking as it were for admittance. But the world of normality does not really return until the very end of the play. The world of hell-gate is not the world of normality. The Porter's words fit the mood of the audience and the play. This time the atmosphere of the play, its combination of what is and what is not, is given us in a grim and coarse form. Those imagined to be crowding into hell, where the Porter has 'old' (or has lots to do) turning the key, are equivocators all of them, from the Jesuit father implicated in the Gunpowder Plot, the farmer who does what he would never expect normal man to do (hang himself on the expectation of a good harvest) and the tailor who could steal material even when making the skimpiest fashion of clothing there was.

The coarseness of his conversation with Macduff repeats the notion of equivocation, this time with reference to drink. It apparently does something for a man, but in reality it takes something away from him. We are told of portents which made the night an unruly one (2. 3. 54–61). 'Accents terrible' of 'dire combustion' (civil strife) and 'confused' (disorderly) events are the fitting accompaniment to a deed whose horror we have seen projected on the stage three times already.

The actual discovery

When the murder is discovered, there is uproar and clamour. The bell rings and Macduff's words (2. 3. 74–80) are a full-throated summons to the world to see the extent of the sacrilege described in lines 67–9. The stage is filled with people in their dressing-gowns, a visual touch which adds to the confusion of the dramatic situation.

The accurate summing up of the significance of the murder comes from the murderer. Macbeth's lines (2. 3. 90–95) are, as we shall see in the development of the play, prophetic. Whether his description of the frenzy in which he slew the grooms is convincing, or whether it betrays its insincerity in the fanciful imagery used, is for the reader to decide. On the stage it would be made clear by the actor. Certainly the conversation between Malcolm and Donalbain in lines 119–26 suggests their disbelief in tears so readily brewed or in sorrow so quick to present itself.

In 2. 4 the murder is again recreated for us, this time in terms of a convulsion of earth, sky and the natural world such as we have noted in the storm which preceded Caesar's murder. Ross's statement expresses what all Elizabethans would believe. The heavens foretold the deaths of princes. Here the predominant atmosphere is of an unnatural world. All the portents speak of a disruption of the natural order: ''Tis unnatural'; the horses turn wild in 'nature'; the suspicion that Donalbain and Malcolm are the instigators of the crime is ''Gainst nature still'.

We know we shall see Macbeth as king, but before that happens Macduff indicates that he is not for the investiture, but for his own castle at Fife. He expresses the ironic hope, in which he cannot believe, that what is going to be done at Scone may be well done, 'lest our old robes sit easier than our new'. We know that they cannot; the king we shall soon see will be wearing what neither belongs to him nor sits well on him.

Second movement

The second movement of the play begins in 3. 1 with Macbeth as king. Its parallels and contrasts with the first are full of meaning. It begins with Macbeth as king; a very different king from Duncan. Once again Macbeth commits a murder; but this time he does not himself bear the knife. Once again there is a meeting between the Weird Sisters and himself; but this time he seeks them out and conjures them to show him the future. Once again the meeting with them leads to evil; this time Macbeth becomes not only murderer but tyrant as well. In the previous movement we were given no hint of coming change; this time there is a plain statement that the light of morning must break through at the darkest point of the play, after the second murder and the appearance of the ghost, in 3. 4. 127.

King Macbeth

Macbeth and Lady Macbeth are presented as king and queen with all the ceremony which was the due of royalty. The Folio stage direction shows this. The business for which the court is assembled is obviously the formal occasion of a council of state. But Banquo's words which are a prelude to the scene state very plainly that Macbeth is no king, but a man who has 'played most foully' for the crown. In the bitterness of his spirits Banquo can ask why if the Weird Sisters' speeches 'shone', or were so plainly proved to be true, with regard to Macbeth, they should not give him hope too. The lines are equivocal. They suggest that Banquo should have acted differently had he been so suspicious. Whatever Shakespeare's views on the matter, this founder of the Scottish royal line could, in a play written in 1606, do nothing else until it had been proved that Macbeth was a tyrant and usurper.

Macbeth's verse. We should contrast the verse spoken by this king with that given Duncan. The latter's is relaxed, easy and full of generous references. Macbeth's here is forced, his anxiety comes out in his repeated questions about Banquo's plans. Both questions and answers are going to take on a sinister significance. There is none of Duncan's graciousness in Macbeth's speech despite his references to the feast and the welcome prepared for his guests.

His council of state is really a colloquy with murderers. They are his councillors and the agenda is Banquo's murder. But before these characters come on the stage, in make-up which must have unmistakeably proved them nefarious, Macbeth in his soliloquy (3. 1. 47–71) confesses the extent of the delusion into which the 'prophecies' of the Weird Sisters have betrayed him. Banquo's observation about the 'instruments of darkness' is shown to be true. Macbeth has been promised the crown; he has it, but it brings neither ease of mind nor peace. So his is an equivocal state: 'To be thus is nothing, but to be safely thus'. He knows he is no king, 'royalty' of nature belongs not to him, but to Banquo.

There is a subtle change in the speech. Up to line 56 Macbeth is occupied with his fears with regard to Banquo, which he feels like nails sticking deeply in his flesh. He then recalls the words of the Weird Sisters, and goes on, as we have noted before, in verse whose obsessive character shows that he is not in contact with the world of reality but with his own imaginings. The repetition of 'my' contrasted with 'him', and then the recurrence of strong stresses on 'them' marks the feverish speed of the poetry, until in its unnatural climax he can take on Fate at the lists and fight a duel with it to the death ('champion me to th' utterance').

The murderers

As he deluded himself before, he deludes himself again. We should note the difference between the man who gave his 'eternal jewel' (his immortal soul) to the devil with Duncan's murder and the politic plotter here. He works alone now, without his wife's prompting or support, and he has become the expert contriver. In lines 127 ff. he undertakes to give the murderers explicit directions. He has advanced in his ability to 'mock the time with fairest show', for he can provide specious reasons for wanting Banquo out of the way and employing these desperadoes to do it. That he deludes himself into believing that this time his crime is mitigated because the murder is committed not actually by himself, but by his instruments, seems to be clear by his remark to the ghost in 3. 4. 50: 'Thou canst not say I did it.'

It is interesting that the man who has deliberately placed himself outside the world of men and order, should yet be dependent on the order he has rejected. It is not just a man whom he needs for his task. The murderers may be men in the 'catalogue' (the mere list which distinguishes men from vegetables). He requires a man of spirit from the 'valued file' (the list which makes distinctions between men and places them in an order). But, with an irony he may not himself realize, his man of spirit, not the tame 'gospelled' creature (the person submissive to gospel precepts), is in reality a murderer. The difference between the reality as Macbeth understands it and the world of human reality is clear.

The couplet with which he leaves the stage recalls the occasion when the bell awoke him from his trance to Duncan's murder. In both will be noticed the resoluteness with which he imagines that destiny is controlled by him.

The banquet

In this scene are concentrated all the suggestions of the equivocal nature of the world of the play. On the stage it must have been presented with the detail conventionally associated with ceremony and formality. The queen sits on the throne (3. 4. 5), and the king moves among his thanes. But we know that both are implicated in murder and that the chief guest will appear as a ghost. Besides, the banquet is prepared for by a scene between Macbeth and Lady Macbeth in which it is clear that all they have gained by their 'success' is the equivocal state of 'doubtful joy' (pleasure continually attended by fear and suspicion).

Lady Macbeth's attitude is one of fatalism: 'Things without all remedy / Should be without regard'—what's beyond our power to change should be put out of our thoughts. But this cannot be his attitude, for he is sick—his is the torture of mind, the state of 'restless ecstasy' which is a frenzied state. The solemn adjuration, in 3. 2. 16ff., that he would rather the whole 'frame of things' (the universe) should break up and the world of the present and the hereafter crumble than put up with 'terrible dreams' proves the feverishness of his condition. To him life itself is a 'fitful fever'—that is, a feverous state which produces fits. The verse of 3. 2. 22–6 mirrors his delirium. And we are to see that he is to have three fits after this preliminary loss of self-possession in this scene.

The dramatic contrast. We should note the strong dramatic contrast between the associations of the royal banquet to which the action is conducting us and the darkness evoked by Macbeth's words in 3. 2. 39–54 and the scene of Banquo's murder. The feast with its suggestions of light and splendour is thrown into sharp relief by the atmosphere of the scenes which precede it. With the mood created by the ominous description of the onset of night and Macbeth's sorcerer-like invocation to night, the banquet can only be a repudiation of all it should be. Played on the popular stage in broad daylight, the two scenes are given the necessary combination of darkness and unnatural evil through the potency of the poetry. 'There's comfort yet', says Macbeth. He advises his wife to be 'jocund', and then launches into a speech calling up the darkness which goes with a 'deed of dreadful note' (a nefarious deed) until she is reduced to a state of horror and fascination (looking at her he says, in line 54, 'Thou marvell'st at my words').

What is needed here is the atmosphere of unnatural darkness, and it is provided both by statement and by implication. The image in line 46 of night 'seeling' or sewing up the eyelids of tender day, as the eyes of the falcon to be tamed were seeled, brings in the suggestions of cruelty and of blood. Perhaps, too, the word 'seel', followed by 'bloody' and 'bond', recalled the bright red of molten sealing-wax dropping on to a legal document, and hence the world of law and order which Macbeth wants destroyed. He himself is as strongly moved as his wife is, for he thinks of himself as 'pale', with the pallor of sickness and of fear at the action that is to follow. The 'great bond' is both the natural tie which binds man to man, and also Banquo's life.

The murder follows (3. 3). Once more the kindly associations of evening in which the late traveller spurs on towards the inn are denied by the horror and confusion of the murder.

At the banquet (3. 4) we see Macbeth seeking out a place convenient enough for him to be apprised of the deaths of Banquo and Fleance without betraying the presence of the murderers. That such characters should appear on such an occasion would be shocking. Much more shocking then is Macbeth's callous remark (l. 14), ''Tis better thee without than he within' (better the blood on your face than in Banquo's body), and the first 'fit' which seizes Macbeth on hearing the news that Fleance has escaped. There is strong irony, too, in his claim that had he known Fleance had been killed, he would have been 'perfect' (both physically fit and also completely satisfied), as firm as a rock on its base, and as 'broad and general' (free and unrestrained) as the air in the heavens (ll. 21–3).

The ghost. It is not Fleance who troubles him, but the dead Banquo. The actor playing the part must have entered with his hair and face 'boltered' or clotted with blood. According to the stage convention of the time, if the others on the stage behaved as if they did not see him, he was assumed to be invisible to them.

In the moment of remembering Banquo and uttering the falsehood that if only he were there as 'graced' or honoured guest, Macbeth does not know that he is there all the time, sitting in the place reserved for the king. As he turns and sees the ghost, his second 'fit' occurs. It must have been a physical paroxysm for Lennox asks, 'What is't that moves your highness?' (l. 49), and Lady Macbeth draws attention to his distorted face with her 'Why do you make such faces?' (l. 67).

The reality which Macbeth tries to beat down by his passionate verse does not exist for the others. The world—as he states it in 3. 4. 75–83—has been transformed by his act, and so unnatural has it become that even the dead now are not dead. The reality of death has been suspended and another level of reality has taken its place.

In his third 'fit', at the second appearance of the ghost (l. 88), he tries to change the supernatural reality of the ghost into some physical reality—of the Russian bear, or the mythical Hyrcan tiger— which he can face. But it fails, and he remains trembling and un-manly, like a baby girl (3. 4. 99–106).

The banquet, which started with the lords taking their traditional and ordered places, has to break up in just such 'admired' (amazing) disorder (l. 110) as Macbeth has brought into the world by his evil.

Alone on the stage with Lady Macbeth he is overpowered by his guilty obsession that blood will have blood. When he asks what the time is, we see from Lady Macbeth's reply that we have reached that stage in the play when at the moment of what seems to be an equal balance of night and morning, night being 'at odds', or disputing, with morning, there is a promise of change, and of the counter-movement which brings light to overpower darkness. This is the equivocal state which must resolve itself into one in which good tips the balance of the scales now held almost equal.

From king to tyrant

The depressed, heavy verse with which Macbeth tries to rouse him-self (ll. 130–40), the insistence on the determination to allow nothing to stand in his way, should be contrasted with the decisions taken: to send to Macduff and to seek out the Weird Sisters immediately. His own picturing of his state recalls the ambiguous character of his world: he has stepped so far into a pool of blood that to return would be as heavy an effort of spirit as crossing over. He has become the tyrant, for now no 'causes' (considerations) can restrain him. The couplet which closes the scene is a piece of self-deception, for he thinks of his 'fits' and his 'self-abuse' (hallucination) as nothing more than the fears of the novice in need of the practice which will harden him. 'We are yet but young in deed' is a prophetic warning which we shall see fulfilled both in the murder of Lady Macduff and her son and what is reported of Scotland in the next scene and in the English court in act 4.

Counter-movement. We can neglect 3. 5 and take 3. 6 as the clear beginning of the counter-movement. It announces, first of all in Lennox's sarcasm about the murders and then in the plain statement of the Lord (3. 6. 24–39) that from England where the pious king (referred to again in line 30 as the 'holy king') rules, Duncan's son, Malcolm, and Macduff will bring relief to the kingdom of Scotland lying 'under a hand accursed'. The deliverance of Scotland from Macbeth, now named as tyrant, is seen as an enterprise which God will ratify. Its effect will be to restore order. To 'free from our feasts and banquets bloody knives' (3. 6. 35) is literally to rid Scotland of such horrors as we have seen demonstrated on the stage twice.

Third movement

In the third movement of the play (acts 4 and 5) the counter-movement develops, so that in terms of plot the play ends in the struggle between the dwindling forces of Macbeth and those of the deliverers bringing health and restoration to Scotland. In this final movement the main contrast is between a diseased country, symbolized by two characters both sick, and the state of health of a country ruled by a gracious king. In the course of this final movement Scotland is 'purged' and restored to its pristine health.

In addition, we see how the world of evil, now deliberately willed into being by Macbeth, at his conjuration presents a show which seems to promise the truth, but in reality dupes him again. The darkness and unnaturalness of this world is contrasted with the light and greenness of the natural world.

Finally, we see how Macbeth as king turned tyrant uneasily wears his robes of state. Neither of the roles he has played so far, as warrior or as king, has sat easily on him. He is no king, and for a moment he refuses to fight when he knows that the charm on which he has relied protects him no longer. He begins the battle with the desperation of an animal; he ends it, as a head brought in on a pole, both tyrant and monster—the armed head of the apparition he himself had conjured up.

A changed Macbeth

The Macbeth we see now is a changed person. He proceeds further in his trafficking with evil, and now himself wants the 'masters' of the Weird Sisters called up. Because he is unsure of what is and what is not—he has just seen the dead Banquo face to face—he must be assured of the reality. So Shakespeare, using the belief in a world of evil presided over by the devil, provides on the stage what must have been an impressive recreation of the rites of magic.

4. 1 is preceded by the Weird Sisters rising (through the trap-door) and preparing their magical brew in a cauldron. Macbeth in his robes of state enters as the stage-door flies open. His blasphemous conjuration (4. 1. 50–61) sets the tone of the scene. It is blasphemous because he states explicitly that though the whole world tumbles in ruins, Nature's 'germens' being the seeds of all created matter, and though destruction reaches the point of satiety, he must have his will. The 'masters' must appear. 'Call 'em, let me see 'em.'

The three apparitions presented on the stage and the show of eight kings, both warn Macbeth and give him confidence. The first, of the armed head (perhaps the stage property used at the end of the play for Macbeth's head was used here too), confirms his fears. The other two give him assurance, but the show again plunges him into doubt and insecurity. Even though assured by these 'sweet bodements' (pleasing prophecies) (l. 96) he has to make assurance doubly sure. His is the counterpart of the dubious sickly state in which his actions have plunged the world. As soon as the show vanishes and the Weird Sisters disappear, he knows that one person has eluded him, for Lennox arrives to announce Macduff's escape to England.

The final murder

He therefore plunges further into the tyrannical course for which his earlier lines (3. 4. 139–40) have prepared us. The murder of all Macduff's family is the illustration of the aphorism, 'the very firstlings of my heart shall be / The firstlings of my hand' (ll. 146–8).

This murder, which can truthfully allow his opponents to describe him as 'butcher', is played in the atmosphere of doubt and uncertainty which hangs over the play. Lady Macduff cannot understand why her husband has left his family; his conduct seems as unnatural as that of the bird that does not fight in defence of its nestlings. To Ross (4. 2. 18–22) the world in which they live is one in which they seem to move and yet do not. It is also a sick world. Macduff's justification may be that he 'best knows the fits o' th' season' (the periodical fits of a feverous time) (ll. 16–17). Whether this is valid or not, we can see how dubious Macduff's position must be to Malcolm in 4. 3. Before he can be accepted, he must be tested by Malcolm.

The boy player who takes the part of Macduff's son has all the pertness and readiness of speech associated with children on Shakespeare's stage. His lines combine pathos and a precociousness which cuts down to the simple reality through the false show. It is a world in which the liars and swearers have beaten the honest men and hanged them. To Lady Macduff it is clear that she lives in 'this earthly world' (4. 2. 74) in which evil and good have lost their distinct characters. The murderers enter to work Macbeth's last murder.

England: the contrast

The long scene in England provides a strong contrast with the diseased and benighted Scotland. But it opens with as ambiguous a passage as we have had throughout the play. To Malcolm, Macduff must be an uncertain quantity, of whose intentions and character he has to be assured before the army which will purge Scotland can gather its forces. The evil Macbeth has brought into being not only turns Scotland into a country whose sorrows echo in the heavens, it transforms everyone who comes from it. Malcolm has therefore to convince himself that Macduff is not a hired assassin. His situation is very aptly put in 4. 3. 22 ff., in the difficulty of distinguishing between evil which can, and does, wear the garb of an angel and grace which must 'still' (always) look gracious even though evil would wear its looks.

The testing of Macduff. The probing of Macduff takes the form of a deception played upon him by Malcolm who describes himself not only as singularly lacking in all the good parts and graces required of a king, but also as full of all the evil passions which disfigure the ordinary man (4. 3. 50–5; 57–66; 76–84; 91–100). Why does Malcolm describe himself in this way? Why are such things as his 'ill-composed affection' (his disordered passions), his total lack of the 'king-becoming graces', his resolution to act like Macbeth, to 'pour the sweet milk of concord into hell', so insisted upon? Dramatically these slanders he puts upon himself are the most efficient test of Macduff's integrity he can devise. But there is more in it. The contrast between these 'taints and blames' and the kingly attributes called up serves two ends: we are given a catalogue of the ills of a country where evil bears sway; we are also given a picture of what should be the state of grace, so to speak, of the country ruled by a true king. These lines may have had the additional purpose of paying a compliment to James I, who believed in the divine right of the king.

When Malcolm has revealed his deliberate deception and the reality is clear to Macduff, the doctor arrives on the stage to relate how the saintly English king, through his God-given power, heals those whose sickness 'convinces' (defeats) medical science (4. 3. 141–5). Though there may have been another compliment here for James I, who was at that time 'touching' for healing, what is more important is the recurring contrast between the sick country suffering under a tyrant and the blessed country ruled by a sanctified king. As the good king cures those who are the 'mere despair of surgery' (given up as utterly hopeless cases by the physician), so the forces gathering here will cure Scotland of her disease.

Scotland recalled

Ross's entry, with fresh news from Scotland where violent sorrow seems a 'modern', or ordinary, ecstasy or seizure, brings Scotland on the stage once more. His tidings for Macduff ought to be howled out in the desert air where no human ears would hear them (ll. 193–5). Once again it is the unnaturalness of Macbeth's crime which has to be stressed. He has destroyed, like the bird of prey 'at one fell swoop', all the nestlings and the mother. We see how natural is the link between what Macbeth's castle promised to Banquo in 1. 6 and the reality here. To Malcolm it is important that Macduff should relieve his 'o'er-fraught heart' in words, for this is the natural way in which the patient ministers to himself. We shall see that Macbeth and Lady Macbeth do speak, but give themselves no relief.

At the end of the scene when Malcolm leaves the stage, he goes as the instrument of the Powers above, of the hierarchy of angels fighting to protect man from the evil one (ll. 237–9).

Its sickness. The scenes which follow recreate vividly the sickness, physical as well as spiritual, of Macbeth and Lady Macbeth and the country they have involved in their evil. Both the sleep-walking and Macbeth's sickness at heart are poetic renderings of something more than the warning of the retribution of crime. Shakespeare's words, his prose no less than his poetry, suggest a spiritual state beyond measurement by yardsticks such as this.

The sleep-walking

The sleep-walking scene (5. 1), besides being a fine piece of stage craft, takes up at almost every point of reference the main poetic images of the play. Lady Macbeth is asleep, and yet she is awake. This 'great perturbation in nature' (constitutional disorder) is like the disturbed state of the country and of the whole world of which the characters are conscious. She is queen, yet here, with a 'night-gown' thrown about her, she wanders about the stage. 'She has light by her continually', quite plainly because the dark has terrors for her. And she speaks 'what she should not'.

Dramatically the scene is an ironical refutation of everything which gave her confidence. She is as much gulled as Macbeth was by the Weird Sisters, for to her it was clear that 'a little water clears us of this deed'. Like him, she can sleep no more, for we see her here afflicted by a 'slumbry agitation' (l. 11), the ambiguous state of slumber marked by a nervous disorder.

Everything the doctor has seen and heard calls up disease, an unnatural condition. The word 'unnatural' is repeated in 5. 1. 70 and 71. The foulness of the condition is communicated by an image of the purulent discharge from the infected ear on the pillow (ll. 71–2).

So the play continues to its close, the poetry lighting up with its images the sick and infected country, and the tyrant unable to 'buckle his distempered cause within the belt of rule' (5. 2. 15–16). The suggestion here is not only of the inability of the belt to keep the clothing on, but, in the words 'distempered cause', a dropsical ailment for which the patient needs dieting, 'rule' being the regimen without which the sickness cannot be cured. A similar image of clothing hanging loose is to be found in 5. 2. 19–22; while the sickly suggestions of blood sticking on the hands of the murderer recall the Macbeth who stared at his bloodstained hands. Finally, the troops gathering to meet Malcolm go out to meet 'the med'cine of the sickly weal' (5. 2. 27)—the true king, who, like the good physician, will purge the country and cure it, as cures were effected then by the letting of blood. The action takes up alternately the representatives of infected Scotland and the health-giving forces of Malcolm.

Macbeth transformed

5. 3 shows us Macbeth trying to bolster up his confidence by remembering the words of the spirits who know the future and immediately after, upset by the pale and frightened face of the servant, plunging into despair. His lines to Seyton (5. 3. 19–29)

have a slow, deadened rhythm, as if he speaks not as a living man but as one already dead, or in a drugged state. In his review of all he 'must not look to have', he calls up all the positive values of the state of nature he has disrupted. His attention is fixed upon himself. When he asks the doctor about his wife, in a moment his attention shifts from her to himself. The 'mind diseased' (5. 3. 40) of which he speaks is his own mind. The verse, in its heavy repetitiveness and the acceptance of the impossibility of the task set (ministering to a mind diseased), calls up the picture of a man far gone in ill-health. Despite the seemingly brave call for his armour, the fatalistic rhetorical questions to which the only answer can be 'no': 'Canst thou not minister', 'What rhubarb, senna...', strike the mood of the scene, to be taken up again in 5. 5.

5. 4 shows us again a state in which what seems to be so is not so. Birnam wood will seem to advance to Dunsinane when the soldiers march forward with the boughs in their hands. But it is clear that, in Siward's words, the time is coming when we shall know how things stand, 'what we shall say we have and what we owe' (5. 4. 17–18) being a clear statement.

Despite his warlike preparations which recall the Macbeth of the opening of the play, his words on hearing the cry of women off-stage (5. 5. 7) show that he is not in the natural state of a living and healthy man. The time has been, he says, when he was alive and sensitive. Normal reactions are not to be expected of him now (ll. 9–15).

His epitaph on Lady Macbeth

His 'epitaph' on his wife in 5. 5. 17 ff. should be taken as spoken by a man who goes through the motions of living, but is no longer alive. He says nothing of her, but everything about himself, and what he does say of her remains ambiguous and uncertain. 'She should have died hereafter' might mean either she must have died at sometime or another, as all of us must die, or, she ought to have died at some other time, not the present. Whatever sense we give this line, we see that it is linked up with 'There would have been time for such a word'; that is in the state in which he is now, such words as death and time can have no significance.

What follows is a poetic statement of meaninglessness. Time is confounded. 'Tomorrow'—the future—creeps as if in the present; and the past—'all our yesterdays'—he sees in the present too in the series of images to which he likens life. The shifts of the imagery are natural, for the mind of the speaker is concentrated on the dull repetition and meaninglessness of the process of time which is life. So from senseless tramping in the darkness through link-boy to candle and actor dressed up and saying words that are not his own to the inarticulate sounds of the half-wit.

Greeted with the news of the wood which seems to be a 'moving grove', for the first time he sees that he might have been deluded by the devil. He begins 'to doubt' (to fear) the 'equivocation of the fiend' (l. 43). As he is no more a man, there can be nothing more for him but to fight with the instinctive reactions of the animal: 'at least we'll die with harness on our back' recalling the horse in armour (l. 52). When he appears again in 5. 7 to meet Young Siward, he sees himself as a bear tied to the stake and baited by dogs (5. 7. 1–2).

But before this the 'leavy screens' (5. 6. 1–2) are down, and for the first time in the play something shows itself as it really is. There is no more equivocation. In the next scene Macduff reveals the circumstances of his birth, so nothing is left Macbeth but to surrender. His 'better part of man', his manly spirit, is cowed and he curses the devil who betrayed him with equivocal words (5. 8. 17–22). But, rather than be treated as a monster on show at fairs (ll. 25–6), he rouses himself to fight, and is killed off-stage.

The true king acclaimed

The play ends with the true king, Malcolm, surrounded by his soldiers and nobles, remembering those who, like God's soldiers, gave their lives in the action (5. 9. 47–50). The head of the tyrant who usurped the throne and afflicted the country is brought in on a pole.

'The time is free' (5. 9. 55), not only the world and society, but times and seasons too. The kingdom has been cleansed of the evil which infected it. With newly created earls round him, the king undertakes to rule, with God's grace, according to 'measure, time, and place'. So order supplants disorder.

To Malcolm, quite naturally, Macbeth and Lady Macbeth can be nothing more than 'this dead butcher and his fiend-like queen' (5. 9. 87). Yet the play has made us aware of much more than this. *Macbeth* is much more than the straight record of the defeat of the agents of the evil one by the instruments of the 'powers'. In Macbeth's sensitiveness to the evil in which he is caught, in Lady Macbeth's process of education, in which she learned that a little water does not clear her of this deed, is to be found the play's real significance. *Macbeth* may illustrate a moral maxim or lend support to our observations of human beings, but these, as we set them down, do not seem to be as meaningful as the living experience of the play.

APPENDICES

Richard II, 1601. From (Francis Bacon's) *A Declaration of the Practises and Treasons...by Robert late Earle of Essex.*

That afternoone before the rebellion, Merricke, with a great company of others, that afterwards were all in the action, had procured to bee played before them, the play of deposing King Richard the second. Neither was it casuall, but a play bespoken by Merrick. And not so onely, but when it was told him by one of the players, that the play was olde, and they should haue losse in playing it, because fewe would come to it: there was fourty shillings extraordinarie giuen to play it, and so thereupon played it was. So earnest hee was to satisfie his eyes with the sight of that tragedie which hee thought soon after his lord should bring from the stage to the state, but that God turned it vpon their owne heads.

Julius Caesar, 1599. From the account of the travels of Thomas Platter. (Translated by J. Dover Wilson.)

After lunch on 21 September, round about 2 o'clock, I went with my companions across the water, and in the straw-thatched house saw the tragedy of the first emperor, Julius Caesar, excellently performed by some fifteen persons. At the end of the play, according to custom, they danced with much grace and in wonderful combination, two clad in men's clothes and two in women's.

Twelfth Night, 2 February 1602. Middle Temple. From *Diary* of John Manningham.

At our feast wee had a play called 'Twelue Night, or What You Will', much like the Commedy of Errores, or Menechmi in Plautus, but most like and neere to that in Italian called *Inganni*. A good practise in it to make the Steward beleeve his Lady widdowe was in love with him, by counterfeyting a letter from his Lady in generall termes, telling him what shee liked best in him, and prescribing his gesture in smiling, his apparaile, &c., and then when he came to practise making him beleeue they tooke him to be mad.

Macbeth, 1611. From Simon Forman's *Booke of Plaies.*

In Mackbeth at the Glob, 1610 (1611), the 20 of April ♄ (Saturday), ther was to be obserued, firste, howe Mackbeth and Bancko, 2 noble men of Scotland, Ridinge thorowe a wod, the(r) stode before them, 3 women feiries or Nimphes, And saluted Mackbeth, sayinge, 3 tyms unto him, haille Mackbeth, king of Codon; for thou shalt be a kinge, but shalt beget No kinges, &c. Then said Bancko, What all to Mackbeth And nothing to me. Yes, seid the nimphes, haille to thee Bancko, thou shalt beget kinges, yet be no kinge. And so they departed & cam to the Courte of Scotland to Dunkin king of Scotes, and yt was in the dais of Edward the Confessor. And Dunkin bad them both kindly wellcome, And made Mackbeth forth with Prince of Northumberland, and sent him hom to his castell, and appointed Mackbeth to prouid for him, for he would sup with him the next dai at night, & did soe. And Mackebeth contrived to kill Dunkin, & thorowe the persuasion of his wife did that night Murder the kinge in his own Castell, beinge his guest. And ther were many prodigies seen that night & the dai before. And when Mack Beth had murdred the kinge, the blod on his handes could not be washed of by Any meanes, nor from his wiues handes, which handled the bloddi daggers in hiding them, By which means they became both moch amazed and Affronted. The murder being knowen, Dunkins 2 sonns fled, the on to England, the (other to) Walles, to saue them selues, they being fled, they were supposed guilty of the murder of their father, which was nothinge so. Then was Mackbeth crowned kinge, and then he for feare of Banko, his old companion, that he should beget kinges but be no kinge him selfe, he contriued the death of Banko, and caused him to be Murdred on the way as he Rode. The next night, beinge at supper with his noble men whom he had bid to a feaste to the which also Banco should haue com, he began to speake of Noble Banco, and to wish that he wer ther. And as he thus did, standing up to drinke a Carouse to him, the ghoste of Banco came and sate down in his cheier behind him. And he turninge About to sit down Again sawe the goste of Banco, which fronted him so, that he fell into a great passion of fear and fury, Vtteryinge many wordes about his murder, by which, when they hard that Banco was Murdred they Suspected Mackbet.

Then MackDove fled to England to the kinges sonn, And soe they Raised an Army, And cam into Scotland, and at Dunston Anyse overthrue Mackbet. In the meantyme while Macdouee was in England, Mackbet slewe Mackdoues wife & children, and after in the battelle Mackdoue slewe Mackbet.

Obserue Also howe Mackbetes quen did Rise in the night in her slepe, & walke and talked and confessed all, & the doctor noted her wordes.

An extract from Leonard Digges's commendatory verses of Shakespeare's *Poems* (1640).

> So have I seene, when Cesar would appeare,
> And on the Stage at halfe-sword parley were,
> *Brutus* and *Cassius*: oh how the Audience,
> Were ravish'd, with what wonder they went thence...
> The Cockpit Galleries, Boxes, all are full
> To heare *Maluoglio* that crosse garter'd Gull.

II. SHAKESPEARE'S SOURCES

It was not necessary for Shakespeare to invent the subject-matter of the plays he wrote, for originality as we know it today was not expected of the playwright. Plays at that time, often put together by writers hired to revise and patch the work of others, were scarcely regarded as literature. We do not know to what extent surviving Elizabethan plays derive from earlier plays which have disappeared.

Some playwrights invented their stories; most did not. Though companies of players were afforded some protection against unauthorized printing of the plays they owned, there were no copyright laws to restrict the writer. What was popular as a contemporary novel or poem could be turned into a play. So Shakespeare used contemporary romance for some of his plots. In a few cases he invented his story.

There is no need to think less well of him for not having been original in this respect, for it is still quite common for dramatists to use well-known material for the subjects of plays. In recent years there has hardly been a dramatist of note who has not based one of his plays on a classical Greek original. Only those whose interest in a play depends entirely on their ignorance of the sequence of events in it would think badly of the playwright who repeated something already known in the plot of his play.

What matters is not what the writer ostensibly takes from his predecessors or contemporaries, but the particular use he makes of his borrowings. We all live in a particular culture, and we share through tradition, literary and oral, in what we ourselves have not created but has been passed on to us. A great deal of Shakespeare's education was given him through the culture he shared with the people of his age. There are numerous traditional beliefs and attitudes to be found in his plays, which he would not have had to borrow from any specific source, since they were in the air he breathed. Certain things he would have inherited as the common possession of all educated people of his time, evidence of which would be abundantly clear in the plays: his knowledge of the classics of Rome and Greece, and of the new literature for the first time being made available to Englishmen through translation from French, Italian and Spanish.

By the sources of Shakespeare's plays we mean those texts from which the main outlines of his plots and characters were derived. Most important in the background of the six plays studied were North's translation of Plutarch, translations of Italian stories, and Holinshed's and Hall's chronicles of English history. In every case Shakespeare treats his source with freedom. In the histories he is naturally much more bound to the salient events of the chronicles, but even within their limits he arranges his material to suit his own purposes. This is not strange, for he was a playwright, using a more concentrated form than that of his originals. He was a creative artist and his attitude would have forced him into moulding his material as he wished.

As our attention is focused on the plays, there is little to be gained by studying their sources in any detail. It is sufficient to know where Shakespeare took his plots from, and what important departures from his originals are to be found in his reworkings of them. It has to be repeated that one probable source may not exist any more—an earlier play he used which has since been lost.

Richard II. The main source was Raphael Holinshed's *Chronicles of England, Scotland and Ireland*, which Shakespeare must have read in the second edition of 1587. He also knew the earlier chronicle of Edward Hall, *The Union of the Two Noble and Illustre Families of Lancaster and York*, published in 1548. Shakespeare compresses the events of the reign. The scene of the gardeners, and of the last meeting of Richard and his queen are his own invention.

The Merchant of Venice. Traditional material may have given him some points in the story of the bond and the caskets. A story resembling that of the bond made with a money-lending Jew, the wooing of a lady, and the trial of the borrower is to be found in Ser Giovanni Fiorentino's *Il Pecorone* (1558). This was not translated into English during Shakespeare's lifetime. The casket story is to be found in the medieval *Gesta Romanorum*. Anthony Munday's *Zelauto* (1580) has a story resembling the elopement of Lorenzo and Jessica as well as that of a bond with an usurer. Shakespeare combines these three stories.

Henry V. Both Holinshed and Hall must have been used. An earlier play, *The Famous Victories of Henry V*, must have provided some hints too; the wooing of the French princess and some part of the humours of Pistol and the low life characters. The concentration of interest on the character of the king is Shakespeare's own development of his material.

Julius Caesar. Sir Thomas North's translation of Plutarch's *Lives of the Noble Grecians and Romans Compared* (1579) from the French of Amyot gave Shakespeare most of his material, which he took from the *Lives* of Caesar, Brutus and Antonius. The events of some years are compressed into a period of a few days before Caesar's murder. The most notable additions of Shakespeare's own are the speeches of Brutus and Antony.

Twelfth Night. Various Italian, Spanish and French plays had developed the subject, derived ultimately from Plautus, of twins separated by shipwreck, the female disguising herself as a boy and taking service with a lord with whom she falls in love. Bandello in his *Novelle* tells such a story which he took from an Italian comedy *Gl'Ingannati* (The Deceived). This was translated by Belleforest in his *Histoires Tragiques* and retold by Barnabie Rich in his *Farewell to the Military Profession* (1581). The subplot of the practical joke played on Malvolio and the characters concerned in it are Shakespeare's invention.

Macbeth. Popular ballads may have provided some material, but the main source once again is Holinshed. Shakespeare combines three episodes: the murder of King Duff by Donwald and his wife; the later story of Macbeth who supplants Duncan; and the story of King Kenneth. Some details about King Edward the Confessor are also taken from Holinshed. Shakespeare alters both Macbeth's character and Duncan's and Banquo's role in the play. The Macbeth of the chronicle was a good king, and Banquo was his accomplice in the murder of Duncan, a weak ruler. Shakespeare invents the ghost at the banquet, the testing of Macduff by Malcolm, and the sleep-walking scene. The Porter scene is, of course, original. For witchcraft and its rites he must have been indebted both to local superstition and legend and to Elizabethan and Jacobean treatises on demonology.

III. SOME TERMS EXPLAINED

ACTING AREA: That part of the stage on which the players are for the time being performing. On the Elizabethan stage there could be several sharply defined acting areas, such as, for example, the main stage which could be divided into front and back; the 'upper stage'; 'inner stage'.

ACTION: The events or happenings of a play which could be abstracted from it for the purpose of reference or study. 'Plot' is the term generally used, both in novel and in play, for this. 'Action' is more generally used of the events as represented on the stage.

BACKSTAGE: or upstage is that part of the stage furthest away from the audience.

BUSINESS: or stage business is those actions and movements performed by the actors interpreting their roles on the stage, which might not necessarily be set out in stage directions. *Richard II* would require a great deal of formal movement and gesture which would be 'business'.

CONVENTIONS: Conventions, both dramatic and theatrical, are those modes of writing plays and performing them on the stage to which we naturally give assent, since they have become through tradition and custom the accepted ways of doing things. Of course these conventions can be modified and changed as the conditions which brought them into being change. Stage conventions depend very much on the physical conditions of the stage. Soliloquies and asides are familiar Elizabethan conventions which are not common on the realist stage today.

DENOUEMENT: The untying of the complications of the plot of the play, as in *Twelfth Night*, when the twins Viola and Sebastian face each other in act 5.

DOWNSTAGE: That part of the stage nearest to the audience sitting in front; the front of the stage.

EXPOSITION: The opening scenes or scene of the play in which its subject and some indication of its development are made clear to the audience (or the reader).

FOLIO: The term used of a particular paper size—a large sheet—which was folded in two to make two leaves of a book. The name was transferred to the volume itself. Printing in this large size was in the sixteenth and seventeenth centuries generally restricted to books of serious interest such as sermons, eminent translations, works of philosophy, etc. It was unusual for plays to be printed in Folio. Shakespeare's plays were published in a Folio edition in 1623. The two persons responsible were his fellow actors, Heminge and Condell. The volume was dedicated to the Earls of Pembroke and Montgomery, and was prefaced by poems specially written for the occasion, and a letter to the reader by the two 'editors'.

IRONY: Irony arises out of the difference between what the words of a speaker on the stage, if we restrict ourselves to dramatic irony, say and what they can mean or imply to the audience. The spectator knowing more than either the speaker on the stage or those to whom his remarks are addressed, is aware of senses of which the actors on the stage are unaware. When Duncan and Banquo comment on the 'pleasant seat' of Macbeth's castle, their words are full of dramatic irony for the spectators (and Lady Macbeth), for they, and the actor playing her part, must know what that same castle is in reality going to prove to Duncan. Dramatic irony, as will be seen in this example, could lie both in the words and in the situation.

NOISES OFF: Sounds made, not on the stage but off it, as they are required by what is taking place on the acting area or being referred to by players on it. 'Within' in Elizabethan and Jacobean stage directions would indicate off-stage. 'Trumpet within' would require the sounding of a trumpet off-stage to announce the arrival on the stage of characters referred to by the actors. The knocking on the gate in *Macbeth* as well as the ringing of the bell when Duncan's murder is discovered would be 'noises off'.

PRODUCER: A comparatively recent word in its stage sense. There was no person so called in Shakespeare's time, but understandably there had to be someone, or some people, to perform his functions of being responsible for seeing to it that the play chosen by the company was cast, rehearsed and made ready for stage presentation. The interlude performed by Bottom and his friends at court in *A Midsummer Night's Dream* provides some indication of how a play could be organized and rehearsed.

PROPS: or properties, are all objects, excluding the scenery, used on the stage by the actors in the course of the play. The knife which Shylock sharpens in *The Merchant of Venice*, and the leek in *Henry V* are important 'props'.

QUARTO: Half the size of the Folio sheet. Used of the book made up of such printed sheets. A number of Shakespeare's plays, nineteen of them, appeared in Quarto before the Folio was printed.

STAGE DIRECTIONS: The instructions provided in the script or text of a play, generally printed in italics, about the location of the scene and the movements of the actors. The simplest stage directions would be 'Enter *X*' and 'Exit *X*'.

SUPERS: or supernumeraries, a modern term for all those appearing in a scene to make up the number required on the stage, with no lines of their own to speak. In *Julius Caesar* in the crowd scenes besides the speaking parts of First Citizen, etc., there would have been supers who were certainly vocal on the stage, but for whom the dramatist composed no lines or words.

IV. RECOMMENDED READING

Bibliographies can be both oppressive and tiresome. The following brief list may be found useful. Books in group A could be used in the classroom for illustration and occasional reference. Group B is indispensable to the teacher.

Group A

G. B. Harrison, *Introducing Shakespeare* (Pelican Books).
J. D. Wilson, *The Essential Shakespeare* (Cambridge University Press).

Group B

For the general background the following chapters in *The Age of Shakespeare*, vol. 2 of *A Guide to English Literature*, ed. by Boris Ford (Pelican Books):

Part One, 'The Social Setting', by L. G. Salingar.
Part Three, 'Shakespeare: The Young Dramatist', by D. A. Traversi; 'Shakespeare: The Middle Plays', by J. C. Maxwell; 'Shakespeare: *King Lear* and the Great Tragedies', by L. C. Knights.

H. Granville-Barker, *Prefaces to Shakespeare*, First Series (Sidgwick and Jackson). The Introduction.
K. J. Holzknecht, *The Backgrounds of Shakespeare's Plays* (The American Book Co.).

For studies of the six plays discussed here:
H. Granville-Barker, *Prefaces to Shakespeare*, Second Series (*The Merchant of Venice*); First Series (*Julius Caesar*).
L. C. Knights, *Explorations* (Chatto and Windus) for 'How many Children Had Lady Macbeth?'
E. M. W. Tillyard, *Shakespeare's History Plays* (Chatto and Windus) for *Richard II* and *Henry V*.
G. Wilson Knight, *The Wheel of Fire* (Oxford University Press), ch. I and ch. VI.

V. CHRONOLOGICAL TABLES

English sovereigns		*Important events*
	1476	Caxton starts printing in Westminster
1485 Henry VII	1492	Columbus discovers the New World
	1496	Cabot's voyage to Newfoundland
	1498	Vasco da Gama reaches India via the
1509 Henry VIII		Cape
	1534	Henry VIII declared Supreme Head of the English Church
	1535	First English Bible
	1536–9	Dissolution of the Monasteries
1547 Edward VI	1549	First Prayer-Book in English
1553 Mary	1560	The Reformation in Scotland; Wars of
1558 Elizabeth		Religion in France
	1568	The Revolt of the Netherlands against Philip II of Spain
	1570	Pope Pius V excommunicates Elizabeth
	1572	The Massacre of St Bartholomew in Paris
	1587	Execution of Mary Queen of Scots
	1588	Defeat of the Spanish Armada
	1598	Edict of Nantes ends the Wars of Religion in France
	1599	Globe Theatre built; Essex in Ireland; East India Company founded
	1601	Essex's rebellion and execution
1603 James I	1605	Gunpowder Plot
	1613	Globe Theatre burnt
	1623	First Folio published

Shakespeare's work		*Works of other writers*	
		1579	North's translation of Plutarch's *Lives*
		1587	Second edition of Holinshed's *Chronicles*
		1588	Marlowe, *Tamburlaine*
		1589	Spenser, *Faerie Queene* (I–III); Kyd, *Spanish Tragedy*; Marlowe, *The Jew of Malta*
1590–1	*Henry VI*, Parts 1, 2 and 3	1591	Marlowe, *Edward II*
1592	*Venus and Adonis; Richard III; The Comedy of Errors*	1592	Marlowe, *Dr Faustus*
1593	*Titus Andronicus; Sonnets* (between this date and 1599); *The Rape of Lucrece*		
1593–4	*The Taming of the Shrew*		
1594	*The Two Gentlemen of Verona*		
1594–5	*Love's Labour's Lost*		
1595	*Romeo and Juliet*	1595	Daniel, *Civil Wars*
1595–6	*Richard II; A Midsummer Night's Dream; King John*		
1596–7	*The Merchant of Venice*		
1597–8	*Henry IV*, Parts 1 and 2	1597	Bacon, *Essays*
1598	*Much Ado About Nothing*	1598	Jonson, *Every Man In His Humour*
1598–9	*Henry V*		
1599–1600	*Julius Caesar*	1599	Jonson, *Every Man Out of His Humour*
1600	*As You Like It*		
1601	*Twelfth Night; Hamlet; The Merry Wives of Windsor*		
1601–2	*Troilus and Cressida*		
1603	*All's Well That Ends Well*	1603	Florio's translation of Montaigne's *Essays*; Jonson, *Sejanus*
1604	*Measure for Measure*		
1604–5	*Othello*		
1605	*King Lear*		
1606	*Macbeth*		
1606–7	*Antony and Cleopatra*		
1608	*Coriolanus; Timon of Athens; Pericles*	1608	Fletcher, *The Faithful Shepherdess*
1609–10	*Cymbeline*	1609	Beaumont and Fletcher, *Philaster*
1610–11	*The Winter's Tale*	1610	Beaumont and Fletcher, *The Maid's Tragedy*
1611–12	*The Tempest*	1611	Authorized Version of the Bible
		1612	Webster, *The White Devil*
1612–13	*Henry VIII*	1613	Webster, *The Duchess of Malfi*